# No Jail for Thought

# No Jail for Thought

## LEV KOPELEV

✦✦✦✦✦✦✦✦✦✦✦✦✦✦

TRANSLATED AND EDITED BY
ANTHONY AUSTIN

Foreword by
HEINRICH BÖLL

Afterword by
ROBERT G. KAISER

SECKER & WARBURG
LONDON

Printed and bound in Great Britain by
Cox & Wyman Ltd
London, Fakenham and Reading

# Contents

# List of Illustrations

# Foreword

BY

# HEINRICH BÖLL

While reading this book, which has some of the characteristics of *Simplicissimus*, the seventeenth-century German novel by Grimmelshausen, we should not for a moment forget its keynote: TO BE PRESERVED FOREVER. In the Soviet Union that has been the standard notation on all court documents relating to offenses under Paragraph 58 (Crimes Against the State). There follows the personal notation of the author: 'This is the story of *one* such case—and it is also an essay in confession.'

If the concepts of 'eternal' and 'eternity' lie outside all Marxist categories and point to a surprising turn toward the almost metaphysical, the book itself offers far more surprises. Contained between these two themes are an extensive compendium and bestiary describing various interlocking and overlapping processes in the double sense of that word: in the sense both of legal process and of developmental process; and each of these is in turn to be understood in a double sense: a legal process of the authorities of the Soviet Union against the author and a process of the author against the Soviet Union, the development of the Soviet Union and the development of the author, as well as the development of Soviet society and of awareness on the part of the most diverse (in fact practically all) levels of that society, from prostitutes and thieves to generals and public prosecutors.

Nor should we forget, while reading this book, how it all began for this Major Kopelev—a convinced Communist who never confuses, much less identifies, conviction with dogmatism and refuses to swallow the accusation that he has no Party backbone. It begins in 1945 during the conquest and occupation of the first German province, East Prussia, by the army to which Kopelev belongs. He becomes an eye- and ear-witness to events which not only are repugnant to his *socialist* conscience and instincts but for which there is no justification in any Marxist theory. He protests, and eventually is denounced 'for having saved Germans and their property, preached sympathy with the Germans.'

Before quoting a crucial passage from the first part of the book, which is devoted to this conflict, I would like to point out that this problem is not merely a Russo-German one, not merely a national one, although on both sides it has become a source of national sensitivity. The Federal Republic of Germany and the German Democratic Republic unquestionably play a certain role in international politics, and it is important to know that many a Russo-German rapprochement has developed *across* the German Democratic Republic and thus bypassed it. It is impossible to understand the emergence, we may even say creation, of these two German states, or their politics, without knowing that one of them, the German Democratic Republic, has simply denied or ignored the events leading to Kopelev's trial, while the other, the Federal Republic of Germany, has almost consistently ignored the prehistory, i.e., the war against the Soviet Union with its indescribable devastation (including twenty million dead!) and only begins to think and to react with the events that took place during the occupation of Germany. If we constantly refer back to the wording of the charges against Kopelev, the background to the denunciation, the proceedings against him which extend throughout the book, we will understand how important the problem is from an *international* standpoint; for as a result of these events in East Germany in 1945 a process of rethinking has begun in the minds of many Soviet intellectuals, a process that is important, interesting, and painful for the internal development of the Soviet Union and thus for the entire world—and we also understand why this process of rethinking is being systematically suppressed, or rather, why a confrontation with it is being repressed. A similar process is occurring, or being suppressed, in all Socialist countries: reflections not only on the treatment of the Germans after 1945 but on the treatment of every kind of traitor and 'traitor.'

In most countries involved in the Second World War, that war slowed down or even halted developments which were already brewing when it broke out, and there followed on all sides that essential 'unity' whose primary purpose it was first to defeat the external enemy and only then to turn to domestic problems. For most of the world it was a surprise, almost a shock, when, shortly after the end of the war, Churchill was voted out of office, and it seems to me that an internal transformation of the Soviet Union was due long before the problem was personified in such concepts as Stalinism or de-Stalinization. In dictatorships, eras can, as we know, end only with the death or overthrow of the dictator; in parliamentary democracies, eras end by defeat in election. As far as Russia and the Soviet Union are concerned, there is an additional factor: fear of foreigners and fear of contempt by foreigners. To this day, thirty years after the end of the war, Soviet troops in, say, the German Democratic Republic live in almost total isolation from the population. Porosity exists only in the International of intellectuals. It is possible to read in or deduce from Russian and Western literature all the mutual admiration, all the influences, as well as all the suspicion, hatred and fear that have existed through the ages, fluctuating levels of rejection, arrogance and admiration; and to me one of the most important discoveries to be found in Kopelev's confession is that he is a true internationalist whose love and admiration for Russia, for the Soviet Union, whose knowledge of the great Russian culture, cannot for one moment induce him to judge other peoples and their cultures indiscriminately, in traditional clichés, let alone in clichés provided by any kind of propaganda. As a Germanist, an expert on German language, literature and culture, he was active as an educator on the German-Soviet battle lines in the struggle against Fascism.

Kopelev knew exactly under what conditions, after confronting what experiences, the Red Army marched into Germany: 'Our Army consists of 20 million fighting soldiers. It is obvious that among them there are a number of good-for-nothings. Moreover, many of our compatriots have been maltreated in the most brutal fashion. We came here from Moscow, from Leningrad, from Stalingrad, across scorched earth, through smoking piles of rubble. In every family there were victims of war and abduction.'

On the other hand, there are the words of Zabashtansky, Kopelev's superior and arch-enemy: 'Above all, the soldier must hate the enemy, that is why he wants to take his revenge, and not just a little but in such a way that everything is exterminated, rooted out. And besides this it is essential for him to have a vested interest in the battle, to know why he is climbing out of the trench and exposing himself to machine-gun fire and mines. So now everything is clear and intelligible, he comes to Germany and everything there belongs to him—everything he finds, even the women, and do with it what you like—get rid of it, so that their grandchildren and great-grandchildren may still feel the terror.'

Kopelev: 'What? Does that mean killing women and children?'

Zabashtansky: 'Now wait a minute. What you're saying there about children, you crazy fellow you, that's extremism. Not all of us will kill children, you won't and I won't. But to be honest, if you like, let those who *will* do it also kill the little Fritzes in their frenzy until they've had enough—that's war, Comrade, and not philosophy or literature. Of course in books there are such things as morality, humanism, internationalism. All O.K., theoretically correct. But right now we want to let Germany go up in smoke, and when that's done we'll behave correctly again, we'll write nice little books about humanism and internationalism. Right now it's essential for the soldiers to want to fight, for them to go into battle, that's the main thing.'

After this excerpt from *one* of the many dialogues between Kopelev and his superior, it becomes clear that the transformation of Man into Socialist Man has not yet taken place; the man who knows neither revenge nor nationality has not yet emerged; the man who does not 'forgive' but 'thinks historically' according to Marxist maxims and would tell himself: these people, although many of them may be Fascists, although they may be stupid, still have a lot to learn, but they've been subjected to their own historical process, and it's up to us to show them that Socialism knows no revenge.

Kopelev then goes on to describe horrifying individual cases which unfortunately conform to an overall trend, and he also quotes the order of the day of Marshal Rokossovsky, the supreme commander in this sector of the front: 'For looting, rape, robbery, murder of civilians—court martial; when necessary—shooting on the spot.' And there are indeed cases of such offenses being punished, but that does little to alter the policy toward the Germans.

Has anyone ever wondered, has anyone ever realized, within the western Communist Parties, within the entire 'left' international scene, why Germany, which once had the strongest Communist Party, the repository of so many hopes, has had the weakest Communist movement since 1945, *despite* all awareness of the madness of Fascism? Is it not conceivable that, for the surviving and returning German Communists, this object lesson was a far greater deterrent than all the anti-Communism being preached—and how many former Communists have joined in that preaching? Can such events be absorbed without contortions, without convulsions, in a country possessing not only specialists in the sense of informed people but profound experts on foreign culture and literature? After all, there was not only this one Major Kopelev, there were many Germanists, and there are many Soviet intellectuals who are better informed on the history and cultural history of Germany than many an intellectual who comes from that culture to Moscow and finds himself—often to his embarrassment—confronted by quotations, analyses, and an accurate knowledge of his own culture. It is the awareness and knowledge of their own great literature and culture that make it possible for Soviet experts to be so supremely well-informed on foreign cultures, and this explains Soviet readers' astonishing addiction to books. Moreover, it is this knowledge, this erudition, and this insight that intensify their sense of shame as well as their sensitivity.

There is little justification for a German to reproach Soviet citizens with failing to come to terms with unpalatable historical events; as a nation we are still too inclined to stress what was done to us *after* 1945 and to forget too easily what we did to others *before* 1945, and if we accept Kopelev's confession on this basis, let alone exploit it for propaganda purposes, we shall misunderstand Kopelev in a manner comparable to that of the Soviet authorities.

The *entire* context must be established, jointly discussed and analyzed, and for this Kopelev's book is better suited than many other publications; for his point of entry is *not* a confrontation with internal processes in the Soviet Union: his reflection, followed by a whole series of other reflections, starts with the *historically* important moment at which the Red Army for the first time occupies a foreign country and must prove the extent of its Socialism, or whether it is Socialist at all. What took place in the minds of the Red Army officers and soldiers during the occupation of Poland in 1939 after the Stalin-Hitler pact, how this totally unsocialist, purely imperialist action was digested, would be a matter for special analysis, as a psychological preparation for the later events. The reaction of the Poles to this Marxist-Fascist-induced fourth partition of Poland (a fifth one followed after 1945!), the consequences it has had, the effect it is still having on the traditionally poor Polish-Russian relations: all this remains virtually unaffected by brotherly hugs and kisses at airports and railway stations.

With his report, Kopelev puts the Soviet Army and the Soviet Union on trial; it is the report of a man accused who becomes the accuser because he has been charged with something that in terms of humanity and every Socialist theory is axiomatic: of having spoken out against hatred, revenge, rape and looting. Not until he has himself become a prisoner does this trial lead him to the recognition of the problematic nature of the Soviet practices of indictment and punishment, and from this point of view he concerns himself in his own fashion with what is familiar to us from other publications dealing with the Stalinist era. He is a Russian, but not *Russo-centric*; he is not confined to internal

Soviet problematics; he is thrust onto them from the outside in, he sees them in their international context, and this is what makes his confession so internationally important.

The whole immeasurable gamut of absurd 'offenses' and accusations, Soviet society 'turned upside down' in cells and camps where the victims of an insane mistrust await their trials or serve their sentences—from general or public prosecutor down to private or dairymaid—serves to demonstrate the 'classlessness' of this insanity. Here the Soviet élite, the entire privileged class (in which Kopelev himself can be included) comes face to face with itself and the unimaginable fates of their less-favored fellow-countrymen, and we begin to comprehend the fear that must have reigned in the camps and cells—and outside.

Here we meet Valya, who has been sentenced to seven years for pocketing two spools of yarn, and someone else who has been given five years for 'praising the enemy's equipment.' We meet the public prosecutor who—like so many whom *he* would not believe—protests his innocence. Every variety of political prisoner, white, red, red/white. Germans, Poles, every variety of Vlasov supporter, every variety of traitor and informer and 'informer' and 'traitor', of criminals who may in turn be subdivided into 'genuine', who do not act as informers, and 'false', who are both at the same time—genuine criminals and genuine informers: a jungle in which no one—regardless of his point of view—is 'genuine'.

'As a soldier at the front,' says one man, 'at least one knew where the enemy and his men were, but here one is surrounded by riff-raff. And it is impossible to gauge where anything is likely to happen.' Is the camp commandant 'genuine', in the sense of being a convinced Socialist who will behave more or less predictably in a given situation, or is the thief who has sunk to the status of informer genuine? There are battles, indeed wars, among criminal and semi-criminal groups, between criminal and political groups and every possible variety of 'coalition'. The number of permutations and combinations is incalculable.

In describing his route from his arrest through various prisons, cells, and camps, with an eye for human beings (all of whom have remained vividly in his memory) and their fates, equipped with an insatiable curiosity and an unbelievable measure of recklessness, the victim not only of denunciations but also of jealousies (in many places, in fact nearly all, one might write in the margin: *cherchez la femme!*), Kopelev slithers from misfortune into still greater misfortune, back again into some better fortune or lesser misfortune, on again into some worse fortune or greater misfortune—it must be borne in mind that it is the Germans who have caused his misfortune, after having first plunged his country into misfortune!—and he continues to slither along this slope of paradox such as can befall only a stubborn and unreasonable intellectual, and he strikes no moral pose other than that of the Socialist and Marxist who refuses to hide his weaknesses, his lack of discipline, his highly dangerous spontaneity, his naïveté, and his recklessness. In his account he does not exclude his entanglements, knowing as a 'materialist' that they belong there. Thus Kopelev suffers and is made to suffer a great deal, yet his confession is not a tale of suffering. He himself is by no means the centre of his story—yet he stands out in every sentence.

It must not be forgotten that this book was written by a man who is protesting against his expulsion from his own party, who is experiencing the ludicrously mendacious 'correctness' of a series of court proceedings, with voluminous documents, numerous sworn statements in which good friends prove to be denouncers and others, whom he had underestimated, prove trustworthy. It is this thicket of mendacious formalism that Kopelev indicts with his book, and yet—this is the surprising part—he is not a Don Quixote, nor is he a Sancho Panza: he is both at the appropriate time; in him, in Kopelev the man as I know him personally from numerous conversations and meetings, the classic dichotomy has been eliminated, and to my mind this is what makes him so 'dangerous', because—each at the appropriate time—he is both. And in this sense he is not an intellectual either, which is to say: of course he is an intellectual, yet he understands the 'people', ranks himself among them, belongs to them, understands their language and their problems—and probably that, too, is what makes him so dangerous. Ideologically, as a theoretician, he is unreservedly a Don Quixote: he discusses and argues according to his conception of internationalism, lets nothing pass, nothing at all, and this he does fearlessly and tirelessly and logically in the face of those all-powerful, boring windmills, those cruel, unimaginative functionaries. As a private person he is confessedly at the mercy of his human weaknesses; in his almost metaphysical materialism he is aware of what a cigarette, or even just a few puffs from a stub, means to someone who for a long time has had nothing to smoke, and he still knows and still remembers what water means to the thirsty and bread to the hungry. His Dulcineas—there are several of them—are not Platonic figments of imagination but—something he by no means spurns—flesh and blood. He omits none of his weaknesses, he acknowledges them (at times he even regrets them!), yet his confession is still not a statement of defense, it still remains an indictment.

All the problems of the Soviet judiciary and penal systems are laid bare in careers, in trial documents, and analyzed in both international and Marxist terms, not only 'humanistically' but—and this is a further dimension of Kopelev's dangerousness—humanly! The fact that all this has happened since 1945, after a glorious final victory, proves the extent of mistrust.

The trial of Lev Kopelev has many preliminary stages: interrogations, solitary confinement, transportation, long before the first official proceedings against him begin, and in the course of his confession the true nature of the 'new man' becomes plain: it is the smoothly functioning functionary, the model of the *apparatchik* (who meanwhile has become internationally established within the sphere of other ideologies as well), a formalist of a very special and especially charming kind: one who abuses the defendant for being a formalist the moment the defendant invokes his rights while at the same time applying a functionary's formalism against him! Is that why the high priests of culture are so terribly angry with 'formalists'? In the final analysis, what proves to be Kopelev's undoing, as well as his salvation during his imprisonment, is his unbroken naïveté, his humor, and his insatiable curiosity for all forms and manifestations of human life, right down to every proletarian and even criminal form, and every form—mixed and otherwise—of prostitution. Finally, one quality which seems to be of Eastern European origin and which perhaps tends especially to develop in prison camps: a staggering memory.

The reader also learns, from the lips of a professional forester, how economically senseless, how wasteful, how absurd, is the slave labor in the camps. This is demonstrated in detail, and to the many absurd dimensions a further one is added: that even from an economic standpoint this gigantic apparatus of mistrust has yielded nothing. And then the 'amiable and accommodating Fedya', a thief, calmly relates a case of cannibalism. The fact that, despite the official prudishness, despite the puritanism of the war—and postwar years in the Soviet Union as well as in its prisons, every variety of 'camp love' existed, plus the rudiments of a permissive society, is a further surprise; and it becomes apparent (yet another surprise) that the rooms provided in the camps for twenty-four-hour conjugal visits were for the use not only of *married* partners. One dimension of the disastrous trend toward rule by functionaries also becomes evident: that it is the functionaries who separate the intellectuals from the people: it is the sensitivity which allows them to be both Don Quixote and Sancho Panza, i.e., clergy and laity, that probably renders the intellectuals so dangerous.

But Kopelev's confession has one further dimension, of which I am reluctant to speak because its designation is so misleading, one of the most misleading of all: a religious one. However we shake up the word 'religion' it still denotes a tying-up, a commitment, and this confession of Kopelev's reveals a commitment to man, to human nature and all-too-human nature, and further, I might almost say, a new sacramental doctrine of man's most elemental ties, a doctrine that perhaps was only possible following upon the experience of materialism which, after all, does not exclude cognition of that matter of which human nature consists.

And in later parts of the book there is mention of a strange and remarkable service, totally unchurchlike in nature, inspired and organised by Aunt Dusya, in which the question of whether a person *was* or is a believer, or whether he was or *is* an atheist, and the transition from one to the other, presents itself in a new humanity of brotherly compassion; and at this Communion service the traitor (who in this case is called Stepan) is, of course, also present. In this new feeling for religion and sacrament we might also include the various forms of 'intercourse', licit and illicit, as Kopelev describes one form that is full of tenderness. Such seemingly rank materialism yields more, far more, than does any abstract, totally desensualized sacramental doctrine if brotherly love and compassion are received *with* it, beyond all legality, for these situations are invariably 'illegal'. Kopelev's religious feeling is neither assumed nor imposed, it is experienced: not like some *deus ex machina* who puts everything right and insists on his 'legality'. Into this new category of religious feeling I would also place the rebellion of the women and a few war-cripples at a railway station who, *against* the orders of the military guards and functionaries (whom they even revile: 'You were stuffing your stomachs while they were at the front') distribute food to the prisoners.

Kopelev's confession contains many instances of inhumanity, yet serves to prove the existence of a profound, ancient reserve of humanity as exemplified by this scene at the railway station.

(*Translated by Leila Vennewitz*)

# AUTHOR'S NOTE

'To be preserved forever.'

These words were stamped on files containing material gathered by the competent authorities in cases brought under Article 58—the statute that deals with 'crimes against the state'—of the Criminal Code (1926) of the Russian Soviet Federated Socialist Republic, the principal republic of the Soviet Union.

This is an account of one such case, prosecuted during the years 1945–47. It is also an essay in confession.

The events recounted are factual. The names of some of the people involved have been changed. However, those who cannot be harmed either by their kindness to the author or by his gratitude, and those whom he regards as confirmed scoundrels, are identified by their proper names.

# TRANSLATOR'S NOTE

This edition of Lev Kopelev's memoir has been abridged. The Russian-language edition, published by Ardis, Ann Arbor, Michigan, is a long, detailed book whose many anecdotes and portraits fill a 729-page volume. This shorter work is intended to remain faithful to the language, spirit and flavor of the original and to preserve the central elements of Lev Kopelev's narrative. Of necessity, some material had to be rearranged, but I have tried to keep all such interventions to a minimum.

All the footnotes in this edition were written by me; they were not cleared with the author and are not to be taken as necessarily reflecting his views. For any mistakes of fact or interpretation that may appear in the footnotes, the responsibility is wholly mine.

New York                                              —ANTHONY AUSTIN

*This book is dedicated to:*

Nadezhda Kolchinskaya, my first wife and constant friend.

Maya and Lyena, my eldest daughters.

Sofia Borisovna Kopeleva† and Zinovy Iakovlevich Kopelev,† my parents.

Elena Arlyuk, Berta Korfin, Inna Levidova, Maria Levina (Zinger),† Galina Khromushina, Mikhail Arshansky, Abram Belkin,† Arnold Goldstein, Boris Izakov, Alexander Isbakh, Mikhail Kocherian,† Mikhail Kruchinsky, Valentin Levin,† Yuri Maslov, Vladislav Mikesha, Ivan Rozhansky, Victor Rozenzveig, Boris Suchkov,† Nikolai Telyantz; without them, I could not have survived.

Raisa Kopeleva (Orlova), my wife and friend; without her, this book would not have been written.

†Deceased.

I shall weave a memorial pall for their grave
From their own simple words that I heard and saved.
                                    —ANNA AKHMATOVA


              I read my life, the painful sum of years;
                I shudder and I curse—but nay:
              For all my grief, for all my bitter tears,
                No wretched line is washed away.
                                    —ALEXANDER PUSHKIN


History provides us with ready-made thoughts, novels with ready-made
feelings. But the text, which gives us only the material, demands that we
work it over for ourselves—that we make an independent effort.
                                    —GOETHE

# 1

I REMEMBER the exact date. April 5, 1945. A luminous morning. One of those mornings that make you feel, no matter what, that life is good and everything will turn out all right. The field hospital was in a clump of brick buildings in a village southeast of Danzig. My fever was down; my back injury was hurting less; the headaches were letting up.

I'd been in there for two weeks. The hospital commissar had proved to be a sympathetic listener. I told him of the whole stupid business. My dismissal from the Party. My suspension as a senior instructor in the army's Political Administration for the Second Belorussian Front. All on the same day that I came down with that blinding pain where I had been struck in the explosion of the enemy barricade at Graudenz. He promised to have me evacuated to Moscow. 'You'll get better care there, and these Party matters will be sorted out.'

That morning he was as friendly as ever. 'We're moving up the line. The orders are to sign out everybody who can walk. Some of them'll hitch rides and catch up; the others can make it to the rear. About you—I'm putting you in the reserves for a while. You can have a car; you can catch up with us at our new base, and we'll complete your treatment there. Who knows—maybe we'll still manage to get you off to Moscow.'

I put on my uniform, got my suitcase, pistol and overcoat, and my 'personal dossier,' a large package secured by five wax seals. The commissar let me use his cot while I waited for an available car. I glanced through a batch of captured German newspapers: panicky communiqués, desperate exhortations, absurd military claims. I switched on the radio: music. The room was bathed in sunlight. The air from the open window smelled of warm, damp earth.

Two officers entered without knocking—a captain and a first lieuten-ant. They saluted respectfully. 'Excuse us, are you Comrade Major Kopelev?'

'Yes.'

'Our general asks if you could see him about a new assignment.'

'What unit are you from?' Every unit at front-line headquarters—air, artillery, engineers, armor—had its own intelligence section, and they were all on the lookout for officers who spoke German. So I wasn't surprised that these two had come for me without waiting until I joined the reserves.

The captain gave a twisted smile. 'It's all the same to us where we spend the war.'

I let it go. Intelligence people love to make a mystery of everything.

A large room, the usual bustle of headquarters. Someone said, 'The general asks you to wait a few minutes.'

In the next room, the first lieutenant, a round-faced, amiable young man, blurted out, 'Comrade Major, what kind of pistol is that? Sure is a funny holster!'

'It's a Belgian Browning, Number One.'

'You mean the kind that takes fourteen rounds? Can I have a look?'

It wasn't the first time that people had shown envious interest in my big, heavy, but handy and dependable 'Belgian.' I handed it over. That same instant, the captain said, in a new, official voice, 'And now read this.'

A small piece of paper, a printed form. 'Warrant for Arrest.'

My first sensation was that of a blow on the head. Then confusion, outrage. 'Why did you wheedle that pistol away from me? What did you think I was going to do—start shooting?'

'All right, all right. Hand over your papers. Take off your insignia. Take everything out of your pockets.'

A soldier brought in my suitcase. Underwear, letters, manuscripts, books, tobacco—everything poured out onto the table.

I forced myself to think calmly. Of course, I had to thank Zabash-tansky for this. But what could he have invented to justify arrest?

I asked them what the charges were.

'We don't know. We're just carrying out orders. The arrest was approved by the commander of the front. You'll find out the reasons during the investigation. We don't go around arresting people without reason.'

They rummaged through the reading matter from my suitcase—

Hitler's *Mein Kampf*; articles by Goebbels, Ley, Rosenberg; several SS journals. They threw these aside and examined my notebooks, diaries, manuscripts, letters. The beginnings of a book about the methods and forms of Nazi propaganda and my 1943–44 diaries were examined with particular care. I was afraid that they might be lost and started to explain that they were important not only to me personally but for their historical value.

'They'll be safe enough. We'll put it all in the record.'

My daughters' letters lay to one side. The captain glanced at them carelessly. 'Ah, children's—' He started to tear them up.

I bellowed, 'No, you don't!' The blood rushed to my head. I made for him, swearing, ready to hit out, and was grabbed from behind.

'Take it easy,' the captain faltered. 'What's so special about this stuff? Don't forget you're under arrest.'

'You don't have any children of your own if you can ask what's so special!'

At my insistence they recorded the number of 'miscellaneous letters.' I wanted them to list the notebooks and manuscripts as well, but they waved me aside.

While I was taking off my own medals, the lieutenant calmly cut off my shoulder boards with a penknife. They took away my cigarette case and matches and placed them in the suitcase with my other belongings. 'No smoking in prison.'

The instincts of a prisoner stirred in me for the first time. While signing the search record, I sneaked my other hand into a pouch of tobacco lying on the table and dribbled some of its contents into one of my pockets.

They took me to another room, empty except for two stools. A young sailor sat on one of them, chewing on a piece of bread. His name was Petya; he said he had been stationed in the rear but had gotten bored 'hanging around with a shore crew' and had taken off on his own for the front. They had arrested him as a deserter.

I could hear the captain's voice in the next room. 'Let me speak with Zabashtansky.' A pause. Then, 'We've got your boy. No, he didn't put up any resistance.'

It was getting dark by the time Petya and I found ourselves being driven along a highway in a Studebaker truck. What would they accuse me of? From the beginning of the war I had kept copies of transcripts of our interrogation of war prisoners and copies of some of my own reports. Technically, these were classified as secret. But when we sent anti-Fascist Germans across the front lines, we gave them maps that we recorded as destroyed. Some of the anti-Fascists returned and sometimes the maps were in fact destroyed then, but sometimes they were given to other German agents or kept for our own scouting across the lines. If they could find some map that I had listed as destroyed, they could accuse me of falsifying reports.

But they hadn't asked about maps; they hadn't shown any interest in transcripts or reports. Was that a ruse? They seemed to be looking for manuscripts. I recalled now how the hospital commissar kept looking the other way that morning. Ah, I thought, how could a crude liar like Zabashtansky have succeeded in reducing me to this, especially after Graudenz, where my propaganda unit had scored such an unprecedented success—nothing less than a mutiny in a German regiment?

Sense had to be made out of all this. How could it be happening to *me*? How did this kind of thing become possible in our army in the first place? How did it all start?

# 2

THE MASTER SERGEANT was almost apologetic—'You know, regulations'
—as he patted me all over. 'No knife. No gun. Well, we trust you, of
course. Give the major a smoke.'

Someone held out a piece of newspaper with a generous sprinkling
of makhorka.* I rolled it; someone gave me a light.

'No matches in the cell,' the master sergeant went on cordially. 'Now,
into quarantine, if you don't mind, and tomorrow the commanding
officer will be here, and he'll make better arrangements.'

A soldier led me downstairs into a pitch-dark corridor. We passed a
guard pacing the corridor and stopped at a door. A key clicked; a bolt
rasped. I went in, and the door clanged shut behind me.

Blackness. At the opposite end of the cell a hint of gray suggested a
window. The air was close, with an unpleasantly familiar odor. Sourish,
moldy, with something in it of stale cigarette ashes, sweaty underwear,
filthy toilets—the smells of captured German dugouts. With us, the
acrid reek of makhorka and the smell of bread overpowered all else.

I hadn't taken two steps before I stepped on someone.

'*Was ist los? Wer da?*'

'*Verdammt!*'

'*Wer trampelt da?*'

I flung myself at the door and pounded at it with my fists and my feet.
'Guard! Where in hell did you stick me? Don't you know there are
Fritzes in here?' I bawled; I swore; I was furious. 'I'm a Soviet officer!
I won't be humiliated like this!'

I could hear the Germans muttering anxiously to each other. One
of them said, 'It's a Russian officer. He doesn't want to be in with
us.'

* A low-grade domestic tobacco.

The guard came up to the peephole. 'What are you yelling about?'

I demanded that he call the master sergeant.

'Anything else? Look—you sit out the night. The commanding officer will be here tomorrow.'

'I'm going to pound on this door all night!'

'Go ahead. It's made of iron.'

I heard him pace unhurriedly to the other end of the corridor. I kicked at the door and shouted after him.

Then, from behind me, came a clear, young voice: 'Hey, buddy, hey, Uncle, stop that racket, will you? We've got some Russians here too.'

I made for the voice, stepping on limbs and stomachs, to a protest of oaths and groans, and found myself by the window. 'How many of you here?'

'Two.'

'Who are you?'

'We're from Leningrad.'

They weren't much more than sixteen years old. We began to talk. It's interesting how meeting your own kind in a political prison calms you down and brings you out of yourself.

It appeared that when the two boys were twelve, they were thrown out of a Pioneer camp near Luga. They wandered about, hungry, and worked in Germany, where they were recruited for an espionage school; but after crossing the front lines back into the Soviet Union, they surrendered to the first Soviet patrol they ran into. . .

'Do you think they'll let us go? Or do you think they'll try us?'

I assured the boys that of course they'd be released—and so I thought. They said that there were seventeen Germans in the cell, members of the German army field police, and knowing this made the fetid darkness all the more repellent. My cigarette had gone out. One of the boys had some matches, and we shared what was left of the makhorka.

'*Pan, pan, prosze, bitte, Tabak!*'

It was one of the Germans. I pretended that I didn't understand. Spreading my greatcoat on the floor, I stretched out.

Another fine morning; bars against the sky. The *feld-polizei* squatted along the walls. Though stripped of their epaulets, they addressed each other as *Hauptmann, Oberleutnant, Wachtmeister*. One of them, red-haired and shifty-eyed, tried talking to me in broken Polish. '*Pan*\* is what— captain, lieutenant?' I saw the brown police insignia on his sleeve and

\**Pan*: Polish for 'Mister.'

collar and cursed him out in my strongest Russian. He explained to the others, 'Doesn't want to talk to us. They have their own notions of honor.'

The door rattled. 'All out!' Two guards led us out into a yard toward a trench latrine off in a corner, alongside a heap of trash. I announced that I would not go with the Germans. The guards were young soldiers; they laughed. 'Aren't you the one who was hollering last night? Well, go to the other corner.'

Back in the cell, which seemed doubly gloomy and stifling. At last, the prison commander. He was a first lieutenant with shiny new gold shoulder boards, his sharp features gathered into a constant frown, probably to make him seem older and more important.

'What are you carrying on for? You're in prison, not at your mother-in-law's for blini.'

I explained that I was an officer, that I had been at the front for four years, and that I didn't want to be in the same cell with the Germans.

'You're all equal here; you're all prisoners. I can't make any distinctions.'

I tried to speak calmly, even ingratiatingly. 'Listen, Lieutenant, if you have any respect for the uniform you're wearing, you cannot permit this. I am wearing the same uniform. I have not been tried; I have not been cashiered. I am an officer in the same army as you. How can you insult the honor of our army by putting me in with Fascist butchers?'

I was close to tears. The lieutenant looked at me with surprise—with a certain respect, even.

'Take him to number eight.' To me he said, 'That's the best cell I have. But there are all kinds of people in there. I have no special quarters. You must understand—this is a field prison, a transit prison at the front. We are soldiers; we carry out orders. They put you under arrest—we have you under guard. As to what it's all about, that's up to the investigation to straighten out.'

Cell 8 was lighter and roomier. About fifteen men sat on the floor along the walls.

A short, bald, wiry old man stepped up to me the moment I entered. 'Well, now, introduce yourself. Name? Rank?' The old man had lively eyes and wore a gray jacket of good cloth.

I gave him my name.

'Officer?'

'Major.'

'What army?'

'The Red Army, of course!'

'Pleased to meet you, Gospodin Major.* I'm the cell boss. Colonel of the White Army Pyotr Vikentievich Berulya. Here's our officers' corner—Colonel of the Yugoslav Army Ivan Ivanovich Kivelyuk, Major of the Yugoslav Army Boris Petrovich Klimov, Lieutenant of the Polish Army Tadeusz Ruzanski. Captain of the German Army Herr Koenig, being the enemy, has been placed in the other corner, near the latrine bucket. These two are Vlasovites,† those men are Latvian saboteurs, this one's an Estonian accused of spying, and the two Germans are an *Obergefreiter* and a private, the Captain's aide. As for *your* army, it has been represented thus far by those two crooks there.'

Thrown off as I was, I could see that this was better than being with the Nazi cutthroats. I even smiled. 'A small but close family, eh?'

'Got any tobacco?'

I took a handful out of my pocket. Ecstatic gasps all around.

'We haven't had a smoke for three days. You're a rich man. But, gentlemen, let us be economical. The officers will share one cigarette between two men. The others will share one cigarette between three men. Gospodin Major, of course, can smoke without limit.'

We lit up. I asked a few cautious questions. Someone said that he'd been in there for six weeks, and I was overcome by cold, clammy fear. I didn't think I could stick it out that long. I'd go out of my mind.

The German captain by the cylindrical clay pots in the other corner stared at me and whispered to the other Germans. He had a chestnut beard and wore a flier's tunic.

I addressed him in German. 'Why are you looking at me like that, Captain?'

'Forgive me—I thought I recognized you. Weren't you the Russian truce envoy at Graudenz?'

'Yes. I was.'

Strange, having him see me again like this. It hadn't been a month since Graudenz.

The first interrogation took place in a large room strewn with scraps of wood and heaps of paper. At a small desk in a corner cleared of rubbish sat a young captain with a scrubbed face and meticulously combed hair.

*Gospodin: Russian for Mister, dropped after the Russian Revolution in favor of Grazhdanin (Citizen) and Tovarish (Comrade).

†Captured Soviet troops enrolled by the Germans in anti-Soviet military detachments under the command of a captured Soviet lieutenant general, Andrei Vlasov.

'Please sit down. I am your interrogator, Captain Poshekhonov.'

I took the chair in front of his desk. 'I wish to register a protest against my being arrested. Also, against the fact that I, a Soviet front-line officer, was put into a cell with German field police.'

The captain gave me a sardonic look. 'In your place I wouldn't be worrying about protests; I'd be worrying about my case. You have been charged under Article Fifty-eight, Section Ten, Paragraph Two, and Article One Hundred and Ninety-three, Section Two, of the Criminal Code. Under either statute you could well be shot.'

My stomach turned cold. He's trying to scare me, I thought; that's their way. The main thing is not to show any fear, not to lose my head, not to be in a hurry to say anything.

'What do these articles cover? I'm not a lawyer.'

He held out a small book, *The Criminal Code of the RSFSR*.* I found Article 58, Section 10—'anti-Soviet agitation and propaganda ... possession and dissemination of ... slander with malicious intent.' Paragraph 2—the same in wartime or during a state of emergency. Punishment: 'up to and including the ultimate penalty': execution. Article 193, Section 2—'refusal to carry out an order on the field of battle, incitement to refusal. ...' Again, 'up to and including the ultimate penalty.'

'None of this,' I said, 'could possibly apply to me. During these four years of war, I have repeatedly demonstrated my loyalty to my country. Never have I failed to carry out an order. Only a month ago, I was recommended for a citation by Major General Rakhimov, Commander of the Thirty-seventh Guards Division, for something he himself and other commanders saw me do at Graudenz. You can easily check.'

'We'll check whatever is necessary. However, as the saying goes, thank you for all the good you've done; now you'll have to answer for the bad.'

'I haven't done anything bad.'

'That's what we'll have to find out. What happened in East Prussia? Why were you expelled from the Party?'

'So that's why I was arrested! But that was all slander, stupid slander!'

'We don't believe in words; we believe in facts.'

The old ritual began. Where were you born? Who were your parents? Do you have any relatives abroad? Any at home who were

*Russian Soviet Federated Socialist Republic, the main republic of the multi-national Soviet Union—in effect, Russia proper.

repressed?* Where did you study? Where did you work? And finally, 'I am authorized to tell you that you have been charged with the following: At a time of decisive battles, when our troops were entering German territory, you engaged in propaganda of bourgeois humanism, of pity for the enemy. You were ordered to gather intelligence on the political situation and state of morale in East Prussia, and on whether there was a Fascist underground. Instead, you spent your time rescuing Germans and weakening the morale of our own troops; you engaged in agitation against vengeance and hatred—sacred hatred of the enemy. And all this not through any haphazard mistake. That much is clear from the facts of an even earlier period: At meetings and in conversations with your comrades, you allowed yourself to criticize, in an unacceptable manner, your commanders, our press, and articles by Comrade Ehrenburg,† to express distrust of our allies; to make statements which in time of war, at the front, can only be construed as designed to demoralize and undermine the fighting spirit of our men.'

'I deny all these charges! I understand now why I've been arrested. I wouldn't have thought it possible! I can understand how a meeting of Party members could be taken in by this ridiculous slander—it so happened that those comrades who could easily have refuted this nonsense were not present. But how could you people in counterintelligence have fallen for it? You could have easily gotten at the truth. After all, that's your duty.'

'We know our duty. Right now it's to conduct an investigation. If the investigation establishes your innocence, you will be released. If it fails to reach a definite conclusion, the case will go before a tribunal. We're not in the habit of condemning the innocent.'

His words had a soothing effect; they almost cheered me up. Maybe it was all for the best. Now the truth would out. Now it would be made clear that Zabashtansky was a shameless liar, Belyaev a cowardly nonentity. The investigation would expose them and their ilk for the mean, miserable types they were. Why did they feel that they had to get me out of the way? They must have reasoned that I had to be working against them personally. And in their world, that meant filing complaints against them, informing against them, intriguing, vying with them for medals and promotions. Yet none of that had ever entered my mind. The main thing for me was the war. What counted most for me was what I could do to weaken the enemy and bring victory nearer.

*Bureaucratic euphemism for arrested, sent into exile, or shot.
†Ilya Ehrenburg, the late Soviet novelist and publicist, whose wartime columns were famous for their impassioned anti-Germanism.

Compared to that, any disagreements in our own camp seemed unimportant, and quarrels that served to distract us from our main goal were inexcusable.

Many years would pass before I began to see that my wavering between unresolvable contradictions—a 'greater' or 'lesser' evil, 'objective' or 'subjective' truth—was a reflection of the central contradiction of our whole life, the heart of the dilemma that had shaped the destinies of several of our generations. For did not thousands of our Old Bolsheviks—the very men who had acquitted themselves so heroically on the barricades, in the Czarist prison camps, on the front lines of the Civil War—debase themselves ten or fifteen years later by lying and toadying and glorifying the 'Great Leader' and betraying their friends and bespattering themselves with false confessions? And not entirely out of fear or selfish calculation—and some for neither of these reasons to any degree— but because they believed that it was necessary for the main cause: the security of the Soviet state and the struggle against Fascism. And in spite of everything they saw and experienced in 1930, 1933, 1937 and 1939, in spite of the famines, in spite of Ezhov's Terror and the pact with Hitler and the carving up of Poland, my own contemporaries volunteered for the Finnish campaign, fought bravely in the Great Patriotic War of 1941–45 and put up sacrificial resistance in the German death camps.

As late as 1953, if another war had broken out, we would probably have marched off as volunteers with the old cry of 'For the Motherland! For Stalin!' And if, as late as then, the planned resettlement of the Jews into a Socialist ghetto in the Far East had actually occurred, even there, on the Amur River, there would have been thousands of young men eager to rush off to Korea, Vietnam, Cuba or Taiwan—any front anywhere—to prove that they 'belonged' and, even more fundamentally, to carry out what they felt to be their duty to the main, great cause.

With the rest of my generation I firmly believed that the ends justified the means. Our great goal was the universal triumph of Communism, and for the sake of that goal everything was permissible—to lie, to steal, to destroy hundreds of thousands and even millions of people, all those who were hindering our work or could hinder it, everyone who stood in the way. And to hesitate or doubt about all this was to give in to 'intellectual squeamishness' and 'stupid liberalism,' the attributes of people who 'could not see the forest for the trees.'

That was how I had reasoned, and everyone like me, even when I did have my doubts, when I believed what Trotsky and Bukharin were saying, when I saw what 'total collectivization' meant—how they 'kulakized' and 'dekulakized,' how mercilessly they stripped the peasants in the winter of 1932–33. I took part in this myself, scouring the countryside, searching for hidden grain, testing the earth with an iron rod for loose spots that might lead to buried grain. With the others, I emptied out the old folks' storage chests, stopping my ears to the children's crying and the women's wails. For I was convinced that I was accomplishing the great and necessary transformation of the countryside; that in the days to come the people who lived there would be better off for it; that their distress and suffering were a result of their own ignorance or the machinations of the class enemy; that those who sent me—and I myself—knew better than the peasants how they should live, what they should sow and when they should plow.

In the terrible spring of 1933 I saw people dying from hunger. I saw women and children with distended bellies, turning blue, still breathing but with vacant, lifeless eyes. And corpses—corpses in ragged sheepskin coats and cheap felt boots; corpses in peasant huts, in the melting snow of old Vologda, under the bridges of Kharkov. . . . I saw all this and did not go out of my mind or commit suicide. Nor did I curse those who had sent me to take away the peasants' grain in the winter, and in the spring to persuade the barely walking, skeleton-thin or sickly-swollen people to go into the fields in order to 'fulfill the Bolshevik sowing plan in shock-worker style.'

Nor did I lose my faith. As before, I believed because I wanted to believe. Thus from time immemorial men have believed when possessed by a desire to serve powers and values above and beyond humanity: gods, emperors, states; ideals of virtue, freedom, nation, race, class, party. . . .

Any single-minded attempt to realize these ideals exacts its toll of human sacrifice. In the name of the noblest visions promising eternal happiness to their descendants, such men bring merciless ruin on their contemporaries. Bestowing paradise on the dead, they maim and destroy the living. They become unprincipled liars and unrelenting executioners, all the while seeing themselves as virtuous and honorable militants—convinced that if they are forced into villainy, it is for the sake of future good, and that if they have to lie, it is in the name of eternal truths.

*Und willst du nicht mein Bruder sein*
*So schlag ich dir dein Schädel ein.**

they sing in a Landsknecht song.

That was how we thought and acted—we, the fanatical disciples of

*And if you won't be my brother
I'll crack your skull open.

the all-saving ideals of Communism. When we saw the base and cruel acts that were committed in the name of our exalted notions of good, and when we ourselves took part in those actions, what we feared most was to lose our heads, fall into doubt or heresy and forfeit our unbounded faith.

I was appalled by what I saw in the 1930s and was overcome by depression. But I would still my doubts the way I had learned to: 'we made a mistake,' 'we went too far,' 'we didn't take into consideration,' 'the logic of the class struggle,' 'objective historical need,' 'using barbaric means to combat barbarism'. . . .

Good and evil, humanity and inhumanity—these seemed empty abstractions. I did not trouble myself with why 'humanity' should be abstract but 'historical necessity' and 'class consciousness' should be concrete. The concepts of conscience, honor, humaneness we dismissed as idealistic prejudices, 'intellectual' or 'bourgeois,' and, hence, perverse.

It was only later, much later, that I began to see things more clearly. Yet in the final months of the war I had already begun to sense a change in me, like some unavoidable oncoming threat. I had already begun to wonder, and had decided that what we lacked was a set of absolute moral norms. Relativist morality—whatever helps us is good, whatever helps the enemy is bad, the creed we proselytized under the name of the 'materialist dialectic'—would debase us in the end, and would debase the cause of Socialism, raising a species of immoral craftsmen of death. Today they apply themselves to killing enemies, real or imaginary; tomorrow they will turn just as willingly against their own.

When I expressed these thoughts, arguing that it was wrong for our soldiers to kill and torture prisoners, to pillage Polish and German villages, I was concerned primarily, if not exclusively, with our own country and our own social system. These young fellows who had come to the front straight from school—what would they be like after the war, having learned nothing except how to shoot, dig trenches, crawl through barbed wire, rush the enemy and toss grenades? They had become inured to death, blood and cruelty, and each new day brought them fresh evidence that the war they read about in their papers and heard about on their radios and in their political meetings was not the war they saw and experienced themselves.

Becoming habituated to violence and lies, learning to distrust words that came down from above—all this would injure us in the end. How could this outcome be prevented? It was for ideas like these, expressed out loud, that I was excluded from the Party. It was there that they found 'propaganda of bourgeois humanism and of pity for the enemy.' I fretted and fumed: Why was I so misunderstood?—I pitied not the enemy but our own people! I had worried and worried about it in the hospital; and on that first day of my arrest, when I was in the back of the car, gazing at the starry sky and being rushed off to prison, I thought of it again. A new system of authentic Marxist ethics had to be worked out. There hadn't been time for that as yet—revolution, construction, war. . . . After the war, however, moral education would become an urgent necessity. Millions of people had been brutalized and corrupted by the war and by our propaganda—bellicose, jingoistic and false. I had believed such propaganda necessary on the eve of war, and all the more so for the war's duration. I still believed it, but I had also come to understand that from seeds like these come poisoned fruit.

# 3

I MET Zabashtansky, the head of the Seventh Section of the Political
Department of the 50th Army,* in May 1944 in Roslavl, at the newly
formed headquarters of the Second Belorussian Front, and I liked him
at once. He was of medium height, thickset, with a round head, short
neck and swarthy, full, puffy face. His eyes were dark pellets, sometimes
dull and sleepy, sometimes sparkling and sly. He spoke with a slight
Ukrainian accent. He would joke and pretend to be a simple fellow, but
you could tell that he was shrewd, energetic and stubborn. Reporting
on his section at our conferences, he made sense, spoke well of his men,
didn't boast, seemed sure of himself and appeared to know his business.
The day we met, I invited him to spend the night in the little cottage
where I was billeted, and we talked until morning.

'Call me Milya,' he said. 'The priest baptized me Minei. Some name,
eh?—he must have been sore at my old man. Minei Demyanovich,† if
you want the whole works; try and pronounce *that* without a half-liter
of vodka! My father worked behind the plow. He was as poor as they
come, but, you know, in our part of the country, around Poltava, even
the poor didn't go hungry—we lived no worse than most middle-class
people in central Russia.'

Young Milya was put to feeding the pigs. But he managed to finish
school and was one of the boys in his district to join the Komsomol.‡
In time, he became secretary of the village cell.

'And that's how it went. Instructor at the regional committee, then

*The Seventh Section of the Political Department was responsible for propa-
ganda and psychological warfare against the enemy and indoctrination of selected
enemy war prisoners.

†Demyanovich: the patronymic, derived from his father's name, Demyan. The
formal mode of address in Russia is usually by the first name and patronymic.

‡The Communist Youth.

section head, first one place, then another, then into the secretariat. You remember the change of Party cadres in 1937.'* By 1939 he was secretary of the Lvov Party committee. 'Then the war broke out.'

We lay in the dark, smoking, talking about the war, about our lives, our families.

'For a long time,' he told me, 'I didn't have any—you know what I mean—personal life. Regional committee, inspection trips around the villages, plenums, conferences. ... When I became secretary I was entitled to an apartment, but who was going to take care of it? I worked so hard I'd often go to sleep without taking my clothes off—sometimes just sitting at my desk. Even so, I was a young man. Girls all around. They know the secretary's a bachelor, so they stick to me like flies. But I couldn't screw around; I was a public figure, and you know how it is in the provinces—everyone knows everything you're up to. Then they appointed me first secretary in another region. I get there, and there's a whole house full of furniture, all for me. But I still eat in a hash house and sleep alone. I decided to get married. But how?

'I didn't have the time for sprucing up and going courting. Besides, you can't marry the first girl that comes along—got to exercise political vigilance, right? But I was tired of my dog's life. So, the very first evening, I decided what to do. I stayed behind at the regional committee office and looked through the personal files of all the girls in the local Komsomol. Well, you know, every file comes with a photograph, so I wasn't choosing blind. It didn't take me long to find what I was looking for. She was a typist in the producers' cooperative—belonged to the co-op cell. Résumé suitable: parents were poor, family record spotless, recommendations good. And not bad-looking either.

'The next day, I ask for her. She comes in, and I can see she's scared. Why does the first secretary want to see her alone, the very first day? I come clean, right away. That's how it is, I say, thus and so. I want to get married, I got all the facts on you, and now I see you'd suit me fine. I haven't got time, you understand, for all that love and romance stuff. I'm not forcing you into anything, of course—I'm putting it to you, comrade to comrade. Think it over. I'll wait until tonight. I'll stay here in this office until nine o'clock. If you decide yes, come.

'I'm looking her over while I'm saying all this, and she really does please me—dusky, clear-eyed, nice figure, and something independent about her, too. She's embarrassed—naturally. I ask her, "Maybe you

*A euphemistic reference to Stalin's great blood purge of the Soviet Communist Party, in which perhaps as many as a million members were arrested, and which struck the Party most heavily in 1937 and 1938.

already have someone you go out with?" She shakes her head, "No." And I say, "If there was anything before now, I don't care; I'm no prude."

'She goes out, quietly. I work all day, run the office, receive people, telephone the area committee, and all the time my heart's in a flutter—will she come or won't she? The day is over, I've sent everyone home, and I'm alone. I can't read anything, can't do anything—just keep looking out the window, which opens on the street. It's getting dark. Well, I say to myself, she's not coming; I'll have to find someone else. And I'm disappointed, sad.

'Suddenly, there she is. I see her from far away. She's walking as though her legs are made of lead. Stops, walks on, stops again. I pull the window curtains open wider, to make sure she'll see my light's on, and I break out in a sweat.

'She enters the front door, and it takes her the longest time to get to my office. I want to rush out to her, but I control myself—I must put myself on the proper footing with my wife from the word "go." Then she knocks on my door, softly, so softly. I'm riveted to the chair, but my heart, as they say, is like a calf's tail. Then, calmly, sedately: "Come in." She comes in, all pale, and I can see the tears in her eyes. I get up from my chair and, without saying a word, I hug her so fiercely and kiss her so hard, smack on the lips, that she almost faints. And the next day she moves in, and we go and get registered, everything right and proper, but no wedding ceremony—I don't go for that nonsense.

'And would you believe it, she was a virgin. Hot-blooded she was, and over twenty, and a good-looker, but a virgin all the same. Maybe it's prejudice on my part, a residue of a bygone era, as they say, but I was glad. And we've been happy together ever since. She stopped working—there was the house to take care of, and we had two sons. But I made sure she didn't fall behind culturally and politically—I brought home newspapers and books, and she went to meetings and political sessions. Now she's back at work in the evacuation program, and because of that they've taken her into the Party.'

He recounted all this with barely concealed pride, as though to say, 'There, that's how real people arrange their personal lives.' He was certainly different from our crowd, I thought, but none the worse for that. We became friends.

Our first clash was over Wilms.

Dieter Wilms was a pilot in the German air reconnaissance. He was shot down over Leningrad at the outset of the war and parachuted right into the Summer Garden. In prison camp he became an anti-Fascist. They sent him to Krasnogorsk for political reeducation, and he came to us as a representative of the National Committee for Free Germany.* He was young, intelligent and brave, with a long face and fair hair and had a Prussian training-school precision that he had applied to a painstaking mastery of the fundamentals of Communism. In the company of women he became soft and tender and would gaze dreamily into the distance.

The National Committee was regarded highly in Moscow as the nucleus of a future German anti-Fascist front. It was essential that the committee win over the trust of the German troops. We were to see to it that any leaflets published at the front in the name of the National Committee be written and edited by Germans and that all radio broadcasts in the committee's name be made by Germans alone. The propaganda conducted by the committee under the black, white and red banner of the Kaiser's Germany was to be free of any foreign flavor. Hence, we could shorten the texts composed by the committee's representatives, but we couldn't edit them.

About the time that Wilms was attached to Zabashtansky's section, Zabashtansky was all fired up about the latest directive from the army's Central Political Administration in Moscow asking for more 'concrete propaganda'—that is, based on specific events and directed at individual units and officers on the enemy side. When one of our German prisoners provided us with some details about the personal lives and relationships of the officers of a German regiment right across the front line, Zabashtansky came up with what he thought was a pretty clever trick. He told Wilms to write a 'personal letter of instructions' to some of those officers—company and battalion commanders—addressing them by name, informing them that we had received their 'reports,' asking whether they had 'carried out our earlier instructions,' and directing them to take their struggle 'out into the open.' A few personal references would lend the letter an air of authenticity; we would make sure that it fell into other hands, and the officers would be discredited. 'We'll let the Gestapo get them in their own sights,' Zabashtansky said. 'It'll weaken their organization.' (The naïve confidence that the Gestapo worked with the same 'sights' as our own security organizations was often the cause of our failures in other more serious and more cleverly planned operations of diversionary propaganda.)

*The committee, which was comprised of German officers and soldiers captured by the Russians, and of German exiles in the U.S.S.R., was formed under Soviet auspices in Moscow in 1943.

Wilms refused to write the letter, saying that the ruse wouldn't work and would only serve to discredit the National Committee. Zabashtansky was furious; he wrote the text himself and had it translated by his interpreter, a young Jewish girl from Belorussia. The poor woman was under the impression that the German language was identical to Yiddish, differing only in pronunciation and some points of grammar. Wilms refused to sign the translation. Zabashtansky made it an order. Wilms objected that he was not Zabashtansky's subordinate. Zabashtansky cussed him out for a Fascist and had him arrested.

I was sent to smooth things over. Wilms was released, and I told Zabashtansky what I thought about the whole affair—and not too diplomatically, either. He didn't put up much of an argument, but he was bitterly offended by my attitude: How could I side with this bourgeois cub against a Soviet officer, a Party member, and a friend? He spoke sadly and solemnly of the danger of losing one's 'vigilance' in dealing with these 'so-called anti-Fascist' Germans and of forgetting the distinction between them and our own people.

We remained friends. I had come to regard him as a true 'son of the people, a soldier of the Party risen to the rank of officer'—as, aping Stalin, we used to put it. Sometimes, hearing him expatiate in hackneyed phrases or intone words like 'Party,' 'Motherland,' 'Bolshevik ideology,' 'the people' and 'Socialism' in a studiedly emotional quaver, emptying them of their essence, I would feel a sudden revulsion, and the thought would occur: Is he putting on an act? Is he just a coarse, wily careerist? But I would dismiss these doubts as the product of that accursed skepticism of the intelligentsia; I would reprove myself again for my penchant for intellectualizing and for complicating the obvious, all from a want of 'healthy class instinct' and 'party spirit.' The ability to see everything—theory and practice, the past and the present, others and oneself—precisely as required by the Party at any given moment; the ability to think and act only in the interests of the Party under any and all circumstances—that was 'Bolshevik partyness,' as we called it. This 'partyness' was an almost mystical concept. The indispensable prerequisites were iron discipline and faithful observance of all the rituals of Party life. By the end of the 1930s a membership registration office had become a holy of holies and losing your Party card had become a mortal sin. To me, at the time, all this made eminent sense.

Zabashtansky was the very embodiment of that 'partyness.' He would remark, as though in passing, that there were, of course, people who were educated, even learned, who knew foreign languages, history and literature, and had read more Marx than he, having spent all their time studying. They had worn out the seats of their pants sitting at their desks, though they hadn't earned the money to buy those pants or even their bread and butter. But he—he had pulled his own weight since he was a boy, and he had served the Party: in the purge of the kulaks, the collectivization program, the five-year plans, the struggle with the Party's enemies. So he didn't envy even the most educated members of the intelligentsia: The experience he had accumulated was the equivalent of universities, maybe even academies, a kind of education you couldn't get sitting behind a desk. I couldn't help rising to the bait—explaining that though I had spent much of my time studying, I had paid for my own pants and had also done my bit in the collectivization program and the five-year plans. But I objected mainly to assert myself; in my heart of hearts I agreed that he, with his class origins, had an invaluable advantage over me. Those very qualities of his that grated on me, I told myself, were part and parcel of his straightforwardness, his common touch.

One day he dropped in on our section. Our field kitchen was in a ravine, and he and I sat on a slope, eating out of pots. I said something about Wilms, and Zabashtansky flared up.

'He's a rat, a Fascist! He's the enemy, the son of a bourgeois and a bourgeois himself, and German besides. Use him, then get rid of him—that's what I say!'

Just then Wilms walked up to us, and Zabashtansky, with hardly a pause, exclaimed, 'Ah, Dieter, hello! *Guten Tag, lieber Genosse, wie geht's?*' He held out his hand expansively, with a big smile. Wilms was pleased: the major who had him arrested admitting that he had been wrong, and so naturally, without any more fuss.

When Wilms moved off, I said, 'Well, Milya, you're quite an actor.'

'You've got to be,' he said. 'The enemy is treacherous. You can't let him know you're on to him. Better let him think we're fools—we'll catch him quicker that way.'

That summer, when we began encircling the German armies in Belorussia, I was assigned to Zabashtansky's section and put in charge of a group equipped with two loudspeaker systems. Two representatives of the National Committee for Free Germany, Dieter Wilms and a man named Hans Ries, joined us, each with a Soviet officer attached. We went off on our own, setting up one loudspeaker in the woods and urging the Germans to surrender. They would come out one at a time or in small groups, and we would send them to the rear without guard, with a note identifying them as German prisoners heading for the assembly point.

But in a few places there were pockets of enemy resistance, with tanks and heavy artillery, and we ran into one near the village of Drachevka, north of the Minsk highway. We played some somber music, and Wilms and Ries spoke over the loudspeakers, but there were no deserters—only, from time to time, cannon and mortar fire from the wooded strongpoint.

After one of these barrages, the captain in charge of one of the loud-speakers told me that his equipment was out of order. No, it hadn't been hit—it was simply malfunctioning. It had struck me earlier that the captain was overly solicitous of the safety of his gear; but I didn't know anything about these machines, and so I couldn't see for myself if he was telling the truth.

It was evening, and we drove into the village, exhausted. Hardly touching our food, we collapsed on the straw-covered floor of a large hut and fell asleep.

Just before dawn, Wilms and one of our majors shook me awake. The major was shouting, 'The Germans are here—in the village! Our vehicles are leaving without us!'

Out in the street, we caught up with our loudspeaker bus. Groups of soldiers passed us, running; horse-drawn transport carts clattered by; motor transports raced through the melee. From behind them came the thud of hand grenades and the chatter of automatic weapons. Wilms grabbed an abandoned submachine gun, lay down on the fender of our bus, and opened up toward the sound of firing.

We got out of the village to a line of defense at the edge of a nearby wood. The firing had ceased. We formed a party—the major who had awakened me, another officer, several soldiers, and myself—to go back and reconnoiter.

On the road to the village everything was still. Here and there we saw traces of panic—bags, sacks of grain, an overturned cart, several discarded rifles. The village was empty. We crept, bent double, along the sides of the houses. Suddenly I saw a sentry marching back and forth before a barn, a middle-aged soldier with a red mustache, wearing a formless army cap and a ragged coat. I approached him.

'What's going on? Who put you here?'

'What do you mean—who? The commander of my unit.'

'And where's your commander?'

He pointed with his glistening submachine gun. 'There—at the edge of the village, by the guns.'

'Did you run far?'

'We didn't run at all.' And, with a show of pride, 'We're the artillery.'

I flushed with discomfiture. We had just been breaking our necks to get out of there.

'And where are the Germans?'

'Who the hell knows? They came from there and tried to find the road. We gave 'em something to light their cigarettes with.'

We reached the other side of the village. He was right. One artillery unit had thrown back an armored German column. Some of the captured Germans said that they had tried to break through to the Minsk highway, not knowing it was already in Russian hands.

It took me almost two hours to reassemble our group. One man, Captain D., was missing. The officers in charge of our vehicles made excuses for running away. 'Captain D. ran out, shouting, "Beat it! We're surrounded!" We thought it was an order.' It turned out that Captain D., who put on someone else's boots in the rush, hadn't stopped until he got to headquarters, where he complained that he had been ditched in the panic.

We got back to headquarters the next day, and I gave Zabashtansky a full report. I was a bit caustic about the overcautious captain with the loudspeaker. I suggested that we look into the mysterious damage to his equipment.

'You're wrong to be suspicious,' Zabashtansky said. 'He spent the whole war under fire, so he's cautious. With you it's the other way around. The men say you go swaggering where you shouldn't be, to be closer to the enemy. That's old hat, you know. All right during the Civil War, when we were combating indiscipline, but in this war you should be protecting our equipment and not sticking your neck out. All I have in my section is one loudspeaker system and you stuck it right on the front line. That captain was right. He was acting out of a sense of responsibility, not cowardice.'

I felt reproved. I knew how frightened I was each time I heard that ominous rumble or that cross between a whistle and a roar, each time the earth shuddered with explosions and the sky overhead was rent by the heart-stopping whine of a bomb loosed from an enemy plane. And to hide my fear from my comrades and from myself, I had to curse all the more strongly, tell stupid jokes, do something definite, like running up to a tree or a ditch or a dugout or, if I was broadcasting under fire, repeating each sentence several times. I had acquired a reputation for bravery on the Northwestern Front, and, fearing to lose it, I often exposed myself unnecessarily to enemy fire.

It was childish, of course, testing oneself that way—not the quiet, prudent courage of real soldiers. Knowing all this, and silently agreeing with Zabashtansky, I let the matter drop. But Captain D.'s behavior could not be condoned. His cowardice made him dangerous to be around in times of battle. I, and others as well, said that he ought to be court-martialed—for one thing, he had been responsible for Wilms, who at all costs had to be kept out of enemy hands; but if trying him was going too far, he should be discharged for desertion under fire. I addded that I would willingly go on a dangerous mission with Wilms who had shown his true worth more than once, but would never agree to go with Captain D.

Zabashtansky was pained. 'How can you talk that way—comparing a Soviet officer, a Communist, with a German, a bourgeois, a Fascist! How will it look—just think! D. is bad and Wilms is good. Our officer is cowardly, and that damned Fritz is brave. Does that sound like something we would say?'

In the end, Captain D. was simply transferred from Zabashtansky's section, and from the Political Department, into regular army ranks.

4

GENERAL OKOROKOV, Chief of Political Administration for the Second
Belorussian Front, called me in for a 'private talk.' The general was
unhappy with the head of the Political Department of the 50th Army.

'He's so insipid. No initiative. I talked to Moscow about it, and they
didn't have anyone to send me. They told me to promote one of our
own men.'

I defended our department head, but without much conviction. He
was a decent old fellow, but there was no denying that he was limited
and lacking in initiative. When the general asked who I thought could
take his place, I suggested Zabashtansky. I thought that was quite
clever of me: Zabashtansky was my friend and would be considerate of
my views. Besides, I really regarded him as being among the best, if not
the best, of the various possible candidates.

I'm sure that the general consulted others as well; still, when
Zabashtansky got the appointment, and a promotion to colonel, at
the end of summer, I had reason to feel that it wasn't without my
help.

Our next clash came soon afterward.

I had written several leaflets addressed to the civilian population of
East Prussia—the *Volksturmer*, the young people, the women who
were digging trenches and antitank pits. We could see them digging
from our observation posts; our pilots reported that tens of thousands
of civilians were working along the Polish-German border.

The leaflets weren't printed. Zabashtansky said, 'Forget it. We and
the Poles are dividing East Prussia between us, so we aren't issuing any
promissory notes to anyone. No addresses to the civilian population.
Our business is with the front, not with the enemy's rear. And don't
argue. This is an affair of high-level diplomacy. Suppose we write

something and it turns out to be a diplomatic blunder?' I argued that the German rear was shakier than the front—just as in 1918, when uprisings broke out in Berlin and other cities while discipline in front-line units was still unimpaired. I argued that we didn't have to promise anything except peace and respect for civilian life. But there was no budging him. It wasn't up to us to decide these matters, he said, hinting meaningfully at a directive from above.

Two weeks later, after returning from a routine mission, I learned of an angry telegram from the army's Central Political Administration in Moscow, taking Zabashtansky to task for not initiating any propaganda 'into East Prussia' and sending him texts of leaflets addressed to the German population. Like most of the material written at that level, the leaflets were verbose and heavy with bureaucratic rhetoric. I pointed this out at a conference, saying that we needed livelier, more effective texts—and that we had them ready.

Zabashtansky interrupted; he was furious. 'I see you're gloating again because our section got it in the neck. Instead of gloating, you should be doing a better job yourself.'

'What do you mean—gloating? You're making that up!'

'I am not making anything up. I am giving you an order as your superior officer, inasmuch as the Party and the high command have placed me in charge here. So just relax, and don't make any speeches, and don't try to show us you're smarter than we are. We are not going to print your cheerful little leaflets; it's not our job to console or entertain the Fritzes. We have texts cleared by Moscow, and that's what we'll use. And we're not going to discuss it any further!'

He went onto something else. Yet, a minute later, he turned to me amicably and complimented me on my work on a recent assignment.

Not long afterward I accompanied Zabashtansky on a trip and fell ill. Dosed with aspirin and a glass of vodka with pepper, I lay, covered with a sheepskin, in the same room where Zabashtansky was having supper with the head of the Political Department of the 49th Army. They asked me if I wanted another drink; I didn't answer.

'He's asleep,' our host said.

Zabashtansky started talking about me, obviously for my benefit—he didn't believe that I was asleep. 'Take Kopelev, now. A difficult fellow. Egotistic, and with intellectual, anarchistic tendencies, and he doesn't like me. He doesn't trust me and he doesn't like me, but I like him. And not just for his work. He's first-class in his work, you know. Hot-tempered, of course, and gets carried away, but he knows his business, he's educated, he's experienced, and he tries—he tries with all his heart and soul. But it's not only for this, you understand, that I like and respect him as a friend. But he doesn't like or respect me.'

Did he want me to respond, to object? How obvious, I thought. I didn't wish him ill, and I still thought that, as our new chief, he was the lesser of various possible evils. But I could no longer be his friend. And I certainly couldn't simulate friendship. I couldn't even tell him how good I thought he was in some ways. Considering our strained relationship, it would seem like obsequiousness.

Zabashtansky had remarked on several occasions that he wondered how Wilms knew the locations of the command posts of some of our divisions, as well as their generals' names. Once, accompanying Zabashtansky to 50th Army headquarters, Wilms even led the way. 'He shows off in front of me,' Zabashtansky fumed. ' "There's the rocket battery, and there's General So-and-so's command post." '

'What's surprising about that?' I objected. 'He's served in those divisions. Those generals invited him to their quarters, drank with him. They were probably curious—a Fritz, but he's on our side.'

'How can you be so sure that he's not spying, collecting information, that he won't sell us out?'

'That's absurd. Wilms is no spy. If only because he doesn't hide the fact that he's well informed—he makes a point of it.'

'There—that's just what he wants you to think. And Hans, that other German—he was a real Fascist big shot. He was a political general in their army. And you leave it to him to arrange everything in our school. He goes out with Wilms; they study all our positions—'

'Look, Hans hasn't gone anywhere for a long time. And I haven't forgotten who he is. And I don't trust him all that much. And he doesn't arrange anything in the school.'

'Well, there's no getting through to you. For every word I say, you come back with ten. But I'll give my right arm if these Fascists aren't making fools of us.'

'All right, then ship them back to Moscow, if you feel that way.'

'All right, let's ship them off.'

The next day they sent Wilms and Hans R. off to the rear, and Zabashtansky, as though casually, showed me the accompanying report. There, over his signature, were the words: 'There are reasons to believe that they may have engaged in the collection of espionage material.'

I couldn't control myself any longer. This was not simply a malicious lie; a report like that could be a death warrant. I told Zabashtansky that he had no grounds for such accusations; that this was baseness, not vigilance; that he should simply say he was transferring them from the front because they knew too much. If he insisted on sending this slanderous report, I would consider it my duty as a Communist to disavow it, and I would write to Manuilsky and Burtsev and Weinert.*

He gave way, leaving it to me to write the report. As a precaution, I gave Wilms a personal letter to Weinert and another letter to a well-placed Moscow friend describing in detail how well and bravely Wilms had conducted himself in difficult circumstances and how conscientiously he and Hans R. had performed their work.

A month went by. Zabashtansky went to the All-Army Conference in Moscow and returned in a very good mood. By this time our relationship was confined to official business, but he was affable when we met.

At a meeting of our section, he said that we were thought highly of at the Central Political Administration. Our leaflets, he recounted, were praised. 'Oh, yes,' he added, as though in passing, 'they also commented on our vigilance. Wilms has been arrested as a spy. As for Hans, they haven't got the goods on him yet, but he's been expelled from the National Committee and sent to a penal camp.'

Everyone looked at me.

'Where did they find out about them?' someone asked. 'Here, at the front?'

Zabashtansky gave some vague reply to the effect that there were still things to be cleared up.

A few weeks later, we received a visit from Major General Burtsev of the Central Political Administration. From his adjutant I learned that Wilms was working on the editorial board of the National Committee newspaper and Hans was a committee representative in an officers' camp. Zabashtansky had invented the whole story.

The next time I saw Zabashtansky with others present, I said, also as if in passing, 'Comrade Colonel, you were incorrectly informed about Wilms and Hans. Burtsev's adjutant tells me something quite different.'

'Then he's the one who has been incorrectly informed,' Zabashtansky

*Dmitri Manuilsky, a high Soviet official in the Comintern, the organization of world Communist parties that was formed in 1919 and disbanded in 1943; Major General Burtsev, then head of the Seventh Section of the Central Political Administration; Erich Weinert, a well-known German Communist poet who became head of the National Committee for Free Germany.

said. 'Or maybe he has reasons not to tell you what isn't supposed to be revealed.'

'He told me where Wilms and Hans are working in the most specific terms. Why should he lie to us? Why would he be heaping praise on a couple of apprehended spies who have already been arrested?'

Zabashtansky's eyes narrowed. A vicious note crept into his voice. 'So you're still defending your Fritz friends, are you? And you still want to show us you're smarter than anyone else. All right, now—enough of this conversation. I told you what I know to be so. And it's not for you to be checking up on me.'

'I am not defending anything except the truth. I don't have any Fritz friends, and I'm not checking up on you.'

'I think I said quite clearly that this conversation is at an end. Do you understand military discipline?'

# 5

IN MY very first conversation with Zabashtansky as the new department chief, I told him that I felt he should know that First Lieutenant Lyuba N., one of our instructors, was, so to speak, my wife. True, I had a family, which I had no intention of abandoning, and Lyuba knew about it. She herself had a husband to whom she would return after the war. But here at the front we loved each other, and I hoped he would keep that in mind in drawing up battle groups and making assignments and housing arrangements.

Zabashtansky gave me a sidelong glance. 'You said yourself the main thing was the good of the cause?'

'I said so, and I believe it. But Lyuba and I work very well together.'

'All right, I'll keep it in mind, though I don't like these front-line families. But, of course, for you I'll make an exception.'

Lyuba and I had been together for more than a year, starting with the Northwestern Front. She had graduated from an institute just before the war and had joined the volunteers as a machine gunner. When all the women in her unit were transferred to the medical corps, she cried and made a scene; but she quickly got used to her new work, and rescued several dozen wounded men while under fire. When they heard that she spoke German, they made her an announcer on a loud-speaker truck. In February 1943 she was made an instructor. She fought against being sent back to the rear but was won over by promotion to the rank of officer. Intelligent, brave, proud and more than a little vain, Lyuba cultivated the manner of a front-line veteran, which contrasted quaintly with her slight frame, freckled face, and two locks of hair that stuck out stubbornly from under her cap. Among friends, when she didn't have to keep up appearances, she could laugh and prance about like a child, but she could also be thoughtful and calculating; she knew how to turn her meek, imploring gray eyes, with their fluffy eyelashes, on stern quartermasters and uncouth generals, importuning them for gas, or for extra pairs of felt boots or sheepskin jackets or vodka for the men.

The head of the army unit in which she was serving in February 1943 shot himself. It was rumored that they had had an affair and that he had grown jealous of certain higher-ups. Lyuba went around for several weeks as though ill, hardly speaking to anyone, hardly eating. Finally, she was assigned to me. I tried to distract her with work. Taking me gradually into her confidence, she told me they'd been no more than friends. She showed me letters to her from his wife, and letters from her husband with greetings to the unit commander. It wasn't long before we became intimate, though in the beginning there was no question of love between us. I told her that since we had to work together day and night, we couldn't avoid sleeping together, so why put it off?—perhaps we would be killed together by the same shell.

At that time, the spring of 1943, people were quite relaxed about such things at the front. A year earlier, front-line affairs had been considered a disgrace—the guilty parties were punished and separated, and the initials P. P. Zh., for field-camp wife (a play on the initials of a sub-machine gun, P. P. Sh.), became current as a term of opprobrium. Then a rumor went the rounds: Stalin had said, 'I don't understand why they're punishing the commanding officers for sleeping with women. After all, it's quite natural for a man to sleep with a woman. Now if a man sleeps with a man, *that's* unnatural—he *should* be punished.'

At that point, all persecution of 'natural' relations ceased. Many commanders suddenly acquired 'front-line girl friends,' which sounded better than P. P. Zh. Some generals quickly came to regard all nurses, waitresses and women typists and radio operators as fair game. A new dolled-up female type sprang up—heavy makeup, elaborate hairdos, leather jackets, shiny boots, coquettish caps or fur hats and fitted sheepskin coats. The troops regarded them with a kind of good-humored spite, sometimes with distaste, but mostly with plain envy.

The October holiday came around,* and we all assembled at administration headquarters. There was a meeting of Party members, and General Okorokov made a speech. He mentioned me in passing, saying that I had done a good job and that it was time to cancel the reprimand I had been given in the spring 'for consorting with priests.' Then he

*The anniversary of the October Revolution of 1917 in which the Bolsheviks came to power in Russia.

added, 'Now some of you around here have been saying that his cousin is a Trotskyist and that he was in with him in nineteen twenty-eight. So I just want to tell you that the Political Administration has known about this for a long time. We knew it when we accepted him as candidate-member of the Party. He didn't hide anything. We've known him since the beginning of the war for his military and political work, and we know his shortcomings. He's a bit unrestrained when it comes to discipline, but we are familiar with his political outlook, and we regard all this talk about his cousin as completely unjustified. It's time to stop it, comrades.'

I was sitting on a bench in front of Zabashtansky. Turning around, I saw an intent look in his eyes.

I said, 'Who do you suppose is the bastard who's been exerting himself so on my behalf? I wouldn't mind finding out and punching him in the snoot.'

He didn't reply.

In the evening there was a party. We drank, sang and danced, and Zabashtansky proposed that we continue the festivities at another village five kilometers away. Only the old 'deserving' officers were asked to come along. The idea of being sifted at the boss's whim— 'This one is deserving, that one isn't; this one's an officer, that one is rank and file'—didn't sit right, especially on a national holiday, and I remember saying something about it, and probably none too tactfully, since I'd had quite a lot to drink.

Zabashtansky frowned. 'You're always coming up with something, and it's always against the leadership. You know, there's quite a bit of petit bourgeois anarchism in you.'

I started to argue; Lyuba drew me away, telling me that I shouldn't make an issue of everything. Then she went off in Zabashtansky's car. The rest of us—officers and soldiers, drivers, typesetters, printers— went on with the party.

Two hours later Zabashtansky and his group returned; Lyuba was not among them. 'You see,' Zabashtansky tweaked me, 'you wouldn't come with us, so your girl friend stayed on there. The colonel took her to his place. She'll probably be there all night now. Yes, my friend, these women—they know how to get even.'

I was muddled with drink, and his words stung. The colonel was a fine figure of a man—polished, pomaded, perfumed, self-satisfied, and an ass. I started drinking more and more. I danced, and sang sentimental folk songs with Zabashtansky, exchanging toasts and pronouncing a curse on all women.

Suddenly Lyuba was back—running toward us, without her overcoat, one shoulder board half torn off, and gasping for breath. 'I ran all the way, through the woods, through the mud. It was dark; I was frightened. Why didn't you wait for me, Comrade Colonel?'

Zabashtansky smirked. 'Well, you didn't tell me you'd be coming back.'

Lyuba's presence made me even angrier, somehow. I drank and danced even more feverishly. When I finally left, she caught up with me in the street. I tore loose from her with a curse.

The next day I tried to avoid her, but she forced me to hear her out. It seemed that Zabashtansky had sat her down next to the colonel. When they were ready to leave, the colonel invited them all to his place, to listen to his records. She declined, but Zabashtansky said to her, 'Now, why? The colonel is inviting all of us—why are you being so rude to him?'

They all walked to the colonel's house, but when they got there Zabashtansky and another man turned around and went back without saying good-bye. The colonel tried to pull her inside. She wrenched free and ran, leaving her overcoat, which had been thrown over her shoulders, in his hands.

I had to see Zabashtansky the same day about another official trip. He listened to me, looking tense, then said, 'All right, enough. Let's have a chat.'

Whereupon, icy with indignation, I said, 'Comrade Colonel, you are my superior officer. I am your subordinate. Please be good enough to speak to me only on official matters. There can be no question of any further personal relations between us, since I consider you to be a scoundrel.'

He gave me a mild, quizzical look. 'What are you doing—declaring war?'

'There's only one war for any of us—the Great Patriotic War. Don't worry; I'll do my job no worse than before. Of course, it would be better if you transferred me to some other command, or into the reserves—anywhere you wish.'

'People don't leave me that easily. When they go, they go with a bang, and without their Party card.'

'I have never been afraid of threats, and I don't propose to start now.'

'All right. Enough. You're clear on your assignment? You may go.'

We didn't see much of each other after that. By the time I got back, three weeks later, Zabashtansky had transferred Lyuba to Moscow for courses in German.

New Year's Eve. A large house in the village of Byalaya—some sort of school or club—a hall turned into a banquet room, with a long table on the stage for the senior officers. The general and the heads of the various sections seated at the table with their wives and girl friends; Zabashtansky sitting with modest dignity at one of the far ends. The rest of us sat at rows of tables weighed down with pots of potatoes, cabbage and pickles, plates of pork fat and stew, a profusion of bottles. We drank vodka from enamel cups. The general delivered an endless toast to the wisest of the wise, the greatest of all geniuses, the most brilliant of all commanders, the coryphaeus of all the sciences. . . . He kept repeating himself, recalling still other feats and historical achievements credited to the Great Stalin—the routing of the oppositionists, the happiness on the collective farms, the unmasking of the enemies of the people, the conquest of the North Pole, the creation of the mighty army, the creation of industry, the creation of everything that existed. And, once again, the ritual of superlatives—'the greatest of the great, the most beloved, the most clear-sighted, the bravest of the brave. . . .'

We stood, cups in hand, shifting from one foot to the other, trying not to look at one another. At last, the toast: Happy New Year, 1945—the year of final victory! Pandemonium. Our own individual toasts followed. 'To the glorious front-line armies!' someone would shout. 'To the gallant forces in the rear!' another would outshout him. Toasts to this or that branch of the service. Toasts to our general.

Zabashtansky, circulating among the tables, came up to me. 'Let's make up. What is this—comrades in arms squabbling over a woman? Remember the song— "I'm not one to bother with a broad . . ."? Let's be friends, the way we were.'

Really, I thought, my head roaring with drink, was it worth fighting about? Lyuba was in Moscow—probably with another man, or back with her husband. We clinked cups, drank and embraced.

Later, in the small hours, I sat pouring out my soul to Ivan Rozhansky, berating my superiors and myself.

Ivan was stationed in another village, not far from ours. I would go to see him when I felt I had to talk. When we first met, he had struck me as being of a contemplative turn, but passionless. As I came to know him better, I recognized in him the ardent soul of a man in love with the poetic and the profound. Bashful, reticent, skeptical, in complete control of himself, he was in many ways the opposite of me. Floundering in my own hodgepodge of knowledge, grasping at contradictory ideals—Narodnik* and Komsomol, Marxist philosophy and Stalinist pragmatism—trying to be honest and at the same time attain the essence of 'partyness,' I often despaired of my ability to combine all this in one comprehensive system of thought, and grew irritable and angry with myself. With Ivan, I found peace. In his company, my fretfulness gave way to the things that were eternal—literature, music, painting, the reasoning of the philosophers, the discoveries of science. He knew and loved everything I knew and loved—the poetry of Tyutchev, Rilke, Pasternak, the great symphonies, the famous canvases —but he also knew what I didn't know. He would show me the constellations of the stars and explain the theory of relativity and the indeterminate equation, speaking slowly, with an occasional stammer, pausing and picking simple words I could understand. And at such moments all the generals and marshals, and all the Orders of the Day that came from the mouth of Stalin, and all the speeches of Hitler, and all the doings of the Zabashtanskys of this world no longer seemed so important.

Toward the middle of January, Lyuba returned. The authorities in the Moscow language school were annoyed with us for sending her there to study German, when she spoke German better than many of the staff. Zabashtansky got a written rebuke. He put it down to some machination on my part.

*A member of Narodnaya Volya (The People's Will), a populist movement of urban intellectuals, formed in 1879, which believed in creating socialism on the basis of the old Russian peasant commune.

# 6

THE OFFENSIVE began. The German front on the left bank of the Narev was ripped open within hours.

We in the Political Department improvised a new role for the men enrolled in our anti-Fascist school. 'Commissars of panic,' we dubbed them. They were to pretend to be German soldiers who had lost contact with their units or who were trying to break out of encirclement. Their job was to spread rumors about the Soviet advance, to yell, 'The Russians have broken through!' 'Tanks behind us!' and the like at opportune moments, and generally to spread confusion in the German ranks.

I spent several days with the advancing armor, selecting fresh candidates for this operation from among the German prisoners. The first prerequisite was that they still be unshorn: our army made a practice of shaving their heads as soon as they were captured.

I was accompanied on this mission by Alexander Belyaev, the commanding officer at the school. A government functionary who had spent most of the war at the rear, he did not know a word of German and left all the training and educational work to Ivan Rozhansky and me, relieving us of the administrative chores, for which he seemed to have a bent. We gathered a sizable batch of prisoners, picking up three wounded Germans along the way. I thought we'd turn them over to some field hospital on the way back; but all the hospitals we passed were full, and I had to take them to our own base. Belyaev, half-asleep when we reached the school after driving all night, grumbled about something or other. I had just spent a week almost without sleep in the thick of battle, and his complaining voice struck a raw nerve. That was the first time we had ever had words, so I didn't give it any importance.

The very same day, after I left the village, Belyaev had the three wounded prisoners executed. I learned of it only later. 'They were Fascists,' Belyaev was to explain. 'They showed anti-Soviet attitudes.'

My search for suitable, unshaven Germans continued. North of Ciechanow, the hills rolled gently on, under a thin coverlet of snow spotted by rust-colored grass and intersected by dark, smooth roads. Now and then we drove by farms or small towns, with their dull-red and yellowish tiled roofs. The roads were filled with tanks, motor vehicles, artillery, infantry and horse-drawn transport, all moving north. Hordes of prisoners plodded in the opposite direction. We were advancing faster than anyone had expected; our tanks and motorized infantry were already crushing the German defenses on the East Prussian border.

When I returned from my new trip and reported to Zabashtansky, he said he had just been informed that some of our Cossack divisions had entered East Prussia and were advancing rapidly. I asked that in assigning me there, he send Lyuba along with me. I presented every argument I could think of; I almost pleaded. He was courteous, but said, 'The command doesn't think that's the place for women—not yet anyway. Go with Belyaev; you're friends, aren't you?'

We rode in a Ford truck—Belyaev, the driver (a middle-aged fellow with the fidgety manner of a shady operator), and me. In the back of the truck sat my new orderly, a short-legged, broad-shouldered forty-year-old from Siberia named Sidorych.

We entered East Prussia in broad daylight. There were only a few vehicles on the road. At the border, marked by a little bridge over a snow-covered ravine, we caught up with a soldier of our horse-drawn transport, mounted on a scraggly nag, his puttees half-unwound, his shoes caked with mud. A suitcase filled to bursting was held together by a rope; bits of colored cloth straggled out of a large sack at his back; and a bundle of hay wrapped in a poncho completed his baggage. A most unprepossessing figure in a wrinkled overcoat and a hat with earflaps, riding calmly along, not hurrying, not surprised by anything. Riding through East Prussia. An ordinary citizen of Ryazan or Orlov or Moscow, riding through Germany as though the German lines had not stretched to the gates of Leningrad, as though there had been no Stalingrad, no swastika flying on Mount Elbrus. Here he was, riding through Germany—not a Horseman of the Apocalypse, not a hero of a Russian fable, not some legendary figure of the Civil War, but an ordinary transport soldier with his paltry loot, riding along as if nothing had happened.

I tried to express something of this to Belyaev, moved as I was by so palpable a reality, so tangible a token of our victory. Earlier, we had agreed that when we crossed the border, we would mark it in an appropriate fashion. Having established the line on my map, I gave the command: 'This is Germany. Everyone out and relieve yourselves!' It seemed humorous to us, standing in a row by a ditch, solemnizing our entry onto enemy soil.

Our truck rolled along the snow-covered asphalt of the German highway, bordered by neat rows of trees. We picked up five young soldiers who said that they had fallen behind. Belyaev said, 'Let's keep them for a while. After all, this is Germany, and your Sidorych is the only armed protection we have.'

The first Prussian villages, Gross-Koslau and Klein-Koslau, were on fire. The driver had to keep to the middle of the road; on both sides the tile-roofed houses were in flames. A tall tree in front of a burning church smoldered and smoked. No one in sight. For several minutes we drove through a fiery tunnel along a narrow, crooked street. It was suffocatingly hot and rather frightening; we were in a shower of sparks, with burning pieces of wood falling all around us. Belyaev kept shouting, 'Faster! Give it more gas! We'll catch fire!'

We drove into a square. Several transport men were standing near an army cart, having a smoke. We stopped.

'What happened here—a clash?'

'What clash? They took off—couldn't catch up with them. Not a single civilian stayed behind.'

'You mean they mined the town? Set fire to it?'

'Who—the Germans? No, there weren't any mines. It was our guys who set fire to it.'

'Why?'

'Who the hell knows? Just did it, without thinking.'

A mustached soldier said with a kind of indolent bitterness: 'The word is: "This is Germany. So smash, burn, have your revenge." But where do we spend the night afterward? Where do we put the wounded?'

Another of the men stared at the flames. 'All that stuff going to waste. Back home, where I come from, everyone's naked and barefoot these days. And here we are, burning without rhyme or reason.'

Belyaev spoke up sententiously. 'The Fritzes have plundered all over the world. That's why they've got so much. They burned down everything in our country, and now we're doing the same in theirs. We don't have to feel sorry for them.'

'No, not for them,' I said. 'For ourselves. Senseless destruction does more damage to us than to them.'

We passed through another burning village. Along the highway we ran into a herd of cows. In those days herds of black-and-white cows strayed, unfed, unmilked, along the roads of East Prussia. I felt a twinge of pity for the Prussian peasants, left not just without cows but without a homeland; for it had already been made clear that we and Poland would take everything for ourselves. My principal reaction, however, remained one of disgust with the senselessness of laying waste to all this property, when back home there were villages where the war had passed like a column of fire, or where, invisibly, from afar, it had sucked out the bread and the blood; where only the women remained to plow the land, hitched to plows like barge haulers; where a piece of sugar was a thing of wonder, and the children, with their enormous eyes and their bluish-white faces, choked and chewed on some kind of mud-black, bitter bread made of the devil only knew what. We talked about this during our first hours in Prussia. Belyaev kept yessing me. Then, catching sight of a black-and-white cow on the highway ahead, he yelled excitedly, 'Go on, hit her! Ride her down!'

The driver bumped the cow's side with the Ford's blunt snout and braked. The cow staggered, bawled, and hobbled awkwardly on three legs across a roadside ditch. Belyaev pushed past me out of the truck. 'Come on! Shoot her down! Fire! Roast beef for everyone!'

The five soldiers in the back jumped out. Sidorych eased himself down unhurriedly. They began firing. A black cow on a snowy field fifty paces away is an easy target. But she just wouldn't fall down. And when she did fall on her side, she kept raising her head. They finished her off at point-blank range. Then they fell to quarreling on the best way to skin the carcass.

It was both ludicrous and sickening. We had finally reached enemy territory—to go cow hunting! Belyaev listened to me but brushed me aside. He had come to adopt the patronizing tones of a superior. You're a queer fish, he seemed to be saying, an intellectual; but I'm the practical, down-to-earth kind, and I understand things you wouldn't understand.

# 7

IT WAS evening when we drove into Neidenburg, a small town with tree-lined streets. The place was in flames. Again, the work of our own men. On a side street, by a garden fence, lay a dead old woman. Her dress was ripped; a telephone receiver reposed between her scrawny thighs. They had apparently tried to ram it into her vagina.

Soldiers moved leisurely from house to house, singly and in groups, some of them with bundles and suitcases. One of them explained that the dead woman was a spy. 'They got her by a telephone booth. Why fool around?'

Belyaev was becoming livelier by the hour, issuing brisk commands with an intrepid air. Drawn to the most prosperous-looking homes, he almost came to grief under a falling beam while dragging a huge tapestry of a bucolic scene à la Watteau out of a burning house. In another house he ordered the soldiers to take a huge mahogany grand-father clock; in a third house, a piano; and, here, there and everywhere, all the clothes and bed linen he could find.

I didn't raise any objections: the houses had been abandoned, and many of them had been ransacked. We trampled on broken dishes and heaps of belongings. I was attracted by rows of books and by the desks. In the house of a local judge I came upon a fine library: bookcases to the ceiling; one bookcase all philosophy; another all history; a third, law; a bookcase of 'Napoleoniana'; another, of 'Russiana'—hundreds of books, from Lomonosov to Sholokhov, in German translations; a bookcase of 'German émigré literature'—Thomas and Heinrich Mann, Feuchtwanger, Leonhard Frank. A collection of records: classical music, the speeches of Kaiser Wilhelm, Ebert, Hindenburg, Hitler. In the judge's desk, kept neatly in paper folders, were letters from his son, a war prisoner in Canada.

I knew that the library and the records should be saved. But Belyaev was using the men to cart away the piano and other booty. I finally talked him into having part of the library loaded onto our truck.

Our assignment on this trip, as set forth in the order log, read: 'To conduct political intelligence, to explore the political attitudes and morale of the enemy populace, to uncover the activities of the Fascist underground.' Our first order of business, therefore, was to talk to some German civilians. Our first day in Prussia was ending, and the only civilians I had seen were a few corpses.

In the middle of the street a group of soldiers surround an old woman in a long, threadbare plush overcoat, a mangy boa and a hat wound about with some kind of shawl. I get out of the truck.

The soldiers are good-humored. 'A crazy woman! Keeps babbling: '*Soldat, Soldat, gut, gut.*'

I address her in German. She looks frightened.

'I'm looking for my daughter. . . . My daughter is with the little children, and I have all the ration cards. . . . They're hungry.' She and her daughter are widows, she says. The daughter's husband was killed in Africa. 'We are very poor.'

'Where is your house? I'll take you there,' I offer.

She starts walking, hurriedly, casting frightened glances from side to side. 'We are poor,' she mumbles. 'We don't have anything. My daughter is sick.'

The old woman totters along the street, tripping up in her long overcoat, pressing her handbag to her breast. Our truck eases up to us, and Belyaev leans out. 'Hey! What are you bothering with her for? She's probably crazy.'

'But this is our first civilian in East Prussia!'

The old woman turns a corner, then another. Belyaev yells, 'She's leading you somewhere! She's probably a plant! Shoot her and have done with it!'

She stops before a house with a little garden. In the gathering darkness I make out several of our soldiers and a sentry at the gate.

'This is where my daughter lives.'

The sentry tells me that there are no civilians in this house, or anywhere nearby. The old woman can't seem to understand that her daughter isn't there, and keeps begging us to let her go in. I explain that the house has been turned into a military headquarters. She resumes prating about her daughter, the ration cards, the children, and starts off, back to the center of town.

Belyaev leaps out of the truck. 'She's giving us the runaround! She's a spy!'

He grabs her handbag. The old woman gives a terrified squeal. Belyaev empties her handbag. The flashlight reveals a sorry jumble: photographs, spools of thread. . . .

'She's a spy,' he declares and takes out his pistol.

I shout at him: 'Are you out of your mind?' I grab his arm, argue, curse, cajole. There's a commotion behind us. One of the soldiers gives the old woman a push. She collapses on a bank of snow; there is a shot. She gives a rabbity whimper; the soldier fires his carbine a second time, and a third. The black bundle in the snow is still. The soldier, a mere boy, bends down looking for something—for her boa.

I bellow, 'What are you doing, you son of a bitch?'

I turn on Belyaev. What to do now? Hit him between his stupid eyes? At this point I am not even indignant, just filled with a sense of helpless loathing.

He murmurs soothingly, 'Come, now, don't take on so. Are you going to turn against your own people over a lousy German crone? To hell with her. She was bound to go, one way or another. If that kid hadn't done it, somebody else would have.'

We ride the night streets in the flickering glow of fires: a crimson, sinister, fevered light. We are told at a command post that there are some German civilians in a house by a lake. We find it—a one-story home with a garden and a brick wall. Three of us enter—Belyaev, Sidorych and I. It is dark. We hear a noise, and Belyaev hops back. I am scared, too, and pull out my pistol. '*Wer da?* Come out with your hands up!'

A click as Sidorych releases the safety catch of his submachine gun. Silence, then the same noise: a moan. Belyaev whispers, 'Don't go in. It's a trap.'

I turn on the flashlight and open another door. A kitchen. Empty. Sidorych keeps up with me. In the next room there are a table with a clutter of dishes, a big bed in a niche. My flashlight picks out a woman with a fur hat, covered with blankets and quilts; a white face, eyes closed. She is moaning hoarsely, spasmodically.

I raise the covers. She's apparently wearing an overcoat. Blood on the sheets. A short dagger. Plexiglas. The kind our men make from the Plexiglas off downed aircraft. The blood has collected in puddles. She has been stabbed in the breast and stomach.

Belyaev comes up behind us. 'Let's go. Nothing worthwhile here.'

The rooms show signs of hurried looting. Scattered piles of linen; old clothes; a few books.

'We can't just leave her here.'

'What are we supposed to do? She'll croak anyway. She's probably a spy like the other one.'

Again, a sense of humiliating helplessness. I can't leave her in this state, in agony, with no one to come to her aid.

'Sidorych, finish her off.' I give the order out of pity and helplessness, craven helplessness. Try to bandage her wounds? Run for the medics? Where will I find them? And will they come? And she has already lost so much blood.

I walk out of the house. Belyaev is saying, 'There now, you did the right thing. You're a man after all.'

There is a short burst behind us. We stand in the yard, smoking. Belyaev worries: 'Where's that Sidorych?' He shouts for him. Sidorych comes out carrying a bundle.

'What took you so long?'

'Oh, I spotted these shoes for my old woman. They're worn, but they'll do.'

We stopped for the night in a two-story house occupied by a detachment of army engineers and a 'trophy' squad. We had dinner with three young officers. We helped ourselves to the commandeered food, French cognac and East Prussian liqueur, and fell to arguing.

The booty captain argued in stock newspaper phrases that everything was developing just the way it should. 'Our sacred vengeance . . . And what about what they did to us? Ehrenburg put it well: "Tremble, cutthroat nation!".'

Belyaev ate and drank, occasionally agreeing with the captain. One of the engineers, a first lieutenant, joined me in arguing that we should confine our vengeance to those who deserved it; that not all Germans were Fascists; that you couldn't take vengeance on women, children and old people. But the main thing was that all this pillage was corrupting our own army.

The third officer, a young engineer, his angular face softened by a trace of boyishness, broke in heatedly. 'We're supposed to be a Socialist army! We're supposed to be internationalists!' He turned on the captain. 'How can you talk of vengeance on the German *people*? That's not our ideology—taking vengeance on a whole people! Remember what Comrade Stalin said! "Hitlers come and go. . . ." And don't quote your Ehrenburg at me—he's not a Marxist, and ever since I was in the

Pioneers I have been taught that the workers of all countries are brothers. Marx and Engels were Germans, so were Liebknecht and Telmann; and today among the Germans there are plenty of Communists and plenty of good ordinary people. It's impossible for a whole nation to be Fascist. Only people who are Fascists themselves can think so!'

He paced back and forth in his agitation. 'Pillage and rape—that's contemptible! Anyone caught at it should be shot out of hand. It's *politically* wrong, terribly wrong, to give way to chauvinism.'

We pulled some chairs together to sleep on. Sometime during the night I woke up. It was cold, and Belyaev was shaking me. 'Wake up! They're shooting!'

In the windows the reddish sky quivered like jelly. All I could hear were the rumble of passing vehicles and the sound of matter-of-fact voices drifting by.

'You're imagining things.'

'They're shooting at the windows! Can't you see?'

I got up to inspect. A row of neat, small holes, with cracks radiating from each one, traversed the windowpanes in a straight line. Some passing avenger with a submachine gun had evidently taken exception to the sight of unbroken windows.

We spent the entire next day in Neidenburg. Belyaev rummaged about for booty while I looked for the 'population.'

Counterintelligence was set up in one of the undamaged houses. When I went to them and asked if they had made any contact with the '*Werwolf*,' the Nazi underground, they told me that so far they had detained only one local civilian. 'Passes himself off as a Communist.'

He was a stocky, red-haired fellow with stubby fingers and watery-blue eyes in which his state of alarm and surprise could be plainly seen. He had a bundle of identification papers on him: a certificate from a concentration camp (he was freed in 1938); his craft union card (he was a baker); his marriage license; ownership papers for his bakery (he inherited it from his father-in-law); a tax receipt; a draft card with the notation *Wählunwürdig* (not suitable for military service as politically unreliable, having been in prison). And, in a separate yellowed envelope, a frayed membership card of the German Communist Party, dues paid until May 1933, and a red lapel pin—a clenched fist.

Even without this, a few questions were enough to convince me that he really was a Communist: he spoke of the Party's organization and propaganda in the kind of detail and terminology that could not have been learned on the outside. But perhaps he had gone over to the Nazis? Nothing is harder to counterfeit than the quality of everyday speech, with its store of clues to its origins. Nazism developed a system of concepts that were incorporated into the spoken language not only of the Nazis and those who were brought up under them, but of those who were reconciled to Nazism. They all had gotten used to saying '*der Führer*' instead of 'Hitler' and '*Reichsmarschall*' instead of 'Göring'; they referred to Hitler's coup as '*Machtübernahme*' (the seizure of power), to the Weimar Republic as '*Systemzeit*' (the time of the Versailles system), to the attack on Poland as '*Polenfeldzug*' (the Polish campaign). They seriously spoke of 'socialist' or 'social' factories, shops and institutions. Also part of this specific Nazi lexicon (the German philologist Klemperer called it '*Lingua Tertii imperii*'\*) were such phrases as '*Blutorden*' ('Order of Blood') for a medal that had been given to participants of the Munich putsch of 1923; '*Gefolgschaft*' (literally, 'followers,' 'adherents') for workers and employees; '*Sippe*' ('kinship,' 'clan') in evocation of the ancient German virtues, and '*Volksgemeinschaft*' for the supposed communal oneness of the German people; while words like 'Reich,' 'Wehrmacht' and 'Luftwaffe' were spoken in a special tone.

The Neidenburg baker was not given to any of this. His speech, a harsh East Prussian dialect, was unpolished and careless of grammar, but he spoke the authentic language of a German Communist—the kind of Communist who had not submitted but for twelve years had concealed his Party card, waiting and not losing faith. He did not try to make himself out to be a hero. After his term in the concentration camp he had had no further contacts with the Party: there was no one to have any contacts with. He had moved to Neidenburg, had accepted the bakery as his inheritance, and registered with the Gestapo every month. He did not dare to make new friends; it could have meant trouble for them.

Convinced that he was telling the truth, I gave him my hand and called him '*Genosse*'† and switched to '*du*.' His eyes reddened with tears and his voice shook. I pretended not to notice, pushed some cigarettes toward him, and tried to lie plausibly in response to his questions.

'*Genosse*,' he said, 'explain to me—why are they holding me under arrest? When the panic, the evacuation, began, my wife and I locked the bakery, and we hid in the cellar of our house. Then, when the Red Army came, we heard the tanks. I opened the bakery and went out with

\*Language of the Third Empire.
†*Genosse:* The German word for 'comrade,' used by the German Communists in addressing each other in preference to '*Kamerad*.'

my identification papers and a tray of fresh rolls. But the soldiers took me and dragged me away just the way I was; I couldn't even put on my overcoat. The comrade commissars and the interpreter said, "We'll check; we'll clear things up," but they've been holding me for two days now. I asked them to tell my wife—after all, she must have been worrying about me. And I asked them to bring me my overcoat.

'You understand, I'm not complaining. I know, it's war, there's distrust—maybe I'm sent by the Fascists—you've got to check up. No, I'm not complaining; I understand. And they do give me food, and let me smoke. And the treatment—in general, it's been good. Well, true, one of them hit me. But he didn't understand what I was saying, and probably the Fascists had done things to him and he had become calloused. But after all I have lived here for seven years; everyone knows me and my bakery and my family, and that I was in the camp, and how I live. After all, it's easy to check all this.

'And I'm sure my wife is very worried. She has a bad heart, you know. Please tell her not to worry, and have her bring me my overcoat, my hat, a pillow and my boots, and have her write and tell me how she's getting along and where she's getting the flour.'

'I'll drop in on your wife,' I said. 'But I'm afraid that they might have evacuated her; after all, there's been fighting here, and there may be more. All civilians have been evacuated. The city is on fire.'

'I don't understand how that could be. The Nazis fell all over themselves to get away. The *Volksturm* all took to their heels. There was hardly any shooting.'

'Well, you see, there were some German troops that broke out of encirclement—from Johannisburg. And—uh—among them there were some SS, and—'

I lied, numb with shame, but apparently I lied convincingly. The truth was so monstrous and absurd that almost any lie would be easier to believe.

I gave him the pack of cigarettes, some tobacco and some canned goods. Then I spoke to counterintelligence about him.

A young first lieutenant said sympathetically, 'So you think he's really a Communist, eh? What kind of Communists were they—putting up with Hitler? Well, anyway, he's not a Fascist, from what you say. His house? There's no house left. The bakery and the whole building burned down. As for his wife, you know yourself what's been. .... I would doubt that she's still alive.' (I thought: She could have been the woman I ordered Sidorych to shoot the day before.) 'Let's just tell him we evacuated her to the rear. We'll be sending him off too, soon. To the assembly point for civilians—Dzyaldovo, someplace like that. They'll straighten things out there.

'Clothes for him? All right. Hey, sergeant, go look in the houses that are still standing—find an overcoat for the Fritz. The major here says that he's not a bad Fritz—looks like he's a Communist.'

The interpreter, a thin-faced, pretty boy, smiled superciliously. He spoke German badly, and tried to make up for it with augmented hostility.

'Now they're *all* going to shout that they're Communists. Get some clothes for him? Maybe we ought to get him a featherbed and a bottle of vodka too?'

I restrained myself. I had the sense to realize that if I bawled him out, it would come out of the baker's hide. I tried to speak calmly and circumspectly, keeping a balance between authoritativeness and caution. And I left, lacking the guts for another meeting with the imprisoned German Communist.

Two days later we were in Hohenstein. Nearby, I knew, was Hindenburg's grave—a mausoleum inside an edifice rather like a fortress of the Middle Ages, a monument to the German victory of August 1914 against General Samsonov's Russian armies. I had long planned to blow up this embodiment of Prussian militarism if I ever got to it. We headed for the site. But when our Ford turned off the highway onto a road laid out as straight as a ruler between two rows of tall, straight trees, we became jittery. Belyaev expressed our fears: 'It's mined, I'm sure.' We turned back, but from a distance we could see that the fortress had already been dynamited.

In the fall of 1947, when I met Alexander Solzhenitsyn in a special sharashka* prison near Moscow, he told me that he had been there, too—probably on the very same day.

We arrived in Allenstein that evening. The city had been taken virtually without a fight—so unexpectedly that for some two hours after our troops occupied the railway station, German trains kept arriving from Königsberg, Johannisburg and Lyk with civilian evacuees. It was a scene of utter confusion: train whistles, sporadic shots, bursts of automatic fire, the tumult of a panicky crowd, a

*Sharashka: Camp slang for a special kind of camp, where the prisoners were specialists and technicians put to doing research, and where living conditions were better than those in ordinary labor camps.

child's cry, a woman's scream, a babble of German speech punctuated by the shouts of our men herding the arrivals out of the station.

The city had barely been touched by bombs or artillery. But the fires began the first night. On one of the central squares the flames were consuming a four-story building containing clothing, furniture and food stores. In the windows, sofas, chairs and wardrobes perished in the crackling, multicolored fire. There was a suffocating smell of burned sugar.

'So much waste,' a middle-aged soldier kept repeating gloomily. Even Belyaev was upset.

Not far from the square we came upon three civilians, a woman and two men, hurrying down the street, pressing against the walls, each of them dragging a large bundle.

'*Halt!*'

The woman answered in Russian. 'We're your own, your own! We worked for the *Bauers** here. We're Russian—Soviet. Listen, dear, go over there—that street there. There's a house there, a rich house. You'll find *Fräuleins* there, and *panis*, and clocks and lots of other stuff. No one's laid a hand on it yet!'

Our car turned into a narrow street lit dimly by the flames and came upon a five-story building. Several cars and trucks of German make and two or three of our Ford and Studebaker trucks were clustered before the entrance. Footprints in the snow led into the courtyard. There was no other sign of life, but the doors stood wide open.

A dark staircase. From the floor above, a flurry of activity and a woman's moan: '*Pan . . . pan . . .*'

One of our men: 'Who's there?'

An open door into an apartment. In a large bedroom a flicker of oil lamps and a huddle of civilians—women, children, two old men. A runty Soviet tank captain had placed a little girl on a table and was tempting her with a bar of chocolate.

'What are you doing here, Captain?'

'I came in to warn them. The building's on fire.'

Questioning him, I sensed the fear all around us. Some of the Germans—even the children—had raised their hands in surrender.

'Calm down,' I said in German. 'No one is going to harm you.' I heard a sob.

An old man said, '*Pan Komissar*, we are Poles. *Prosze pana*, we're not Germans, we're Poles.'

I addressed him in Polish. He didn't understand very well and

*Small farmers.

pretended he was hard of hearing. A woman joined in hysterically: 'We're Poles!'

'Calm down! You don't have to pretend to be Poles. You don't have to be afraid. We aren't fighting the German people, but the Hitlerites, the Fascists. We aren't fighting civilians. Don't be afraid. We punish looters and rapists. Has this man done anything?'

'No, no.'

Then several of them started talking at once.

'He says the building is on fire.'

'Mama, I don't want to burn up!'

The captain apparently understood a little German. 'Yes, yes, *brennt, brennt!*'

Our sergeant and driver went off to check.

Everyone began talking at once. A woman, not all that old, wearing a turban and lipstick, spoke ingratiatingly to me, grabbing my hand. 'Save us. You are a cultured, noble man. We hate Hitler. We have children. . . .'

A girl of fifteen or sixteen, a long-legged blonde, the type that's the star student of her class, perhaps a Hitler Youth leader, piped up in broken German—the way Negroes and foreigners speak in the children's books of the Third Reich.

'*Sie gut deutsch sprechen.* You speak German well. You save us from fire. We say you very much thanks.'

Several women led up a plump, handsome young woman with a baby in her arms. 'Look, she's only thirty; she already has ten children. She's won the motherhood award.'

I offered my congratulations. The blonde child on the table turned out to be one of her daughters. The four-year-old stretched trustingly toward me. 'Do you have children, Uncle?' I was asked. 'Yes, two girls, one eight years old, the other five.' I showed them the snapshots. Everyone crowded around. Cries of admiration, a surfeit of falsehood, and yet a sense of genuine relief.

The sergeant returned. 'It's burning on the other end. Take an hour, I'd say, to get this far.'

The tank captain said that he knew where the refugee processing center was.

I interpreted. More cries of alarm. 'Mama, I don't want to burn up!'

We decided: everyone to the processing center. Someone said, 'There are more people upstairs. The Schultzes. They're Communists.'

The star student took charge in a ringing voice. Placing a hand on my arm, she said—no longer in broken German—'Let's go to the Schultzes,

Major.' Mounting the stairs, she held my hand in a firm grasp—too firm, I thought for a minute, but maybe it was because of the darkness.

A thin old man opened the door. 'Herr Schultz,' she said, 'the building is on fire. This is a Soviet major. There are some other Red soldiers here. They're all very nice. They'll take us to a safe place.'

'Welcome, *Genosse*.' The old man grasped my hand. He obviously wanted to embrace me but didn't dare. We entered.

'My wife, *Genosse*. She is very sick. Her heart's failing. I was in prison for three years, then three more years in camp. My son died.'

His wife tried to get up. '*Genosse, Genosse*, at last!'

'And this is my friend, also a *Genosse*, but they didn't catch him. He left his home and came here to help us. He's an old union man, a joiner. A master craftsman, the kind you don't find these days.'

Schultz brought out his mementoes. 'How many years I hid this button saying *Rot Front*,* these portraits of Lenin, Liebknecht, Marx!'

So, I thought ruefully, another encounter with German Communists. And all around us fire, looting, rape. Maybe they weren't Communists at all? Or fainthearted Communists who made their peace with Hitlerism and sat things out? But do you kill people for that? Does that justify us if we let them perish? And what is happening now to the people below? There's that mettlesome tank captain of ours, and the sergeant. What if in all the chaos they start looting, or drag the terrified women off into the darkness? Belyaev certainly wouldn't interfere.

I tried to hurry the three oldsters, but Schultz went on with his stories and his wife wept, barely able to move.

We finally got them all out of the building and loaded them onto trucks. Someone kept asking tearfully about his suitcase. My self-appointed student aide cut him short: 'Now stop it. We have lives to save, and you're crying about a suitcase.'

The fecund young mother wanted to go back to the building's bomb shelter for her baby carriage, and Belyaev offered to go with her. The driver grumbled in a temper. 'How much longer do we have to wait?' He had found time to have a drink somewhere and was snapping at the soldiers who were helping us carry the refugees' possessions. Little Urshel—the four-year-old—had lost her gloves, and I gave her mine. She was delighted and showed them off to everyone. 'The Russian Uncle gave them to me.' I held her in my arms.

Belyaev and Urshel's mother returned. They hadn't been able to find the carriage. The palms of her hands were scratched and bloody. Belyaev bustled about, avoiding looking at me.

*Red Front.

'What happened?' I asked her. In my fury, confusion and shame, my voice was loud and sharp.

'Nothing, nothing,' she replied quickly, with forced cheerfulness. 'I fell down. It's dark down there. Broken glass—I cut myself. I'll bandage it up.'

Bending down to her, I said in a softer voice, 'Did anyone hurt you?' Out of the corner of my eye I saw Belyaev's worried, watchful look.

'No, no. No one hurt me. The officer was so kind. . . . He helped me. . . . No, no. Don't think anything.'

She smiled, but in her eyes I saw a melancholy dread.

At last we were loaded: twenty-eight people in all—more than half of them children. Belyaev, sitting beside me, said, 'You know, I think this is the best deed we've done these last few days. Why, the children are just like ours.'

I handed Urshel up to the back of the truck. She gave me a resonant kiss on the cheek in parting. Belyaev went on talking about nobility and humanity.

The processing center was in a warehouse area by the railroad station. The commanding officer, a first lieutenant, unshaven, his eyes red with fatigue, gave us directions. We stopped in front of one of the warehouses. It was jammed with refugees, with their bundles and suitcases. Several soldiers were on guard at the door. From the street came the sounds of shouts, an accordion, drunken singing. Two tanks stood nearby.

We transferred our charges into the warehouse. Now and then soldiers would stagger out of the darkness. 'Hey, Frau, *komm*. Come here!' We would drive them away, cursing.

Just then there was a frenzied scream and a girl ran into the warehouse, her long, braided blond hair disheveled, her dress torn across her breast, shouting piercingly, 'I'm Polish! Jesus Mary, I'm Polish!'

Two tank men were after her. Both were wearing their black helmets. One of them was viciously drunk. His jacket was unbuttoned; his medals jingled on his chest.

I placed myself before them. 'All right, just calm down now, comrade tank men.'

The lieutenant in command motioned casually with his pistol. 'Go away,' he told the pair, in a languid, practiced tone. 'Orders from headquarters. For rape—execution on the spot.'

Two or three soldiers joined us in blocking the entrance. But the other soldiers around us were sniggering unpleasantly. Several more tank men came running up. I drew my pistol and went cold with dismay: would I have to shoot at our own men, at this brave soldier blind-drunk on vodka? He came at me, hoarse with anger, spraying saliva. 'You fucking officers, fuck your mothers! You! Fighting the war on our backs! Where were you when my tank was on fire? Where were you, fuck your mother, when I set fire to that Tiger?'*

I tried to outshout him. 'Don't disgrace yourself! Leave the girl alone! She's Polish. Don't you have a mother, a sister? Have you thought of them?'

'And what did the Germans think of? Get out of my way, fuck your mother! I need a woman! I spilled my blood for this!'

The other tank men pulled him away, looking sullenly at the lieutenant and me. Voices in the darkness around us:

'Some commanders . . . They'll shoot their own men over a German bitch.'

The lieutenant repeated in a monotone: 'Go away. Orders from headquarters.'

We took the Polish girl to another warehouse, one for 'non-German civilians.' I could make out words in Russian, Polish, Ukrainian, Czech, French. Someone was playing a harmonica. An Italian with a wheezy tenor was singing a sweet Italian song.

Most of them were women, children and old men. I addressed them in German. Immediately there were questions from all sides.

'What will happen to us?'

'How are we going to feed the children?'

'Are you sending us to Siberia?'

Belyaev pulled me toward the exit. 'Let's go. The driver's drunk. He'll pass out if we don't get going.'

Our way was blocked by a woman. Brown hair almost down to the shoulders. Big, glistening eyes. A lazy smile on her thin, bloodless lips.

'*Herr Kommandant.*' She spoke in a whisper. 'They deceived you saying I can't have children. It's not true! I *can* have children. You understand? I *can* have children!'

I was taken aback. 'What is it you want?'

'I'm still young,' she whispered. 'I consent—I want . . . You see, I *can* have children. Order your soldiers to—you've got lots of soldiers . . .'

Her thin fingers tightened on my arm. She pressed against me with her breasts, her stomach.

Several women hurried up. 'Leave the officer alone. You know you're

*The Wehrmacht's heavy Tiger tanks.

◇ 51 ◇

a good girl. Come, come with us. We know some admirers of yours who'd like to meet you.'

One of them explained: 'She's been feebleminded from birth. So they sterilized her, and she went clear out of her mind. Excuse it, please.'

We spent the night in a large residence turned into a press center. There was plenty of booty liquor.

The next day my head was killing me. There was a stench of vomit, of sweaty bodies, of stale tobacco. But Belyaev was in fine spirits.

'Yesterday I did what you wanted. And I'm not sorry. We did a good deed. But today let me handle things. No looting, of course—I won't allow it. But you can see for yourself—stores, warehouses, empty apartments. It'll all burn, or the Poles will carry it off. Are our families any worse than theirs? And why have we been permitted to send parcels home? Headquarters knows what it's about.'

Yes, they had given us the right to send parcels home. The order had come down shortly before the winter offensive. Eight kilograms per soldier per month, twice as much for officers. This was direct and unmistakable incitement to plunder. What else could a soldier send home—his old underwear?

Zabashtansky had called me in for a heart-to-heart talk. 'You can understand,' he said; 'we're all sick and tired of this war, and the front-line soldiers most of all. When we were fighting on our own soil, everything was simple: we were fighting for our homes, to drive the enemy away. But now we're on their soil, and the soldier who's been under fire for four years now, and has been wounded—and knows that his wife and kids are hungry back home—he's got to go on fighting, on and on! Forward, always forward!

'Now, we're materialists, aren't we? So what's needed now? First, for the soldier to go on hating, so he'll want his revenge. And second, for the soldier to have a personal interest in going on fighting, to know why he should climb out of that trench and face that machine gun once again. So now, with this order, everything is clear: he'll get to Germany, and there everything is his—goods, women, do what you want! Hammer away! So their grandchildren and great-grandchildren will remember and be afraid!'

'Does that mean killing women and children?'

'Don't be silly. Why bring in children? Who's going to start killing children? You? Me? But if you want to know the truth, if there are any who will do it, let them kill the little Fritzes in the heat of the moment, until they get sick of it themselves. Have you read Shevchenko's poem "The Gaydamaks"? You remember, Gonta cut up his own children. That's war, buddy—not your philosophy or literature. Of course, what the books say—morality, humanism, internationalism—that's all right, that's all correct in theory. First let's send Germany up in smoke, then we'll go back to writing good, theoretically correct books on humanism and internationalism. But now we must see to it that the soldier will want to go on fighting. That's the main thing.'

I had found his reasoning odious, but he wasn't the only one to take that line. As for me, I did not put up any real argument. It is painful for me to remember that today, but that's how it was. And that day in Allenstein, with hardly an objection, I let Belyaev take over.

First we scoured the railroad station for booty, then went through a huge pile of parcels at the post office, then took in several empty residences filled with expensive furniture. I helped haul the stuff away and took earnest counsel with Belyaev as to what would make a good present for General Okorokov, our overall chief. We decided on a triple-barreled hunting rifle and a big album of Dürer's engravings with a carved wood binding—a limited edition of 300 copies.

I was saturated with French cognac; my shoulder bag was stuffed with Havana cigars. Our German anti-Fascists were startled to see us Russians taking deep drags at the cigars; you're not supposed to inhale, they said. But we went on treating these cigars as though they were our own cheap makhorka. They made you dizzy at first; then you got used to it. The constant inebriation from all the cognacs, schnapps and liqueurs, and the biting smoke of those powerful cigars, seemed to steady us against the nastiness of what was going on all around.

The railroad platform is piled high with crates. Belyaev and the driver have found some axes. The crates contain blankets, mattresses, pillows, overcoats.

Between the blows of the axes, I seem to hear an old woman's voice, soft and calm. '*Soldat. Soldat.*'

Hidden between some crates, there is a little nest of mattresses and blankets, out of which the old woman looks up at me with calm, intelligent, almost smiling eyes.

'How did you get here, grandmother?'

She doesn't seem surprised to hear German spoken. '*Soldat.* Please shoot me. Please—be so kind.'

'What are you talking about, grandmother? Don't be afraid. Nothing's going to happen to you.' How many times have I repeated this meaningless phrase? 'Where are you off to?' I ask. 'Do you have any relatives?'

'I have no one. My daughter and my grandchildren were killed by your soldiers. My son was killed in the war. Everyone killed. I must not live any more. It is not right for me to live any more.' She speaks with an utter, serene calm. No dramatics, no emotion, no tears. Only a great sadness, an utter resignation. '*Soldat*—please. You have a gun. I can see you are a good man. I have asked several other soldiers, but they only laugh; they don't understand me. I am old and sick. I can't even get up. Please, shoot me now.'

I mutter something comforting and go off looking for the station-master. Belyaev and his team have discovered a railway car with suit-cases. All along the platform there are groups like ours, busily at work. A general with a silver-tipped baton gives orders over a mound of radio receivers.

'Don't go too far,' Belyaev throws after me, 'or we won't find you.'

In a little brick station house a bent old fellow sits before a cold stove. He has a long, gray Hindenburg mustache and a German railroad uniform. I tell him about the woman. 'Get her off the platform. Get her to a processing station.'

He listens uncomprehendingly. He seems deathly tired and paralyzed with terror. I repeat the order, with all the military sternness I can muster.

'It would be better for her to die.' The husky rejoinder comes from another German lying prone on a bench. His face is dark, with dirt or with illness. 'It would be better for all of us to die.'

'Nonsense. Everything will be fine. Take the woman somewhere, understand?'

I hear Belyaev calling. 'Where are you? Let's go!'

I leave. I have done what I could. Will they go and get the old woman? Will it do her any good? I don't allow myself to think about it. I don't allow myself to think that, all in all, I too am a coward and a rat.

The street in front of the post office is broad, flanked by a neat line of trees. A woman, clutching a bag and bundle, is walking down the middle of the pavement, holding a girl by the hand. The woman's head is bandaged with a bloodied kerchief. The girl has blond pigtails, a tear-stained face and blood on her stockings. They walk hurriedly, ignoring the catcalls of the soldiers on the sidewalk, but look back and stop now and then.

I walk up to them. The woman throws herself at me in tears.

'Oh, Mr. Officer, *Herr Kommissar*! Please, in God's name! The soldiers kicked us out of our house. They beat us; they raped us. My daughter is only thirteen. Two of them did it to her. And many of them to me. And they beat my little boy. He's only eleven. For God's sake, help us. They drove us out. They wanted to shoot us. But he's still there; he's still alive. She doesn't want to go back for him. She's afraid.'

The girl sobbed. 'Mama, he's dead anyway!'

Several soldiers come over. 'What's the matter?'

I explain.

One of them, an older man with a submachine gun, looks morose. 'Bastards. What do they think they're doing?'

But a younger one objects. 'And what did they do to us?'

I reply sharply, 'That's why they're Fascists, Germans, but we're Soviets, Russians.'

The older one: 'It wasn't the women and children who did things.'

A soldier in a stained padded jacket spits and swears at someone—it's unclear whom—and goes off to one side. Two others look on silently.

I get the woman's address and promise to go find out about her son. I tell her to go to the processing center, which isn't far.

She repeats the street name over and over, the house number, the apartment. The boy's name is Wolfgang; he is wearing a blue suit.

I tell the older soldier to escort her.

'But I've got my wagon and driver here with me.'

I request him to do it (it's pointless to give orders now), reminding him that they could be assaulted again on the way. I give him some cigarettes. The soldier to one side, apparently the driver, observes— sympathetically or sarcastically, I can't tell which—'Go on, see them there, so they don't get laid somewhere in a doorway.'

The older man slings his submachine gun over his shoulder. 'Well, come on, Frau, let's go, *komm*.'

The woman pales, flinching in fear. I explain that he's her escort. She looks distrustful, imploring. The girl presses against her. 'Wolfgang,' the mother repeats. 'Blond, gray eyes, blue suit.'

They go off, down the middle of the street, the soldier in his beat-up overcoat plodding heavily ahead.

Somewhere nearby, the rumble of artillery. Renewed fighting outside the town. And here we are, gathering booty! Belyaev and me and the other looters—all of us in it together. The general on the station platform. The young lieutenant of the engineers' detachment, who believes in internationalism. The tank man who was after the Polish girl. All those caught up in that battle, huddling in the shell holes and crawling through the snow. The men who at this moment are fighting and dying in the assault on Königsberg. All the others, safely in the rear. All of us together. The good and the bad, the brave and the cowardly, the kind and the cruel. All of us in it together, and there's no getting away from it, now or ever. And the glory of it cannot be separated from the shame.

At staff headquarters, the usual flurry of activity. The Germans—it isn't clear how many, but they have tanks and motorized artillery—are trying to break out of encirclement. The staff has other worries as well: the looting, the women, the drunkenness, are undermining morale. One division commander, we are told, personally shot a lieutenant who was lining up a group of men before a German woman spread-eagled on the ground.

Several Russian girls, shipped to Germany for forced labor, have been hired as waitresses in the headquarters mess. 'One of them,' our informant recounts, 'beautiful, young, cheerful, hair like gold tumbling down her back—some soldiers, drunk, I guess, were walking down the street, saw her—"Hey, Fritzie, hey, you bitch!"—and a spray from a submachine gun across her back. She didn't live an hour. Kept crying: "What for?" She had just written her mother that she'd be coming home.'

In our presence they read aloud an order from the Commander of the Front, Marshal Rokossovsky. For looting, rape, robbery and murder of civilians, court-martial; when necessary, execution on the spot. Belyaev nods approvingly. 'You see,' he says to me, 'the people in charge have figured things out—they're making order. And you were so worried!'

We are leaving East Prussia, returning to our base, overtaking streams of civilians, some with carts, carriages, bicycles. We hear Russian, Polish, Ukrainian, Italian, Dutch, French. At a crossroads, an army truck, a crowd around it. Loud, angry voices; women's cries.

A group of soldiers—from the rear echelons, by their uniforms—are wresting suitcases away from the women, who are pleading with them in Russian and Ukrainian. The master sergeant is cursing them out: 'German lapdogs, whores, traitors!'

A young Frenchman's face is bloodied from a blow. He's trying to come to the women's defense. Belyaev and I approach. The sergeant explains: 'This Fritz here keeps babbling *Kamerad, Kamerad.*'

'Stop it!' I shout furiously. 'Who do you think you're beating up, you blockheads? He's not a Fritz; he's a Frenchman, an ally! Give those girls back their suitcases! We've rescued them from Fascist slavery, and you rob them of what little they have!'

Belyaev takes out his pistol. 'Orders of Marshal Rokossovsky— looters to be executed on the spot. Let's shoot this son of a bitch, to make an example for the others.'

The sergeant pales and jumps back into the truck; the others hop onto the back, and the truck races off.

We drive on in silence. Belyaev says, 'What can you do? It's war; people become brutalized.'

'Come on, Sasha, don't try to make excuses. Why did that old woman have to be killed? It was despicable, and I'm despicable for letting it happen. Is this the kind of victory we dreamed of? Can this be the Red Army? Why, it's no better than Makhno's bands.* I've got a book here in my bag published in Königsberg twenty years ago: *Russian Troops in East Prussia.* It's about August 1914. Written by a German historian—a civil servant, a nationalist. He did his best to dig up everything bad about the Russians. And what did he come up with? Two cases of rape. Several cases of robbery, beatings, one or two cases of murder. And in each case, Russian officers stepped in, tried to stop it, handed out punishment. The German author enumerates all the chickens killed, all the fruit trees smashed, all the faces slapped. Whenever he can, he brings in the rudeness, the barbarousness. And do you know, to read that book today is frightening—frightening and humiliating. Those were Czarist armies. And to think how much worse we are! And the shame of it falls on us, the officers, the political instructors.'

'And you think the high command doesn't know? First, they per- mitted those parcels. And now, when it's called for, we have the Marshal's order. It's a question of policy. Comrade Stalin knows.'

'Stop putting all the responsibility on Stalin. He's the commander in chief. He's got a dozen fronts and the whole rear and all our foreign relations to deal with. Here at the front, it's we who are in charge. Another month or two and we'll link up with the English and the Americans. The Germans will start running from us to them. We'll be disgraced before the whole world. And never mind the disgrace—what about those soldiers who queue up by the scores for a German woman, who rape little girls, kill old women? They'll be going back to our own

*Nestor Makhno, anarchist leader of a peasant guerrilla army during the Russian Civil War of 1918–21.

cities, our own women, our own girls. Thousands and thousands of potential criminals, and twice as dangerous, since they'll be coming back with the reputation of heroes.'

Belyaev listened without interrupting, mumbling now and then, 'Yes ... yes, of course ... But all these things—they'll mend themselves, you'll see. ...'

# 8

ON RETURNING from East Prussia, we found that the Political Department of the 50th Army had moved to a place west of Ciechanow. Zabashtansky was off in East Prussia, with Lyuba along as translator. Belyaev busied himself unloading the booty. Our women workers exclaimed and quarreled over the clothing, bed linen and tableware, dividing the stuff among themselves, and putting aside a share for those absent.

General Okorokov called me in. But, officially, Belyaev was the senior officer on our trip; besides, if I went without him, he'd be afraid I would tell the general the whole truth, which, after Marshal Rokossovsky's order on pillage, could bode ill for him. So I asked him to come with me. He thanked me effusively. 'You're a real friend. I always knew you were.'

The general had a colonel from the Central Political Administration in his office. Both were curious about what we had seen. Belyaev was silent, letting me speak. I tried to be dispassionate, matter-of-fact. But, naturally, I told of the plunder, the rape, the senseless destruction of property. The general—and the colonel from Moscow—interjected here and there, 'Yes, leave it to our fellows. . . . Setting fire to houses— hmm, we can't have that. . . . Yes, our brother Slavs seem to be over-doing it. . . .'

General Okorokov summed up: 'There's no need to pity these Germans. Let it be a lesson to them. But there's no place for wanton destruction, either. All this territory will be going to us now, or to the Poles. Well, that's how it is—where there's drink there's trouble.' Our presents he accepted with indifference, almost disappointment, as though he had expected something better. He didn't even look at the magnificent Dürer.

. . . . .

Lyuba was back the same evening and gave us her impressions of East Prussia animatedly and with that self-important, businesslike air she would sometimes assume. She remembered the designations of all the units they visited, and the exact times, without giving the exact places, which we weren't supposed to do. They had spent a day in Allenstein, and she reported her findings: the inhabitants were still keeping fearfully to their homes or bomb shelters; let one of our military walk in, and they all put their hands up, even the children; there were fewer incidents of rape. She spoke with sprightly ease, as though back from an amusing excursion. When I pointed this out to her, she grew silent and sulky.

Going into the next room, I began my written report: 'I request that I be detached from this section and from the Political Department as a whole, and perhaps from the army altogether. The war is ending, and my health is deteriorating. Moreover, I find it impossible to go on working with my immediate superiors in the coming occupation regime.'

Belyaev walked in and looked over my shoulder. Let him read; it was partly because of him as well. He snatched the sheet of paper away, crumpled it up and threw it into the stove.

'Have you gone crazy? You know what could come of this? They could throw you out of the Party. Zabashtansky has it in for you as it is. Don't be your worst enemy. Now you've hurt poor Lyuba, too, for no reason. Come, we've got some French cognac, and some sardines.'

I sat drinking with Belyaev, Lyuba and Belyaev's front-line wife, whom, it developed, I had known years ago in Kiev, where we had attended the same school. I remembered her as a pert little thing and could hardly recognize the coarsened creature she had become. 'Sasha is your best friend, no matter how much you've quarreled,' she confided melodramatically when he was out of earshot. 'No one's perfect, but he isn't capable of anything mean. I couldn't love him otherwise.'

All right, we'll drink! We'll drink to this not being the last time we have a drink on this earth! And so, at length, we collapsed, the four of us, onto a bed of heroic width. Lyuba had drunk more than usual and laughed senselessly. Then, falteringly, she whispered, 'I was horrified at the sight of those German women and children—simply horrified. . . .'

I was soon off on another assignment, as head of a group including a representative of the National Committee for Free Germany, three German graduates of our anti-Fascist school and a sound technician.

Zabashtansky I had seen only in passing; we had not exchanged more than a few words.

One raspberry-colored morning, rolling along with a military column of trucks, artillery and rocket launchers, we came under fire from some German tanks on the edge of Yaroslavl. I sat in the cabin of our Studebaker truck, in the midst of the exploding shells and the bursts of machine-gun fire, and fretted: What if they damaged our truck? If anyone saw our agents in their German uniforms, it could cause a panic—we could come under attack by our own men. A thought occurred: This was a typical situation for me. I wasn't doing the shooting; I wasn't doing the driving; I was under fire; and there was nothing I *could* do but hope that sometime soon, perhaps around the next turn, things would be better and I could do something more useful.

In Torun, for the first time in many months, we saw a city that had not been destroyed. The Germans had retreated without a fight. Here it was like in the pictures in old German books—narrow, winding streets; steep-roofed buildings; an ancient church housing Copernicus's tomb. And, in the suburbs, broad, well-lit boulevards, concrete, glass, steel. The Polish population of Torun welcomed us with joy—not the way it had been in Belostok or Grodno, where the Poles had not forgotten 1939 or 1941, and where politeness had been a mask for fear and distrust.

We helped set up a local government and armed the Polish militia; we found the archives of the local Gestapo and huge stores of food-stuffs, wine and cognac; we drank a lot, and we sang a lot. Meetings would spring up spontaneously—on the square with the dark bronze statue of Copernicus, at the entrance to the Commandant's office, by the Gestapo and prison buildings, and anywhere in the streets. I made speeches until I was hoarse, inspired to oratorical heights by the looks and smiles of the Polish girls—at once exalted and caressing. My speeches had one theme: 'For your freedom and ours ... let us smash the predatory Teutons, the mortal enemies of the Slavs. . . . Russian-Polish brotherhood has been sealed in blood. . . . Onto Berlin!'

Suddenly, a telegram. I am to report back to the Political Department. At once.

We arrived late in the evening. I distributed my presents—cognac, wine, cigarettes, canned goods. Again, the four of us got together. Belyaev seemed uneasy and avoided looking at me. After a while he called me aside.

'We must have a talk. Something's happened. I told Zabashtansky about our trip, and he ordered me—ordered, you understand—made me—write a deposition against you.'

'What deposition? About what?'

'About East Prussia . . . about your report . . . And he turned my deposition over to the general. The general got angry and tore up the citation he had written for you. That's why they called you back. I wanted to let you know, like a friend. Look—he *made* me do it. You know, I'm on pretty shaky ground myself, on account of my brother.'

On account of his brother . . . Several months before he had told me —'Give me your word that you won't let it slip out'—that his brother, who, he thought, had perished, had come back from a German prison camp and had been placed under arrest pending a 'check' on the circumstances of his capture. Belyaev had asked me: 'What do you think? Should I tell them about it or keep quiet?' I had advised him, 'Sasha, you can't play games with the Party. Your conscience will hurt you, and besides, it'll be worse if they find out from someone else. You must tell them yourself. What are you afraid of? We all know you. After a war like this, do you think they're going to change their attitude toward a front-line officer and a Communist because of something that a relative of his did or didn't do?'

But Belyaev couldn't shake off his fears. And, as I realized later, he was nervous about me, about what I might say about our East Prussian trip, especially in the light of Rokossovsky's order. As for Zabashtansky, his tactics were obvious. He had bought Belyaev. The payment was considerable: his protection, with a promise, no doubt, of reward and promotion.

I said disgustedly, 'You poor shit, you. All right, what did you write about me?'

'Everything. How we argued. I didn't think Zabashtansky would take it all so seriously.'

Reporting to Zabashtansky the next morning, I remarked, 'Belyaev tells me he made some kind of deposition about me.'

Zabashtansky started. 'He told you? What deposition?'

'Something like a complaint, to do with our trip in East Prussia.'

Warily, 'Then there was something to complain about?'

'I can't imagine what.'

'Then he dreamed up something, a pack of lies?'

'I don't know, and I don't really want to get into it. I don't know if he lied deliberately or imagined something. Either way, our friendship is over and done with, but I don't want to be dragged through this muck with him. Believe me—you know me quite well; we've quarreled and we've made up—I'm not looking for rank or title or medals. What's important to me is the job, and a clean conscience. The war is ending, and our work becomes more important every day. And I want to work at full capacity and without unnecessary hindrance. I don't need praise or flattery, but I don't need any bickering either.'

'You're a proud one, aren't you?'

'Proud? Well, you can call it that. Everyone has his pride. With some people, pride demands honors, glitter, pictures in the newspapers—'

'And you sneer at that sort of thing?'

'I don't sneer at it—I understand it and respect it. But to me, the chief thing is to be sure, in my own heart, that I am of service—that I am really, as we say, "serving the Soviet Union." I hope you can understand.'

'Don't try to propagandize *me*! I've been propagandized already.'

He stared at me intently as I left.

General Okorokov received me coolly. The colonel from Moscow was with him again. 'Here's a deposition against you, from Belyaev—your best friend, I believe. I am ready to hear your explanation.'

He handed me two sheets of paper covered with neat handwriting: 'I consider it my duty as an officer and a member of the Party to bring to your attention . . . And even before that, he engaged in conversations in which he expressed pity for the Germans and dissatisfaction with the policy of the high command in regard to the Germans. I had not taken his statements seriously. However, in East Prussia . . . defended Germans and went out of his way to save their lives . . . provoked dissatisfaction among our fighting men . . .'

There was even a paragraph about our ride back from East Prussia. 'On the return journey, he cried with pity for the Germans, said that Comrade Stalin doesn't know anything about the situation, since he is occupied with international affairs, compared our army to Makhno's bands, and cursed our command, our political workers and Comrade Ehrenburg with unprintable names.'

'All this is false.'

'How do you mean—false?'

'Simply false, and ridiculous—all the facts crudely twisted, turned inside out.'

'Why should he write falsehoods about you?'

'I don't know. But I suspect it's something personal. Something I'd rather not talk about. Comrade General, have I ever lied to you?'

'No, you're not a liar; I know that. But—' Zabashtansky entered; the general went on. 'But I did believe this deposition. And partly because I know you. You're not a bad fellow; you're a capable worker, a good soldier. But—and everyone knows this—you're too kind. You have this flabbiness of the intelligentsia. Why were you the only one to be so concerned about mistreatment of prisoners?'

'I was concerned, first and foremost, about our army, its morale.'

'All right, all right, you're not the only one to concern yourself with that, but about the prisoners—you were the only one.'

'No, I wasn't.'

'Well, more than most. Tell me, where did you spend your childhood?'

'In Kiev. When I was little, before the age of five, in the village of Borodyanka, near Kiev.'

'And what kind of family were you brought up in?'

'My father is an agronomist; my mother was a housewife at first. Then she worked as—'

'I'm not asking about *your* family. What German landowner brought you up?'

The question was so absurd I didn't understand it at first.

'What nonsense is this? That's the most idiotic invention I ever heard! And it can be checked easily enough. My parents are in Moscow. There are dozens of people who know me from childhood.'

The general glanced at Zabashtansky, who remained silent. I began to feel more self-assured.

'Comrade General, both this lie and the other one can be easily disproved. In East Prussia we were always with others; we spent a lot of time in headquarters. As for this business of German landowners—I think I can guess where it came from. When I was ten or eleven, my father worked as an agronomist on a collective farm, and the director there was a German. We used to visit my father in the summers. I've talked about this many times—to Comrade Zabashtansky, for one.'

Zabashtansky flushed. But he spoke calmly. 'Still, it's hard to understand why Belyaev, your best friend, would lie about you.'

'Obviously, he's no friend of mine if he lies about me. As to why he lies, I don't know and don't want to know. If I try to find out why, there'll be a quarrel and it'll impede our work.'

General Okorokov turned to the colonel from Moscow. 'He's all mixed up, but I can't figure out in what way. It's true he doesn't like to lie—doesn't know how to, in fact. Quite the opposite. Does himself harm, contradicting everyone. Even me, sometimes. A real Don Quixote, or a Hamlet, but a provincial one. Too kind'—he turned to me again—'that's what's the matter with you. Still, you're a Jew. How can you love the Germans? Don't you know what they've been doing to the Jews?'

'What is "love"? I hate the Fascists not as a Jew—I haven't had much occasion to be reminded of that— but as a Soviet Man, a Kievite, a Muscovite, and, above all, as a Communist. And that means my hate cannot find expression in rape or pillage.'

'There goes our Hamlet again. Who's raping them? They're begging for it, and you pity them!'

'Not them so much as us—our morality, our discipline, our glory!'

'All right, enough of that. The Party and the high command will somehow take care of morality and discipline without Major Kopelev's help. Now you listen to me. We won't make an issue of this. If we did, they'd throw you out of the Party. This Hamlet complex of yours comes from lack of partyness. You have a head on your shoulders, but your Party backbone is weak. To pity the enemy is to betray your own. The citation I was going to draw up—I'll put that off. For the time being, Comrade Zabashtansky is not to assign you to German soil. You speak Polish, don't you, and we've still got some fighting to do in Poland. Let the Poles show you how to love the Germans.'

Two or three days passed. We were ordered to translate into German an order of the Government Defense Committee: All German men between the ages of eighteen and sixty would be mobilized into labor battalions. The directive was to be translated at once and distributed as widely as possible.

The work was done by me and another member of our unit, Arnold Goldstein. We took it in to Zabashtansky's office. Two other men of our group, Mulin and Klyuev, were present.

'What do you think?' Zabashtansky asked me. 'What will they do with these Fritzes?'

'Make them work.'

His voice dropped to a confidential tone, as though to denote that he was privy to some state secret. 'I happen to know that they'll all be driven east. Pretty far east, too. What do you think, what does that mean?' He looked me square in the face.

'So? They'll do manual labor. Probably undergo reeducation too, like the military prisoners.'

'The fact of the matter is that for all these men—and there'll be millions of them—we're assigning maybe forty or forty-two political instructors. Well? That's not enough to *begin* to reeducate,

They're being sent to prison camps, that's where—to the end of their days.'

It was a blatant and outrageous lie, an obvious attempt to provoke me into some imprudent statement.

'Well, now,' I said smoothly, 'that strikes me as rather faulty information. Why should we treat civilians worse than war prisoners? Even the prisoners have libraries, clubs, wall newspapers, discussion groups—'

'Maybe sanatoriums too, and rest homes?'

'Let's not exaggerate. But they work; they get rations. A man can earn a kilo of bread.'

'*What*? You hear what he's saying now? Our people, our workers, my own wife—they get four or five hundred grams, and the Fritzes get a *kilo*!'

'Not all of them, of course. The ration is four hundred grams. But a man who overfulfills his norm can earn as much as a kilo. Everyone knows that.'

Mulin and Klyuev were silent. Goldstein tried to say something, but Zabashtansky bore down on me. 'More of your tricks! A kilo of bread for the Fritzes . . .'

'I didn't set the norms; the government did. And Comrade Stalin knows what he's doing.'

'Don't you dare befoul the leader's name with your crap! I won't allow it, do you hear?'

'And don't *you* dare insult *me*! What do you mean "befoul"? *Lies* befoul. *You* are lying! I am telling the truth.'

He jumped up. 'Enough! That's an order!'

Mulin, Kluyev and Goldstein surrounded me. 'Come on . . . let it go. . . . Why get all worked up? . . . Comrades, forget it. . . .'

Zabashtansky, in an unexpectedly plaintive voice, said, 'I just can't talk calmly about these things. Don't you see, I don't want my sons to have to fight this war all over again. All right, let's forget it. Get this stuff printed.'

Two more days passed. I was called in by the secretary of the Party organization within the Political Department.

'There's been new material sent in about you. A serious political accusation. That you've been interceding for the Germans again. That you've been speaking up against the measures taken by the Government Defense Committee.'

'That's a lie.'

'We have a statement here by Lieutenant Colonel Zabashtansky.

How can it be a lie? He is a Communist through and through. He has spent his whole life working for the Party. As for you, we know more than enough about you.'

'This is more slander. I had an argument with Zabashtansky, but I didn't say anything against the Defense Committee. Klyuev, Goldstein and Mulin were present. They heard what I said.'

The secretary said that he would get their versions of the conversation.

I went directly to Zabashtansky and called him a slanderer and a liar. He stood before me, beet-red, his eyes narrowed to slits, leaning on his desk, fists clenched.

'Leave my office,' he said in a furious whisper. 'Leave this instant.'

I went looking for witnesses. Klyuev mumbled something incoherent. 'You . . . don't . . . you must understand . . . can't have political errors . . . they'll know what . . .'

Mulin said that he didn't remember hearing me criticize the Defense Committee. 'But you know yourself—you did say things before this, things you shouldn't have. Zabashtansky got hot under the collar, but he has the Party written all over him, and he's the commanding officer. You keep forgetting you're in the army.'

Goldstein, usually so impassive, was indignant. 'This is nothing but spite! You never said that. That's ridiculous. Of course I'll write to the Party bureau. What a heel that Zabashtansky is.'

Goldstein did write the truth. Klyuev and Mulin wrote that they had left the room before the argument took place. Mulin urged me to write a letter apologizing for insulting my commanding officer. He advised me to refer to the accusation against me not as slander or a lie but as a 'misunderstanding.' 'Tell them that he misunderstood you, but that you, on the other hand, were rude and undisciplined.'

Vladimir Mulin, lanky, long-faced and with a broken nose—a memento, he said, of his one-time interest in boxing—had been with us since the summer of 1944. He was secretive, but now he courted me, swearing friendship and playing the go-between who had my interests, as well as the good of our whole unit, at heart. The war was ending, he said; we had more work than ever; we'd soon be in Berlin. Why let these petty squabbles come between comrades in arms?

# 9

ALL I wanted was to get away, and so I took Mulin's advice and wrote a letter saying I had been 'misunderstood,' acknowledging my lack of discipline (I had been rude to my commanding officer) and offering my apologies. I was at once assigned to a group headed by Belyaev, and we set off across Poland on the heels of our advancing troops, with a large sound truck and several graduates of our anti-Fascist school.

Belyaev and I sat in the front, hardly talking to each other. We passed through tidy little towns and villages. Snow covered the roof-tops and glistened through openings in the woods; the air was soft and damp with approaching spring. I wanted to think about pleasant things—a quick end to the war, how we would enter Berlin, how we would link up with the English and the Americans. I really ought to be studying English in earnest, I thought; I'll have to be propagandizing *them* soon.

By morning we were at the headquarters of the 16th Regiment of the 38th Guards Division, located in a confectionery plant in the suburbs of Graudenz. Some of our artillery pieces were emplaced inside the buildings, and their barrels stuck out of the second-story windows as they pounded away at the center of the city, which was plainly visible in the valley below. Our sharpshooters occupied a railway depot and a workers' quarters just ahead of us, and the Germans were holding onto a road-building equipment factory just beyond that. From the factory the German defense line crossed the highway, in the form of a massive barricade of steamrollers and bulldozers, and ran along a city street.

The siege was in its third day. Our artillery and mortars were firing ceaselessly, and our fighter-bombers swooped down several times a day. The Germans responded with infrequent but fairly heavy artillery barrages.

After their first barrage Belyaev left, and I remained as the senior officer of our group. A week later Zabashtansky paid us a visit, staying several hours.

We conducted our broadcasts from evening to dawn. During the day we interrogated prisoners and deserters, hastily recruiting likely material for infiltration back into the German lines to spread defeatism among their troops.

On the night of February 23, Red Army Day, we moved our sound truck into a damaged building serving as a forward post for our gunners. Impressed by our German- and Polish-language broadcasts, the artillerymen plied us with French cognac and proposed that we celebrate the holiday with a joint operation. Over the field telephones went the order: fire on command from the sound truck. Elated by the notion, I shouted impassioned commands into the microphone. 'For the pristine tears of our mothers, for our wives and sweethearts, for our ruined cities and our ravaged fields—fire! For our friends and comrades fallen in battle, for their eternal memory, for their eternal glory—fire!'

Near and far, behind us and to one side, the guns roared and thundered. The very sky seemed to moan and shriek. From the German lines the flares of rockets chased each other in unending succession. There was an angry bark of German mortars, and our building shook as though under a ferocious lash. Over our loudspeakers, a song boomed out: 'A people's war—a sacred war—'

Life was glorious; victory was near; my comrades around me were all splendid! To hell with Zabashtansky and those others! For me, there was nothing more important than a night like this!

The song ended, and the post commander shouted, 'Come on, Major, one more salute in honor of the holiday!' And, giddy with happiness, I bellowed into the microphone: 'For our homeland—for our Moscow—for our quiet rivers and limitless steppes, for our birch trees, for our children, for our great Stalin—fire!'

The attack began before dawn. We conducted our broadcasts a block or two away from the Germans, sometimes across the street from them. After breaking into the city proper in two days of fighting, our troops were ordered to dig in and rest.

Our crew stayed in a building occupied by the battalion headquarters. That night we joined the headquarters staff in a room warmed by a Dutch tile stove, with all kinds of bottles and canned goods on the table and the carpeted floor. We were eating and drinking, singing and laughing, when the house was rocked by a deafening explosion. The wall was gone. In its place were the fiery sky and a huge advertisement on the wall of the next-door building. We slid and rolled, clinging to each other, and fell out onto a tiled roof, together with a cascade of broken wall, glass, chairs, bottles and cans. The explosion was caused by a bazooka shell, which killed several soldiers and civilians on the first two floors; but in our party no one was seriously hurt. That same night we transferred to the residence of an SS *Obersturmführer*, resplendent with mahogany furniture, velvet drapes, lace curtains, silk coverlets, feather quilts, tableware, silverware, and a cellar stocked with wine, smoked meat and home preserves.

With rumors that Graudenz had been taken, the looters began to make their appearance. The 'trophy hunters' would break into abandoned homes, as they did in East Prussia. Others would march into the cellars, where most of the civilians had taken shelter. 'Inspection of documents,' they would announce, and would demand wristwatches and rings and drag women out into the open.

A second visit from Zabashtansky. Only this time he didn't go any farther than the divisional headquarters several kilometers short of the city. He stayed for about two hours; I heard from him by field telephone.

Zabashtansky ordered me to send our sound truck back to him. We could have a smaller truck instead, with a movie projector and a loudspeaker. It would do, since by now we were broadcasting at close proximity to the Germans, sometimes as close to them as a block or two.

A young soldier in a spick-and-span uniform walked unhurriedly along the sidewalk, carrying a suitcase in one hand and leading a bicycle with the other. Following on his heels was a woman wailing for her lost possessions, with a little girl at her side.

I hit the fellow in the stomach with a pistol so hard that he doubled over. 'Looting, you bastard? Robbing women and children, dishonoring the Soviet Army? We'll shoot you down like a dog! You'll lie here like carrion, with the sign "Looter" hung around your neck!'

A small crowd of Poles gathered—women, young boys, a few men. My companion, a member of our loudspeaker team, told them that our army was merciless with looters and that this soldier would be tried and probably shot.

Compassionate voices: 'No, no, *Pan*, don't shoot him. He's just young . . . foolish . . .'

The soldier, pale and confused, kept repeating, 'I didn't know. . . . They said we could send parcels. . . . I thought it was all right.'

A mine exploded at the corner. The onlookers jumped for the doorways. We led the young looter away and let him off with a cuff and a warning: 'Don't do it again.'

Word soon spread of a group of Soviet officers who 'protected' Polish civilians. Women, and sometimes men, would come to us begging for help against looters or other lawbreakers, and we would go with them.

One night we were awakened by a member of the newly formed Polish police. What was he to do? Several drunken soldiers had broken into a cellar. How could he shoot at his Soviet allies, even if they were stealing? We ran to the scene. At the entrance we were met by a group of frightened women: 'Help us!' Screeches came from the cellar.

Apparently one of the soldiers had fired a burst over the heads of the people in the cellar, and one of the bullets had grazed a young woman in the head. Covered with blood, she moaned, 'I'm dying. . . . I'm dying. . . . Why? Why?' The wound was superficial. Where were the soldiers? What if they opened fire again? I shouted in Polish: 'Everyone flat on the floor!' And in Russian: 'Come out, surrender peacefully, and we'll let you go. If you resist, you'll be shot.'

'There they go!' someone shouted at the entrance. One of the soldiers in our own group swore. His face had been bloodied by a rifle butt.

I pushed my way out. A small truck was making off. I jumped on the running board, pointing my pistol through the window. A soldier entwined by a length of lace curtain shoved me in the face; the truck jerked forward, and I fell off and began firing. The Polish policeman, running up, inquired anxiously, 'Pan Kommandant, may I?' and fired his rifle from a kneeling position. The truck got away.

The day after this incident, Zabashtansky phoned again from divisional headquarters. I was away doing a broadcast, and he spoke to one of my men, Major Nepochilovich, a big, good-natured fellow who didn't let anything ruffle him.

'What have you done, enrolled in the police? You're interfering with military operations, you're diverting soldiers to police duty, and you're neglecting your own mission. The military command is complaining about you. It's not your business to catch looters, or to make a fuss if some soldier grabs a German woman, or even a Polish one. Pass this order on to Major Kopelev: carry out your mission, demoralize the Fascist enemy, and don't distract yourselves with these extraneous matters—with this . . . this *humanism*!

'I'm sending you a representative of the National Committee for Free Germany. Use him, but don't forget about vigilance. Understand?'

The attack was resumed on March 2 or 3. We crossed the Trinka Canal on the very first night, with few losses. The Germans had set up a hospital in a school building. We approached it from the back. White flags with red crosses hung on the railing.

A doctor in a white coat over his uniform met us inside. 'We surrender. We put credence in what you said over your loudspeakers. We believe in the magnanimity of the victorious Russian army.' He spoke flawless Russian with the throaty r's associated with prerevolutionary Saint Petersburg. He had studied there, he explained.

He was the chief surgeon. 'We have two hundred and forty-six wounded in the cellars, some of them seriously wounded. We rely on your nobility and mercy. The German command decided not to defend the hospital. I beg you, don't use the hospital as a fortified position.'

Our soldiers kept filtering into the garden in the back; there were still Germans in the street out front. In the glare of the fires to the right and left of us, two of our soldiers spotted a bar across the street and made a beeline for it. They were pinned down by a hail of small-arms fire; their comrades inside the school building fired back; a machine gun rattled across the foyer. The German doctor was beside himself. '*Gospodin* Officer! I beseech you. . . . This is a hospital!'

A lieutenant in a fur hat swore at him; then, catching sight of Major Nepochilovich and me, changed his mind. 'Stop firing! Don't fire unless ordered.'

We went to take a look at the wounded. While we were away, a new company of troops took the surgeon prisoner, as well as several of the doctors and nurses. We interceded with the colonel in charge of the assault, who ordered all medical personnel released and returned to their duties. In the meantime, some hotheads in counterintelligence had shot one of the wounded because, according to one version, 'he looked like an SS man,' or, according to another, because he said something in Russian and was taken for a Vlasovite.

We restored order in the hospital. Soon some of the less seriously wounded were drinking something potent with our own soldiers and avowing: 'The war is *scheiss*. . . . The war is *kaputt. Russ is gut. Russ Soldat gut.*'

I interrogated some of them, together with Major Bechler, the representative of the National Committee for Free Germany assigned to me by Zabashtansky. We picked out two young fellows, both corporals, and gave them a letter to the commander of our next objective, a fort whose walls came into view, with daylight, on the side of a hillock not far from the hospital.

The two Germans set forth, carrying one of the hospital's improvised Red Cross flags. Firing was still going on in the surrounding blocks. As they passed the bar across the street, the dozen or so soldiers inside cheered them on tipsily.

Several German soldiers in long gray coats emerged on the hillside. Heads with German helmets appeared at windows along the street leading to the fort. Two German soldiers walked out into the street; then another, and another. Soon there was a whole group of Germans in the street, all unarmed.

Bechler, Nepochilovich and I ran across to the bar, afraid that our drunken defenders would take it into their heads to open fire. There were isolated shots: Germans, still firing from the windows. Bechler and I shouted in German: '*Kameraden!* Let the truce team go through! Come down!' More German heads poked out: '*Wer seid ihr?*'

For the first time I was talking to German troops not through a loudspeaker but directly, face to face.

'We are officers of the Red Army, and in the name of our commanders we promise not to harm you! This'—I pointed to Bechler—'is Major Bechler of the National Committee for Free Germany.'

Bechler shouted peremptorily, 'All of you—lay down your arms! Come down at once!'

We walked up the street. More Germans kept coming out of the doorways. Nepochilovich put all the expressiveness he could muster into his few words of German. '*Kameraden—komm, komm! Gefangen— gerretet! Krieg—scheiss! Kameraden—komm!*' With his great frame and good-natured smile, he gave off a sense of calm and friendliness that more than compensated for his linguistic deficiency. He chatted with the Germans in a peculiar mixture of German and Polish.

From a doorway a boy's voice rang out: '*Ruscy przysli!*' 'The Russians have come!'

In Polish, Nepochilovich was in his element. He boomed: '*Niech zyje wolna Polska! Niech zyje radziecko-polska przyjazn!*'

Our emissaries had reached the bulwark in front of the fort. I couldn't see much more, because we were surrounded by Polish civilians. A Polish girl hung on my neck, a gray-mustached man was pumping my hand, a boy had me by my other arm, and someone was shoving a bottle into the pocket of my coat. Nepochilovich was besieged by a group of ecstatically squealing women and children.

A machine gun opened up. There was a sound of breaking glass. Everyone dashed for the walls and doorways. Three German soldiers lay on the ground. The firing came from the German bulwark. Our machine guns began firing back. Soldiers under the command of the lieutenant in the fur hat were taking up new forward positions. I was shouting commands in German.

The fighting ceased as abruptly as it had flared up, and the colonel in charge was more than satisfied. The plan, apparently, had been to storm these few blocks between the hospital and the fort the following night, after moving up the artillery. As it was, we had occupied the area without losses, and the battalion on our flank had also occupied its target area without a fight, since the Germans there, seeing what was going on in our streets, had simply decamped.

Someone shouted: 'Here they come!'

The two emissaries were back. They had been inside the fort. They had a note from its commander, a Captain Findeisen, requesting that the 'German Major'—Bechler—be sent to him for negotiations and that there be a truce in the meantime.

The emissaries were exhilarated. 'All the soldiers there have had it with the war! They kept asking us questions. What are the Russians like? Are they going to run amok?'

I wrote a reply: 'Captain Findeisen! Negotiations can take place only if so decided by the Soviet military authorities. Your situation is hopeless. By continuing to resist, you will be guilty of senseless bloodshed and the senseless death of your men. Our terms are unconditional. All who surrender will be repatriated to their homeland. All who resist will be destroyed without mercy.' Bechler wrote his own note, urging the commander to 'heed the voice of reason, and understand that an officer's duty and honor compel him to think of the fate of his men and of the civilian population.'

The situation remained tense. A young sergeant who took it on himself to walk behind the emissaries when they set off a second time was wounded in the face by a bullet from the bulwark, and it was all that I and the lieutenant could do to prevent him from ordering his men to open fire again.

This time the messengers returned with two Germans—an officer and a soldier, both wrapped in bandages.

The officer, fat and purple-faced, saluted. 'Are you Major Bechler?'

'No,' I said. 'I am a Russian major. Kindly introduce yourself.'

The officer saluted again, swaying unsteadily. He was drunk. 'Captain

Findeisen, commander of the fort. I would like to talk to the German major from the Free German Committee. I request a truce and time to think.'

Our soldiers crowded around us. I told Findeisen that his request would have to be taken up back at our base. The six of us started off, trailed by our men.

When he passed by the bodies of the three German dead, Findeisen saluted. Bechler said, 'They were killed by German bullets. An hour ago. A group of German prisoners came under fire from the fort.'

'Terrible! *Schrecklich! Schrecklich!* I didn't want that. I didn't give any such orders.'

The colonel in charge came toward us from the building that served as his headquarters. He had found time to put on his jacket with the gold shoulder boards, and he looked very impressive.

Captain Findeisen told us that he had telephoned the divisional commander, Major General Fricke, at his barracks headquarters half a kilometer away asking for permission to surrender the fort, and that permission had been denied. He asked us for a twelve-hour cease-fire to give him time to explain the situation to the general.

Translating, I added in an undertone, 'I wouldn't give him more than an hour.'

The colonel sipped his coffee. 'Tell him I can't agree to a long delay. Our troops are advancing all along the front. I can't hold my section back.'

Findeisen said, 'I implore you. If only until tonight. I will explain the hopelessness of the situation to the general.'

'And if your general doesn't accept your explanation?'

'Then I will capitulate.'

'I give you two hours. After that we will attack with everything we have.'

After the two German officers left, together with our two emissaries, I taxed the colonel for giving them too much time. He laughed. 'But I don't have a single artillery piece yet! They've only started pulling up the mortars.'

Less than an hour later, a gray column of Germans marched four abreast out of the fort, behind a Red Cross flag. They were led by our emissaries and an officer in a leather coat. Reaching me, he identified himself as an assistant commandant of the fort and handed over his pistol in its holster. 'The garrison of the fort, seven officers and one hundred and twenty-six soldiers and noncommissioned officers, capitulates.'

'But where is Captain Findeisen?'

'He went to see the commanding general. The officers of our garrison consider his behavior unworthy of a German officer. He gave you his word, but he didn't intend to keep it. He even gave thought to breaking out to the north. But all the officers of the fort refused to obey. Besides, he was swinishly drunk. The soldiers couldn't respect him, or believe him.'

Our colonel positioned his forces closer to the fort and returned to headquarters more satisfied than ever. 'Our orders were to take this area by the day after tomorrow. We're overfulfilling our plan all right! I've reported it to General Rakhimov, and he asked me to thank all of you.'

Bechler and I wrote a letter to Colonel Steidle, commander of the German barracks, as well as of a regiment of the 250th Division and of two battalions of *Volksturmer*, urging the capitulation of these troops. The letter was signed by our colonel, as the local commander; by me, 'at the direction of the supreme command of the Soviet armies'; and by Major Bechler, as a representative of the National Committee for Free Germany. It was night by now, and we escorted the two emissaries through streets that were either pitch-black or lit by flames, to a point halfway between the chatter of our machine guns and the defensive fire of the Germans. From there, they went on alone.

When we returned to our base, I was told that there had been an urgent telephone call from divisional headquarters. Colonel Smirnov, the senior political officer, wanted to speak to me.

The colonel had sent down an order two days earlier: We were to hand over our new sound truck to another division, which was advancing on the city from the north. We had not been able to comply. The truck would have had to cross the Trinka Canal, whose bridges had been blown up by the retreating Germans; even if it could have crossed the canal, no one knew where the advancing division was; and, even if we knew, we were out of gasoline and our own troops didn't have time to replenish our supplies. The best we could do was to leave the truck at the base, requesting the transport officer to get some gas if he could and to ask divisional headquarters for fresh instructions.

Colonel Smirnov, when I got him on the line, was infuriated because his order had not been carried out. I told him why it had proved impossible to do so and reported on the capitulation of the German fort and the negotiations for the surrender of the German barracks, but he wouldn't listen.

Lev Kopelev in 1930

Kopelev in August 1941

1944, Kopelev at the front

April 1943, *left* Major Yuri
Maslov, *right* Major Lev Kopelev

May 1945, *left* Belyaev,
*right* Zabashtansky

Mikhail Arshansky

Ivan Rozhansky in May 1945

'I know what you're up to—boozing in cellars with Polish whores! You ditched the truck—you've got cold feet—and you're trying to make out you're out of gas. I'm going to have you court-martialed for cowardice under fire.'

He sounded drunk. I tried to reason with him, then lost my temper and told him that he had no right to shout at me like that—I was on a special mission, and carrying out the orders of my own superiors.

He grew shrill. 'Now I see why your superiors say you're— All you know is how to slander our own officers and men! We know all about it!'

He could not have made Zabashtansky's role in this any clearer. I was taken aback. The contrast between what we had just achieved and what I was hearing was too abrupt.

The colonel calmed down a bit and said, 'As to who is whose commanding officer—we'll see about that later. Meanwhile, the bridges have been repaired. Send someone to me for gas. Then use the sound truck to broadcast an ultimatum to all enemy positions to surrender at once. I'll have the text for you.'

He didn't seem to realize that our loudspeaker, with its range of 250 or 300 meters, could hardly broadcast 'to all enemy positions' strung out over a distance of ten to twelve kilometers.

Galya Khromushina, a smart and brave kid on my team, always in the center of things, went for the gasoline, with a soldier as escort. I watched her walk off toward the self-propelled artillery moving up across the bridges. The whole area was under fire from German guns on higher ground. She walked toward the bursts of shell shot, under a canopy of orange sky, and I thought, 'If she is killed or wounded now, just as the war is ending, it will be my fault, and that drunken fool's, and Zabashtansky's.'

The emissaries returned quite a while later, unnerved. At the German barracks they had been abused; one officer had torn the Red Cross flag from their hands and had wanted to shoot them as traitors. Colonel Steidle had seemed to be at a loss; he consulted with his staff in another room, and the emissaries could hear them shouting and quarreling. Finally, Steidle told them that there would be no reply: let the Russians address General Fricke, the divisional commander. But the soldiers they spoke to in the barracks yard were angry with their officers and wanted to surrender. Let the Russians come, they said; we won't move a finger.

The messengers proposed a plan. They could go back, together with six or seven of their comrades in the hospital, as a new truce delegation, but with guns and hand grenades hidden under their coats. They could seize the staff officers, and the soldiers would give up. We realized that we could not arm a truce team under cover of a white flag, but it gave us an idea for a counterplan.

The emissaries—five in number this time, and carrying three white flags—would go back unarmed, but would be followed by a commando unit of about fifty men, who would keep out of sight. Two of the emissaries would go in with a letter addressed to General Fricke; the other three would remain in the yard and soften up the soldiers, warning them that in the event of another rejection, the Russians would attack immediately and in force. If Colonel Steidle agreed to capitulate, all five would go out of the gate, waving their white flags and shining their flashlights. If he refused, only two of them would go out, with only one flag, while the other three would try to divert the attention of any soldiers who might be between the gate and the staff headquarters building. The commando team would then rush in and capture the staff officers. A white flare would tell our main forces that the staff had capitulated; a red flare would be the signal for a break-in, whereupon we would rush the barracks, suiting our actions to the circumstances.

Our heavy guns were pulling up by this time. Some of us went together with the commandos. In front of us and to one side, flames like giant tatters gave off showers of sparks. A dull glow covered two-thirds of the sky. The emissaries marched quickly toward the barracks gate. Half an hour passed. We crouched, freezing, in the icy ditches. From the barracks came a cacophony of voices. Then the signal: on the incline, in front of the gate, several men waving white flags and shining their flashlights. The heavy gate swung open, and a mass of men poured out behind a white flag.

We ran forward to meet them. The garrison had mutinied! The first mutiny, as far as we knew, in any unit of the *Wehrmacht*! The officers had left. Our emissaries had ordered the soldiers—more than three hundred in number—to form ranks, and had led them out. We sent up a white flare.

Galya was back with several cans of gas. Colonel Smirnov had sent her back in his own Willys jeep. He had even conceded that he might have been a little rough on me. But he insisted that we broadcast the text of the ultimatum, which he had written himself.

The enemy now held only the northern edge of the city, containing residential houses, factories, and a wooded park beside the Vistula

River—and, dominating the rest, a massive citadel, Korbier Fortress, headquarters of General Fricke.

At one point the distance between our line and theirs was no more than 300 meters—narrow enough for them to hear our loudspeakers. We drove our truck as close up as we could, hurrying before daylight would reveal our position, and broadcast the ultimatum. I laid into Findeisen, accusing him of cowardice and deceit.

The sky grew lighter. We played a sad German song. We noticed, suddenly, that there had been no firing from either side for a whole hour —the first time in two weeks that we had known so protracted a still-ness. A signalman ran up: we were being called back; the Germans had sent another delegation.

On the way we met Bechler. He recounted that Captain Findeisen was back; from his drunken rambling, Bechler made out that General Fricke himself had ordered him to go to the Russians and fulfill his promise, since his conduct had been disclosed in the Soviet broadcasts, and for a German officer death was preferable to disgrace. Findeisen begged Bechler to have him either shot or exonerated.

The authorized German emissaries this time, however, were an officer with a Red Cross armband and a soldier with a hospital flag. General Fricke was inviting the Soviet officers and Major Bechler into Korbier Fortress for discussions.

'Does that mean,' I asked, 'that he is surrendering?'

'General Fricke appeals to the Russian command for magnanimity.' The German officer spoke in a tired, slow, mournful voice. 'In the fortress, we have two and a half thousand wounded. The general asks you to stop shelling and bombing the fortress. We are no longer able to resist.'

'Then you are capitulating?'

'I am not authorized to speak of capitulation. I am a doctor, and I, too, appeal to you for magnanimity and for mercy. General Fricke authorized me to say that the fortress will not fire. It can't. We have no more ammunition. But I am not authorized to speak of capitulation. I convey the words of the general: he invites the Soviet officers and the German major.'

I translated for our captain. He shrugged. 'All right, let's go.' He gave commands over a field telephone, ordering his artillery to stop firing at the fortress, since he was going there for negotiations.

We took a road through the woods, past abandoned barricades and trenches, the snow under our feet littered with helmets, gas masks, bazookas.

Then the high, massive, gray walls of Korbier Fortress. A moat spanned by a bridge with cast-iron railings. Huge iron gates. A small door opened, and two officers came out. One of them saluted; the other extended his arm, Fascist style, then, catching himself, brought his hand to his cap.

'The General bids you welcome.'

Inside, another bridge across another moat, around a wall no less forbidding than the first. We walked through the gate into a courtyard, past lines of soldiers drawn up on parade.

'*Achtung! Stillgestanden! Links um! Augen rechts!*'

A clatter of heels. What do I do—salute? I tried to do it carelessly, as though waving them away.

An alleyway and a second courtyard. More lines of soldiers coming to attention as we passed. Suddenly, a roar of planes from behind.

'*Flieger! Flieger! Volle Deckung!*'

The soldiers rushed to the walls, pressed themselves into niches, fell flat on the ground.

Our party walked on. The German colonel escorting us smiled wanly. 'You didn't inform your fliers?'

'We informed them, naturally. But who knows if the message got through in time.'

I tried not to betray my terror. To perish under our own bombs—and at the very end! Why this show of bravado before an already beaten enemy? Yet we all walked on as though by mutual consent, holding our heads high. And the two German officers with us followed our example.

Two Ilyushins roared by, directly overhead. I felt my collar clinging moistly to my skin. The roar receded. Then it returned, from the front this time, crushing us, tearing at the heart.

'*Flieger! Flieger!*'

Yet, again we did not falter or run—just walked a little faster. Again the dark shadows passed by, leaving the air shaken.

The young soldier carrying our white flag ran to the center of the court. Planted in full view of the planes, he waved his flag at the receding rumble.

'Brave lad,' murmured the German colonel. We walked on, past huddles of soldiers lying prone, crouching, pressing themselves against the walls. The roar overhead approached again, from behind. Would they start bombing on the third pass?

'In here, please.'

Through a door. Down into a cellar. Wood-paneled walls. A brightly lit corridor, with a rug running the length of the linoleum floor.

Another door. A large room. Soft lights. A man sitting behind a desk rose as we entered. Smooth flaxen hair, red-and-gold general's collar tabs. Several senior officers rose from a couch.

'Herr Major General, I have the honor to present the Russian truce team.' The colonel performed the introductions.

General Fricke leaned forward, his fingertips on the desk top. 'Please sit down, gentlemen. Cognac! Cigars! Coffee, perhaps?'

'Thank you, Herr General,' I said, 'but we have come to discuss the terms of surrender.'

'Gentlemen, I have already communicated to you that I have no authority to capitulate. I am under strict orders *not* to capitulate. Orders from the supreme command.'

'Why did you invite us here then?'

'Gentlemen, please understand. I cannot capitulate, but I cannot resist either.'

'So you are surrendering?'

'I appeal to the victors for magnanimity. I count on the fabled magnanimity and nobility of Russian officers. I ask you to call off your artillery and bombers.'

'You don't want to surrender, but you ask us to stop firing. Herr General, we have been at war for four years—a merciless war—and you are suddenly proposing some strange kind of game.'

But our captain interrupted. 'All right. Let him formulate it any way he likes. But I want a yes or no answer to this: Will they resist when our forces enter the fortress?'

General Fricke replied in a voice full of exhaustion and anguish. 'I can only repeat—I am carrying out an order, and for that reason I cannot sign any agreements or discuss any conditions. I rely on the magnanimity and nobility of the victors.'

The captain nodded. 'In that case, I think everything is more or less clear. Give me that!'

He stepped up to the general's desk and with two sharp blows of a German bayonet he cut the wires of the desk telephone. The general sank down in his chair.

Within half an hour our troops were in the inner courtyard. The removal of the garrison began.

Then two days of rest at General Rakhimov's divisional headquarters. On the second day, at a ceremony before an assemblage of troops, the general thanked his officers, the commanders of his regiments, battalions and companies; and, in conclusion, he thanked us of the Political Department for helping his division accomplish its mission so quickly, so successfully and with such small loss of life. His chief of staff read out his recommendations for medals. Among those recommended were Bechler, for the Red Star; Nepochilovich, for the Order of the Great Patriotic War, Second Class; and I, for the Order of the Great Patriotic War, First Class.

# 10

WE WERE walking down a peaceful street. There were more civilians than military in Graudenz by now, and plenty of children. Suddenly there was a roar as a barricade in front of us blew up. I could see a wooden beam sailing down on my head. It crashed on a veranda right over me as I crouched against a wall. There was a cataract of bricks, and I felt something heavy strike me in the back.

Lying spread-eagled on the ground, I was afraid to try to move. What if my backbone were broken? I'd be paralyzed for life. But my legs responded; I got up on all fours, then straightened up. A soldier next to me was groaning. His shoulder had been broken; they carried him away. I stumbled off. Still in one piece! The pain in my back was bearable.

The next few days passed as in a feverish dream. A team of newsreel cameramen offered us a ride back to our Political Department center. I swallowed quantities of German painkillers, washed down by liquor, and walked with difficulty. At a party on the way an old Polish doctor told me that an injured back required plenty of exercise. On the third or fourth night I was feverish again and delirious, and didn't remember how Nepochilovich got me to our anti-Fascist school. Once there, however, I got better and was able to resume giving lectures.

I had no idea that these were to be my last days in the school—our successes at Graudenz were so striking and so undisputed that I was sure they would outweigh any accusations against me—and I threw myself into my lectures with enthusiasm.

I remember one particular day. After discussing the peculiarities of Nazi propaganda and the situation at the front, I asked if there were any questions, and a young graduate said that he did not want to remain a German, that it was shameful to be a German after all that German soldiers had done. The only thing to do, he said, was to go to America or Australia and acquire a new nationality. He was a simplehearted, not particularly intelligent but rather well-educated lad, and as he spoke he got more and more excited and almost cried.

His comrades looked at him glumly. These were German soldiers in March of 1945. They still remembered the bragging announcements of victory, the frenzied speeches of Hitler, Goebbels and Göring, and now they were listening to a call to reject their country.

I interrupted him tactfully, reminding the class of Stalin's words that Hitlers came and went but the German people were eternal. Then I went into how we—Communists, Marxists—understood our national duty.

I knew that other eyes besides my students' were fixed on me. I knew that they would soon be examining my case within our Party organization—the charge of pity for the Germans. But, then, there had been Graudenz; and anyhow, one couldn't very well renounce the truth out of fear of malicious smears. After all, these young Germans were to be our comrades tomorrow.

'One cannot renounce one's nation,' I said, 'just as one cannot renounce oneself. Many Germans today probably feel unbearable shame and despair. This is understandable, but it cannot be approved. When two or three years ago there were German émigrés, and some Germans inside Germany, who wanted to give up their nationality—and this in the days when the swastika flew over the Bay of Biscay and the banks of the Volga, over the Pyrenees, the Caucasus and the Sahara—these gestures were admirable. The Germans who refused to be German in the years of the Wehrmacht's victories were heroes. But to renounce one's nation in a time of defeat is more a sign of faintheartedness. Not since the Thirty Years' War has your country known such disasters. Not since Napoleon's conquests has it experienced such humiliation. Now as never before Germany has need of strong and honest people.'

For a minute, hearing myself speak, I felt that my words were acquiring a life of their own. They were being heeded by soldiers in alien uniforms, hardened front-line men with dimmed eyes and stern, dark faces and new recruits of lighter and softer mien. Some of them didn't know what had happened to their friends and relatives; others knew all too well, and wondered what other anguish was in store for their country and their homes.

I told them that Germany's true greatness had never lain in feats of arms or military victories—that, on the contrary, wars more often than not brought the Germans mortification and woe.

'You were taught that the Prussian, Bismarckian victories created the German Empire and brought it to greatness, but this greatness was sham. Less than fifty years after Sedan came Verdun and the empire's collapse. And now it is clear that the new peace will be worse than Versailles. But there is another and more authentic greatness in Germany, the greatness of the German spirit, the German mind. The German Gutenberg invented printing: it was he who, in the truest sense, conquered the world. The Germans Dürer, Cranach and Holbein created an art that for centuries has gladdened the hearts of people of all races and nations. The German Martin Luther broke the chains of medieval dogmatism and enriched your language and your poetry. The Germans Leibnitz, Kant, Hegel and Feuerbach taught all mankind how to think. The Germans Lessing, Goethe, Schiller, Hölderlin and Heine made German literature the glory of the world.'

I spoke of Bach, Mozart, Beethoven, Wagner; of the wonderful living German writers—Thomas Mann, Berthold Brecht and many others—that had been hidden from them; of the long succession of real German heroes, from the Jacobins to Karl Marx and Friedrich Engels to the anti-Fascists who in our own day were continuing the tradition of German greatness in the German underground, in the Soviet armies, in partisan units behind the Nazi lines. I argued that those who saw Germany's principal merits in terms of imperial power, cannon and a barracks 'order,' those who reposed the main virtues of the German character in blind obedience and unthinking self-sacrifice, were the worst enemies of German culture. Hence, it was not by chance that the highest flowering of the German spirit coincided with periods of administrative, political and military weakening. On the cultural map of the late eighteenth and early nineteenth centuries the capital of the German spirit was little Weimar; and Berlin acquired international cultural importance only after the Reich's defeat in 1918. So today there was no cause for despair: the military defeat of the Third Reich would not mean the defeat of the German spirit and the German mind. On the contrary, only now would Germany's creative potential be fully liberated.

They listened intently. I could imagine what they thought. Long-familiar concepts—the German spirit, Fatherland, national honor, the legacy of the past—but linked to words that were quite unfamiliar or had only yesterday carried a load of hostile associations: proletarian revolution; the great truth of Marxism; scientific Communism born in Germany; humanistic Russian culture. When I finished, the silence was almost tangible. Then they started asking questions.

'What territories will be taken away from Germany?'

'Is it true that they want to turn Germany into one big potato field?'

'Can't we be united with the Soviet Union as one or as several republics—Prussia, Bavaria, Württemburg?'

'But America and England are capitalistic countries; won't they start fighting the Soviet Union now?'

I answered as best I could, falling back on a joke when I had to. The emotional tension gave way to an ordinary chat.

From time to time, while waiting for my case to come up, I was overcome by black, unaccountable melancholy. On March 17 I was called up before my Party peers.

At the meeting Zabashtansky was conciliatory. 'True, the Comrade Major permitted himself a number of politically incorrect statements,' he said mildly, 'but more recently he seems to have come to his senses, and he did some good work in Graudenz.'

Belyaev was terse and even admitted to some mistakes of his own.

I too spoke softly, saying that my comrades had misunderstood me; I did not, and could not, have meant what they thought I did. But I admitted that I had been impulsive, undisciplined, even insubordinate.

A lieutenant colonel whom I knew as a clever careerist kept asking me whether I had told them everything: were there any other reasons my comrades might have misunderstood me? I kept repeating that there was nothing I could add, that I was ready to accept a reprimand, and that I was sure it would be voided by my subsequent work.

My friends Klyuev, Mulin and Goldstein were not there. Zabashtansky had sent them off on various missions the previous day. The Party leadership of our section was represented by Zabashtansky, Belyaev and a Party official named Victor Sborshikov. I had known Victor from the old days on the Northwestern Front. He too counted himself my friend, almost my pupil. I had helped him study German and had pushed him for promotions and awards. We were accepted as candidates for Party membership together in 1943; by now he was a full member, whereas I was still in the candidate-member category. I took his presence at the meeting as a good sign. Yet it was Victor who said in a calm, businesslike tone: 'I move that he be excluded as candidate-member of the Party.'

The next day there was a meeting of the full Party membership. I had a chill and a raging fever and could hardly walk. Asked for an 'explanation,' I spoke rather incoherently, repeating that I had been misunderstood. Why? I could not tell. I had not pitied the Germans; I had been concerned about the morality and discipline of our army. Perhaps, objectively, I had erred, but subjectively I had wanted only the best.

Zabashtansky, on the other hand, spoke quite differently from the previous day. Recounting one of our arguments, he said, 'He wouldn't let me get a word in about the German atrocities in Maidanek*—kept insisting that they killed Germans there too.' He said that I had 'been friendly with the spies Wilms and Hans R.'; that when he shipped them off to Moscow, I gave them letters of recommendation, practically proposing that they be decorated. And now, of course, they were under arrest.

I shouted, 'That's a lie!'

I was told to be still, and General Okorokov said, 'There you see him —the lover of truth! You see his kind of truth? Defending spies!'

Zabashtansky again and again called on them to 'uncover the roots,' 'expose the ideologically hostile soil.' 'All his life, while we worked and struggled, he spent his time studying. Whom did he study with? What did he learn?'

Belyaev confessed that he had been lax. I had admitted to him that I had long had plenty of German books, magazines and newspapers at home, and he, Belyaev, 'had not realized that this was clear evidence of ideological corruption, a link with alien, hostile, petit bourgeois— bourgeois, in fact!—German ideology.' In East Prussia, I had occupied myself with 'saving Germans and their property and preaching pity for the Germans, in spite of the indignation of our officers and men.'

The chairman of the Party commission read gloomily and interminably from the writings of Lenin and Stalin, dissecting my 'demagogic tricks' both 'objectively' and 'subjectively' and tracing them, I believe, back to Bukharin and Trotsky. I felt my mind glazing over. The rank and file Party members present hardly listened; they conversed in an undertone or went out for a cigarette. The chairman had to call them to order.

The last to speak was General Okorokov. 'He gave us trouble on the Northwestern Front too. He had the reputation of being some kind of young, foolhardy type, some kind of Don Quixote. Didn't know much about discipline, but, on the other hand, here was a man who wasn't afraid to look you in the eye and speak the unvarnished truth, whoever you were. And a scholar, you see, spoke different languages, a professor to those—what do you call 'em?—anti-Fascists! The Germans all seemed to listen to him. But now we must ask ourselves: What kind of

*Nazi death camp in Poland.

anti-Fascists did he prepare for us? What did he teach them, if he turns out to be so friendly with spies? All these years we fussed over him, tried to educate him, reprimanded him, excused him. We hoped that he could be reeducated, that his petit bourgeois core, the birthmarks of his bourgeois intellectual consciousness, could be overcome. After all, why all these waverings of his? Because he never went through the forging of a proletarian, he never acquired a Party backbone.

'Now everything is clear. This wasn't wavering or vacillation. These weren't the accidental fragments or remnants of an alien ideology. No, this was a whole system! Yes, a system of viewpoints—what can be called a world view! A world view that is profoundly alien to us—hostile, I would say. Others have spoken here of the subjective and the objective. I see it like this: Subjectively, he may have imagined himself a hero, a scholar, a professor of anti-Fascism. But objectively, he was not a Communist, not a Soviet officer, not a Russian or a Jew, but a German agent in our midst.'

General Okorokov's words hit me hard, but dully, as though through a thick cotton blanket. Pain bored into my spine. My head and eyes ached. I understood only one thing: it was useless to resist. When the chairman asked me, 'Do you have anything to say?' I answered, 'No.' Then, trying to speak calmly, 'I request permission to leave. I am not well.' I seem to remember their taking a vote on that. Walking out, I tripped and fell in the dark. I lay with the cool, wet grass against my face, not wanting to get up. Somehow I managed to get to the house where I was staying.

Next morning my temperature was down, but the back pain was still bad and I was so weak that I could hardly stand. They called me over to the Party commission. The vote had gone against me. I had been expelled from the Party for 'gross political errors, for showing pity for the Germans, for bourgeois humanism, and for harmful statements on questions of current policy.' Belyaev's phrase—'saving the Germans and their property'—was also made part of the official text. (It was to become a formula that would dog me through the indictments and hearings ahead.) My card as candidate-member of the Party was taken from me.

I appealed the decision to the Party bureau of the Central Political Administration. 'I cannot live without the Party,' I wrote, rejecting all the accusations against me and insisting on the facts. Surely the Central Political Administration knew that neither Wilms nor Hans R. was a spy, or under arrest; surely that single lie was enough to open their eyes to the untruthfulness of my accusers!

Toward evening the fever was back. I was sent to the field hospital. Before leaving, I was given a large package sealed with wax—my dossier. As I stood in the yard waiting for the vehicle that was to take me to the hospital, a woman ran up. It was Nina.

Nina was another of my friends from the Northwestern Front, where she had worked as a typist in the Political Department. We had quarreled bitterly over my attitude toward the Germans, and we had made up. Flung together by events, we had been briefly intimate; then she married a handsome lieutenant colonel in the Political Department, who became my friend, and she went to work for counterintelligence. And I met Lyuba.

Now Lyuba was off on some mission, and Nina was standing in front of me, crying and saying, 'How awful . . . I'm so afraid for you. . . .'

I remembered her telling me once, 'I implore you, be careful. Zabashtansky hates you—you have no idea how he hates you. He hates all intellectuals, and he's an anti-Semite. Be careful; don't quarrel with him, don't bare your soul to him, don't drink with him—you say all kinds of things when you drink.'

Seeing her here, her breath coming quickly from running to catch me before I left, I felt a kind of sweet, tender melancholy. We were linked by almost four years of war, and now, perhaps, I would never see her again.

'The worst thing,' she said, 'is that counterintelligence is full of those new people. The old ones from the Northwestern Front, they respected you. But these new ones, they don't like you at all. Please, take care of yourself.'

She kissed me good-bye. The car arrived, and I got in.

**11**

IN THE field prison in Tuchel, where I was taken from the hospital, Captain Poshekhonov, who conducted my first interrogation, seemed quite friendly the second time he called me in. All he wanted me to do was sign the record of my testimony. When I asked him how long he thought I'd have to wait for my case to be settled, he said cheerfully, almost with a wink, 'Who knows—maybe we'll be drinking together on May Day.'

The prisoners were served a watery gruel, made of millet and smelling of motor oil, in used tin cans. I couldn't get it down at first, and ate only the daily portions of bread and sugar. April 9, 1945, was my thirty-third birthday, and that morning our cell boss, the former White Russian Colonel Pyotr Berulya, presented me with a pound of sugar, made up of ten or eleven individual portions. It was a birthday present from my cell mates, and it gave me my first moment of happiness in prison. They, too, were hungry and afraid, yet they did what little they could to provide a bit of human warmth to one of their fellowmen.

Some of them I remember to this day.

For Pyotr Vikentievich Berulya, the Civil War had come as an unavoidable extension of his military service. A career officer in the Czar's army, he had attained the rank of captain by 1914. After the end of the First World War he continued to serve, first under Denikin,* then under Wrangel,* against the new—internal—foe. Orphaned early in life and never finding the time to marry, he knew nothing but the army—the barracks, the social gatherings, the campaigns, the trenches, the field hospitals, the few friends among his messmates, the few

*General Anton Ivanovich Denikin and Baron Peter Nikolaievich Wrangel, White Army commanders in the Russian Civil War.

interludes of mostly drunken leisure. After the Whites' collapse, he found himself in Poland. There, at last, he acquired a wife, a domineering woman who owned a woman's dress shop in the city of Bydgoszcz, where he was put to work as a kind of doorman in charge of polite conversation with the customers. They had children, who grew up under the care of governesses and later in boarding schools; he never felt that they really noticed him; the home was the domain of *Pani Matusia*.

He was never much interested in politics. He subscribed to only one paper, put out by a Czarist officers' union; this kept him in touch with what remained of his world—who had done what, who had died, what anniversaries or other memorable dates there were to be remembered. Now and then he managed to get enough money from his closefisted wife to pay his dues at the officers' union, but he never went to their conferences or receptions. The Civil War had left a bitter aftertaste: vain strivings, vain sacrifices, senseless cruelties, senseless destruction. The Bolsheviks remained an enigma to him. True, he no longer believed that they were all Jews, or Latvians, or Chinese, but he regarded them as creatures of an alien, malignant breed.

In 1939, with the start of a new war, he saw the Hitlerites killing Poles in the streets, hanging them on lampposts and from verandas; he saw the rowdies among the *Volksdeutsch* of their part of Poland driving multitudes of Polish women, children and old people out of the city, which had become a part of the Third Reich. Then came the German invasion of the Soviet Union. He was sure that the Germans would be in Moscow in no time. Instead, with every passing week, with every passing month, he felt the return of a long-forgotten feeling of pride in his own country, his own people, comparable to what he had felt when he was commissioned as an officer. More and more he came to feel that everything had changed. It was from Russia—his Russia!—that salvation was on its way.

He met our troops with tearful rapture, embracing them, inviting them to his home, plying them with food and drink. His wife and children looked at him with new respect. But his spontaneity proved fatal. A month later he was under arrest, and an interrogator of SMERSH* was demanding that he confess how many Red Army men he had hanged during the Civil War and what mission he had now been given by the Germans.

These interrogations continued in the prison where I knew him.

*SMERSH: the Soviet military counterintelligence organization of the Second World War, an acronym for 'Death to Spies.'

Sometimes he was beaten; at such times, this dried-up little old man would return to our cell looking even older, trying to hold himself straight, but with a sad perplexity showing in his pale blue eyes. To keep up appearances, he would bustle about the cell, handing out the cans of gruel and performing his other duties as cell boss. The prison authorities let me have all the tobacco in my suitcase, and I gave it to Pyotr Vikentievich, who established a tobacco ration for everyone in the cell and enforced it strictly while the supply lasted. When he was called for interrogation, he would entrust the day's rations to a specially designated deputy.

In May a military tribunal sentenced Berulya to eight years. He signaled the number with his fingers when they led him past our cell.

He was my first live 'White Guardsman.' I did not try to resist the sympathy I felt for this affable, kindhearted and not unintelligent man. At the same time, I regarded my feelings for him as 'subjective,' and, hence, not as a proper basis for judging someone from the camp of the class enemy. I believed that a real, revolutionary Socialist ethic flowed from 'objective historical necessity,' under which everyone was to be judged in accordance with the interests of the state, of the Party and of the workers' collective. A higher necessity could demand the strictest punishment, including death, for someone you liked person-ally, even someone related to you by blood. We were taught, when we were young, that it was our duty as citizens and members of the Komsomol to denounce friends and relatives, if need be, and to keep nothing from the Party. I never believed that Bukharin and Trotsky were Gestapo agents or that they had wanted to kill Lenin, and I was sure that Stalin never believed it either. But I regarded the purge trials of 1937 and 1938 as an expression of some farsighted policy; I believed that, on balance, Stalin was right in deciding on these terrible measures in order to discredit all forms of political opposition, once and for all. We were a besieged fortress; we had to be united, knowing neither vacillation nor doubt. But to most people—the 'broad masses'—the theoretical differences between left and right within the Party were difficult to understand: both sides quoted Lenin and swore loyalty to the October Revolution. Therefore, the opposition leaders had to be depicted as deviationists and villains, so that the people would come to hate them.

Finding myself among those marked out for such hatred, I did not lose my convictions. I remained concerned with my ability to view everything in an 'objective' light. In prison I became even more consistent a Stalinist. What I was afraid of, more than anything else, was that my sense of personal injury would impair my view of what remained most important to the life of my country and of the world. That vision was essential to me as a source of spiritual strength, of my conception of myself as part of a great whole. Without that conviction my life would lose its meaning—my past life and whatever lay ahead. Let things go badly for me; let me suffer unjustly. I would not give in; I would still be more honest, more enlightened, more worthy than those who accused me and judged me and kept me in jail.

I also believed that the generals, the men of the NKVD,* the judges and the jailers were all blood of my blood, bone of my bone; that we were all soldiers in one army. Only some were more intelligent and conscientious than others, and some were stupider and worse than they should be. Even if a majority of the NKVD men, the prosecutors and the judges were no good, the overall objectives of the sum total of their work were just and historically necessary. And so I believed that no amount of mistakes or miscalculations or injustices could alter the aggregate or halt the coming triumph of Socialism.

Pyotr Vikentievich Berulya had been a 'White Guardsman,' an open enemy of the Soviet cause. Hence, his arrest and sentencing were fully justified. Yet I could see that his enmity had long since given way to other feelings; I could see that he was a good and brave man; and, pitying him, I felt no pangs of Party conscience. Aware of this contradiction in my thoughts and feelings, I consoled myself by saying that contradiction was what the materialist dialectic was all about.

Words! What can they not explain away when you want them to!

The seventeen Yugoslavs in our cell were all of Russian descent. They were in a German war-prisoner camp for Yugoslav officers. When we liberated the camp, they said that they were really Russians, and some of them wanted to join our side and go on fighting. While the other inmates were repatriated to Yugoslavia, these seventeen were detained on suspicion of 'espionage and treason against the Motherland.'

Ivan Ivanovich Kivelyuk had been a colonel of the Royal Yugoslav Army. He had also been a judge, and, he told me, chairman of the Yugoslav Central Military Tribunal; more than the other Yugoslavs,

*The Soviet secret police, whose designations since the Russian Revolution have changed as follows: Cheka (1917–22), GPU (1922), OGPU (1922–34), NKVD (1934–46), MGB (1946–53), MVD (1953 ) and KGB (1953 on).

he was nonplussed by the legal circumstances of their detention. Ivan Ivanovich had rather naive and academic notions of the law. He assumed, for instance, that the legal authorities should know whether the crimes of which the detained was suspected could logically have been committed by him.

'Explain this to me, *Gospodin*—excuse me, Comrade Major.' A big man with a shock of graying hair and a very Slavic face, Ivan Ivanovich spoke Russian with a Ukrainian accent, throwing in Serbian and Polish words. 'How can this be? The interrogator tells me, "We can charge you with betrayal of the Motherland." What Motherland? I was a native-born citizen of the Austro-Hungarian Empire, though of Russian descent. In nineteen-fourteen I didn't want to fight for the Emperor Franz Josef against my brother Slavs, so, at the first opportunity, I crossed over to the Russian lines. They wouldn't take me into the Russian army, so I got back to Serbia via England, France and Italy. So, in all of my life, I spent, maybe, twenty-one days in Russia. After the war I became a citizen of the new Yugoslavia. So tell me, what Motherland did I betray?'

I tried to answer, explaining the special features of revolutionary legality and the workings of the dialectic.

'And there's something else I can't understand,' he would go on. 'This lieutenant colonel of yours—he's well-dressed and looks intelligent enough, and suddenly he hits me on the shoulder with his rubber truncheon and begins to shout and use words a drunken peasant would be ashamed of. And I am senior to him in years and in rank, and I am not under arrest, as he himself admits. How is one to understand this? How can people like that be put in authority?

'And something else, too. The interrogator says, "Confess, how many Communists did you send to the gallows? We know everything," he shouts. "You'd better confess, or we'll have you executed."

'Now, in our army, all my responsible officers had to know the legal codes of all the armies of Europe. Then why don't your responsible officers know that in Yugoslavia, military tribunals had competence only over military offenses—desertion, breach of discipline, and so on— and all political cases and espionage came before the Royal Tribunal? And I was the chairman of the Central *Military* Tribunal—in other words, the Court of Appeals. So I could not have sat in trial over anyone—much less, say, a Communist—in a political case. All of which should be clear to anyone who has ever gone to law school!'

I tried to make allowances for the shortage of qualified personnel. He listened politely, but apparently found my excuses unconvincing and became more constrained in his conversation, turning to other subjects, like literature and education.

Tadeusz Ruzanski completed his education in a Polish underground high school in Nazi-occupied Warsaw. Most of his graduating class joined the Resistance. Tadeusz commanded a platoon during the Warsaw uprising of 1944. They were retreating through the sewage system in the final days of the battle when they received General Bor-Komorowski's* order to capitulate.

It was rough on the Warsaw rebels in the German camps. They were treated as badly as Russian prisoners in the most difficult times, and perhaps even worse. The first four days they were not given anything to eat or drink; their wounded were shot, and everyone was beaten. They were guarded by German and Ukrainian SS from the 'Volyn' Division, which had suffered severe losses in the Warsaw street battles.

Tadeusz still carried visible reminders of that time. All his front teeth had been knocked out; he had scars on his head and body from rifle butts and hobnailed boots. That's why his appearance struck me as so extraordinary at first—youthful, almost childish, gray eyes; a youth's unwrinkled brow, but an old man's face with drooping skin; a fallen, toothless mouth; and sparse graying hair.

There followed a month of hunger and beatings. Dozens of prisoners died every day. The Germans waited for the corpses to pile up before letting the prisoners carry them out of the camp. Then, one day, came a visit from a commission of German and Polish doctors. The healthiest prisoners—those who could still walk—were moved to another camp, with clean barracks and good medical care. There the Germans began to feed them—not just adequately, but intensively; they even got chocolates and wine.

When the prisoners had recovered sufficiently, they were put through a course of training in guerrilla warfare. They were issued training weapons (such as rifles with the locks removed so that they could not be fired) and Polish uniforms (except for German-made boots), and their instructors were Polish officers who had fought against the Germans in the early days of the war. German officers would often stand and watch, saluting when they came and went. No one could understand what was going on, but the prisoners were glad to be eating so well.

In January 1945 the Germans issued excellent winter uniforms and formed the Poles into military units. One day they were drawn up in ranks and addressed by a colonel of the German General Staff:

*The leader of the Polish underground and the Warsaw uprising.

'Gentlemen, up to now we have been enemies. But the German army knows how to respect the military valor of its enemies. We respect you for your patriotism and your daring.

'The German army is being forced to leave the territory of your Fatherland. We know that many of you have reason to be dissatisfied with us, and with what you have experienced during the occupation. But, gentlemen, you are all soldiers, and I don't have to explain to you that this is war, a war unprecedented in scale and intensity. After the victory of the German Empire, a reasonable and just order will be established over all of Europe, an order worthy of the traditions of our all-European culture. Because, no matter how much we may have fought each other, we are all Europeans. And now, Asiatic hordes are moving against your Fatherland from the east—those same barbarians who slaughtered your comrades in Katyn, who drove hundreds of thousands of Poles to Siberia, who betrayed you when you fought in Warsaw—those bands of kikes and Mongols, those swarms of coarse, cruel Muscovites who kept your nation under a one-hundred-fifty-year yoke.

'Yesterday, we were enemies. But today, history has decided otherwise. By the will of history, in the interests of all the peoples of Europe, in the interests of your Fatherland, we have become allies. And because of that, we are giving you our best weapons and our best equipment and are presenting you with the opportunity to defend your long-suffering Poland against the Soviet invasion with the same valor with which you fought against us.'

Tadeusz was part of a thirty-man platoon, under the command of a Polish major. They were loaded onto two trucks—a third truck was filled with automatic weapons, pistols, bazookas, mortars, grenades, explosives, food rations, medical supplies and even cases of cognac—and they set forth under the direction of a four-man German escort team. By evening they encamped in a wood west of Bydgoszcz. From the east came the sound of artillery. As soon as they began to unload the weapons, the Poles seized the Germans, who did not try to resist.

Digging in, the platoon scouted the rear with the object of attacking the German communication lines. But the Germans had fallen back, and by morning Soviet tanks were rolling along the highway. The Poles marched out toward them, singing, and were greeted by the Russians like brothers. They shared their bottles of German cognac and exchanged pistols as souvenirs. But as other Soviet units moved up, the Poles were first disarmed, then interned, and finally told that they were under arrest on suspicion of 'treason against the Motherland.'

We all coached Tadeusz on what he should say at the interrogations. But the interrogator held to his own: 'The Soviet army is allied to Poland. The Germans are our common enemy. You took up German weapons in order to attack the Soviet troops. Hence, you betrayed your Motherland. You say you are subject only to Polish courts. But we are Poland's allies and must try you as traitors to Poland.'

One of the Germans in our cell was a soldier from Hamburg, a man with a pale, intelligent, bearded face who was a Communist. At first the German authorities wouldn't take him into the army as politically unreliable; then they put him in a rear-area unit. He talked about what had happened to him with amazing objectivity. He was not angry at our people for arresting him; he did not complain about being kept in prison and under interrogation. He said that he understood the mistrust and harshness of the Russian *Genossen*; he thought that he would be sentenced to forced labor; he only regretted that he would see Russia in that way. Still, it was good that he would be taken to Russia—he had long dreamed of going there—and would participate in the construction of Socialism.

He discussed all this the way many of the German Communists I had known reasoned—in logical sequence, basing every deduction on the previous one, all in the abstract: Hitler's armies caused your people much suffering, and ordinary people cannot distinguish an army from its nation and people; the German people put up with the Hitler regime for a long time, and, hence, the Soviet people distrust all Germans, especially Germans in military uniform; therefore, I became an object of mistrust and hatred among the Soviet people. Since I have no way to resist this, and since, at the same time, I was and remain a Communist, I am duty-bound to work as hard as I can for the good of the Soviet nation, for this means working for the good of the world, and therefore for the good of the German proletariat.

The trials took place in May. Tadeusz was sentenced to eight years, his comrades to terms ranging from eight to fifteen years. All the Germans, including the Communist soldier, were sentenced to be shot. I don't know if this monstrous sentence was carried out.

There are two others I remember. They were Russians in German army coats—a somewhat older man with a reddish beard and darting eyes, and a younger fellow steeped in silence. The redhead would come back from interrogations beaten up, moaning, looking as desperate as a hunted animal.

They were Vlasovites—traitors who had served under the Nazis. At least, that's what they were known as. Later I learned that they weren't Vlasovites but *hiwi*—from *Hilfswillige*, 'willing to help.' That was what the Germans called a special unit formed in 1942 of Soviet war prisoners who volunteered to work in the Wehrmacht as grooms for the dray horses, kitchen help, hospital orderlies, drivers, maintenance men, and so forth. They were given German uniforms without insignia, the same rations as German soldiers, and somewhat lower pay. They were not, as a rule, issued weapons.

I came across the *hiwi* for the first time in the summer of 1944 in Belorussia. Our soldiers, when they captured them, would sometimes deal with them on the spot.

I knew that the *hiwi* were not Vlasovites; I didn't think it right to kill them out of hand. Even the Vlasovites, I knew, had, for the most part, 'signed on' only to escape from starvation—and some of them, I had heard, had volunteered with the idea of getting German arms and joining our partisans. Nonetheless, I regarded both the *hiwi* and the Vlasovites as creatures of a lower order, worthy only of contempt.

The *hiwi* were recruited only from among Soviet prisoners. The soldiers of all the other armies at war against Germany were left to their own devices in the war-prisoner camps. They were treated as rightful citizens of their countries; they would get packages from their relatives and from the International Red Cross; they could send and receive letters, and they knew that after the war they would all go home. With our men the situation was different. Even before the war it had been drummed into them that to be taken prisoner was tantamount to betrayal of their country. Many of them knew well enough what had happened in 1937 and 1938, and how our rules of 'vigilance' ordained distrust of anyone who had had any contact with the 'enemy,' or just with foreigners. They knew, too, that none of the men who had been taken prisoner in the war with Finland or the clashes with the Japanese in the 1930s had come back to their families. All this made it much easier for the Germans to persuade their Soviet prisoners that Stalin had written them off; that that was why they did not receive any letters or packages; that the Soviet government was the only power in the world not to have recognized the Hague Convention on the treatment of war prisoners, and that it regarded them all as traitors. Why, I would often be asked maliciously by the Germans and Poles I met in my subsequent years in jails and prison camps—why was it that not one of the bourgeois countries conquered by Germany could furnish Hitler with more than, say, a battalion of troops while in the Soviet Union hundreds of thousands—almost a million—soldiers and officers enlisted with the Germans in Vlasovite and Cossack units; in the various 'legions' of the Tatar-Chuvash, Caucasian and Turkestan minorities; in two divisions associated with the SS; and, as *hiwi*, in the Wehrmacht itself?

What could I say? Of course, no war prisoners of any other country produced as many martyrs and heroes—men who remained loyal in spite of everything, organized resistance groups in Vlasovite barracks and Nazi death camps, and faced torture and death with unflinching courage. But even those who were not heroes and who broke under torture—even they could not have later been judged and condemned the way they were except by callous bureaucrats for whom all concepts of truth, law, common sense, even their own nation's best interests, took second place to a rigid compulsion to act 'by the rules,' in accordance with the 'current situation,' and so as not to risk the displeasure of 'higher authorities.' This compulsion was the motive power of that huge, many-faced, insatiably hungry machine whose different parts were called 'organs of state security,' 'prosecutors' offices,' 'courts,' 'military tribunals,' 'Gulags.'* Hundreds of thousands who survived the war, the German camps and the Gestapo were fed into the maw of this Kafkaesque machine—crudely primitive, yet incredibly complex; blind and deaf, yet armed with a thousand eyes and a thousand ears—and were crushed in its gears. And so absurdly was the machine constructed that it did not differentiate between those who had actually served the Nazis as police agents, executioners and informers and those whom harsh circumstance and the cruel indifference of the Stalin government had driven into the ranks of the *hiwi* or the labor battalions of the prison camps—between the luckless flotsam of war, like the young 'spies' I met on my first night in prison, and the real heroes of German captivity. To all of them, the interrogator put the same questions:

'Why didn't you shoot yourself instead of surrendering?'

'Why didn't you die in the war-prisoners' camp?'

'What state secrets did you pass onto the Germans?'

'What assignments were you given by the Gestapo and the Abwehr?'

For those liberated by the English or the Americans, there was an additional question: 'What assignments were you given by the Anglo-American intelligence?'

One former war prisoner told me: 'If the Germans had said, right off, "Serve under us, or we'll shoot you," most of us, I think, would have replied, "Then shoot us, you bastards; we're not traitors." But when

*Gulag: acronym for Central Administration of Corrective Labor Camps.

you're starving, week after week and month after month, when you can't think of anything except food, when you eat grass and chew on an old belt, when you're marched off in formation and the sight of a turnip in the ground or a piece of carrion makes you break ranks, no longer caring if the guards shoot you down—when you've reached that state, there's no need for threats or blows to make you into a Vlasovite or a *hiwi*—a plate of swill or a piece of bread will do it, without your knowing how it happened. Starvation is worse than death—it sucks out your brain and your character and your conscience. Anyone who has stood up against that kind of starvation is a superman—or, as they used to say in the old days, a saint.'

I was to hear such explanations again and again. The more I knew of hunger, the better I understood them and the more admiration I felt for people whom hunger had not deprived of bravery and conscience. The interrogators and prosecutors, who knew nothing of hunger or conscience, could not understand them—nor did they particularly want to.

An order: Everyone out. The prison was being moved to keep up with the front. We were packed together in an open truck, with our belongings. Two guards with submachine guns sat on wooden benches on either side of us, and two others, with police dogs, guarded the back. 'No talking! No squirming about! Any move to get up will be taken as an attempt to escape! The guards will shoot without warning!'

We drove for a long time in the warm spring sunshine. Craning my neck, I could see the tender green of the fields and the roadside trees. Now and then we would be overtaken by columns of vehicles filled with our soldiers. Some of them would shout, 'Vlasovites! Spies! Hang them all!' Little German towns flitted by. We were driving through Pomerania. Less and less destruction. German civilians, men and women, walking placidly along the streets.

Turning off the highway into a wood, we drove through a gate and stopped before a long, white, two-story structure adorned with little towers and with a shattered marble crest over the entrance. We were herded into a large basement room and told to sit down on the floor. Roll call. By surname. In reply, you were supposed to give your first name and patronymic; specify the statute under which you were arrested; state whether you had been sentenced or were awaiting trial; and, if sentenced, specify the number of years. The prison commander, the lieutenant with the shiny new shoulder boards, sat astride a chair, a cigarette between his teeth, supplying the substance of each statute—

whether to educate his subordinates or for the sheer sound of it, I could not tell.

A prisoner would respond: 'Article Fifty-eight, Section One-B, awaiting trial.'

Prison commander: 'Traitor to the Motherland.'

Prisoner: 'Article Fifty-eight, Section Six, ten years.'

Prison commander: 'Spy.'

'Article One Hundred and Thirty-six, awaiting trial.'

'Murderer.'

'Article One Hundred and Ninety-three, Section One, eight years.'

'Deserter.'

My surname. I responded: 'Article Fifty-eight, Section Ten, awaiting trial.'

'An anti-Soviet.'

'That's a lie! I am a victim of slander—as the investigation will show!'

The lieutenant raised himself from his chair. 'Ah, it's you. Still trying to prove your innocence?'

'And I'll prove it!'

'All right. But without any interruptions here.'

We were led up to a semicircular hall, its walls hung with stags' horns and boars' heads. Over the door to the inner quarters, a quotation in black-and-gold Gothic lettering proclaimed the glorious mission of the Prussian nobleman.

Our cell: a bare room off a long corridor. Two windows, without glass, boarded up except for a tiny opening on the top. A jagged peep-hole cut through the door. An empty gasoline can with wooden handles—the latrine bucket. On one of the walls, another black-and-gold inscription boasting of Prussian exploits.

Of the men I had spent two weeks with in our previous location, only the 'White Guardsman' Beryula and the Pole Tadeusz Ruzanski were allocated to this cell. Tadeusz and I lay down on his overcoat and covered ourselves with mine.

The next day I felt as though a hot iron hoop were being tightened around my head: my sinus trouble, developed in the marshy damp of the Northwestern Front, was back with a vengeance. And I had a vile cold. A medic took my temperature and gave me some pills. The next morning Tadeusz told me that I had been delirious all night, cursing in Russian and German. That night I was called in for an interrogation.

A darkened room. A desk lamp turned toward me, so I could not see who was seated at the desk. A harsh, unfamiliar voice.

'Don't come any closer. Sit right there.'

A chair, in the cone of light, was placed about ten paces from the desk. I sat down.

'The investigation of your case is continuing. I am your interrogator, Major Vinogradov.'

He continued in a dispassionate monotone. 'I must inform you that your attempts to mislead the investigating authorities and conceal your criminal activities are all in vain. We know everything. Only a frank confession can save you and lighten your lot. You know the words of the great Soviet writer Maxim Gorky: "If the enemy does not surrender, he must be destroyed." Do you understand?'

This was a turn for the worse. What were they after now?

'No, I don't understand. I don't understand a thing. I didn't engage in any criminal activities.' My eyes swam from my sinus headache, and I was nauseated.

'I see you persist in your obstinacy. You have already given false evidence. We know that you defended the Germans and spread anti-Soviet slander. Only if you confess your guilt and help the investigation uncover the ideological roots of your bourgeois humanism—'

'Not bourgeois humanism! Socialist humanism! It wasn't the Germans I defended, but the Socialist morality of our army. I have explained all this to Captain Poshekhonov. He wrote it down in his report, which you must have.'

'What we have is our business. The investigation is starting from scratch.'

Another voice came from behind me. I looked around. A tall man in shiny boots; a lieutenant colonel with a cap of the rear-echelon forces. White gloves. A rubber hose in one hand, being flicked meaningfully against the palm of the other.

'What, he doesn't want to confess?' he said in a loud, disdainful voice. 'You'd better confess voluntarily, or we'll find other methods.'

I felt hollow—cold and feverish and hollow. Were we really back to the *Ezhovchina* of 1937?* Were they going to torture me? They'd make me 'confess,' inform against others, after which I'd die anyway—a miserable death, and a slow one. I saw his white, smoothly shaven, contemptuous face above me; the rubber hose in the white glove.

Suddenly, without being fully aware of my actions, I reared up and swung the chair over my head. With a thrill of exultation, I saw him cower, an arm over his face. I heard myself bellowing hoarsely.

*Ezhovchina: 'The time of Ezhov,' the period of terror that took its name from the then secret-police chief, Nikolai Ezhov.

'So you're going to strike me, fuck your mother, are you? Then do it right, you rear-echelon rat! Strike me dead with a bullet, not with that rubber shit! Or else you'll get your own back, in your clean-shaven snout, goddamn your fucking soul! German shells didn't scare me, and you're going to scare me with your little piece of rubber? Kill me, you worm! But the Soviet government will pay you back for it!'

My voice rang in my ears. There was a clatter of feet in the corridor. The room was filled with other men. The overhead light was on. A colonel with a red, jowly face was holding a glass of water to my lips. 'Come now, come, enough. Here, drink this. No one's going to beat you. Now, really, Barinov, what a silly trick. This is one of our own guys. From the front, too. He slipped up a little, that's all. We'll fix him up; we'll help him.' And, addressing me again: 'No one is about to beat you, or kill you. Now sit down, calm yourself, have a cigarette.'

I sat down, but this time with my back to a corner of the room. The cigarette I rolled with the tobacco he gave me was sweetly aromatic. To my humiliation I realized I was sobbing, unable to stop.

The colonel—it seemed he was the chief of the investigating unit, Rossiisky by name—walked back and forth in front of me, his belly spilling over his belt, waving his stumpy arms. 'I'm an old Cheka hand. I'm a veteran. I used to work with Felix himself.* I've had business with the SRs,† and the Trotskyists, and the Bukharinists. I interrogated the man who killed Kirov.‡ You can't slip anything past me, my friend.'

He coaxed me. 'Don't fight, my friend, don't fight. We know you. We know you better than you know yourself. You know what we're interested in? We want to see if you're sincere. We want you to bare yourself ideologically.'

To all my objections he would say, 'Come on, come on. You won't convince me that this stove is black when I can see it's white. No, brother, you can't plow a field with your prick. Better give in—you're not going to outsit us, you know.'

It wasn't the last time I was to hear from him about the white stove, the impracticability of plowing in that original fashion and the unlikelihood of my outsitting my jailers. He too liked to cite Gorky, though it

*Felix Dzerzhinsky, the first Soviet secret-police chief.
†The Social-Revolutionaries, an agrarian Socialist party which got the most votes in the elections to the Constituent Assembly at the end of 1917; opposed to the Bolshevik government, the party was later destroyed.
‡Sergei Kirov, Party boss of Leningrad, whose assassination in December 1934 led to the great terror of 1937–38. There are grounds for suspecting that Stalin instigated the assassination himself.

wasn't his strongest point. 'You know, as Gorky says—Gorky himself!
—the personal friend of Lenin and Stalin—how did he put it? "If you
don't confess . . ." No, "If you don't surrender, we'll destroy you."'

But on that first night Rossiisky was gentle, for the most part. 'We
only want what's best for you. We want to correct your mistakes. We're
not against you—we're fighting *for* you. Look, we've given you our
best interrogator: Major Vinogradov, an old Party member, chairman
of the Marxism-Leninism department of the Yaroslavl Pedagogical
Institute, a Ph.D. You see, we understand.'

Calming down, I began to talk. They listened. I began to think that I
could convince them. I told them about East Prussia, about my relations with Zabashtansky. I told them how grossly I had been slandered,
how adroitly I had been jockeyed out of the Party. They listened attentively—even, it seemed to me, sympathetically. I talked on and on,
inspired by their compassionate silence. Sometime during the night, my
fever abated.

When I was done, Rossiisky said, 'Well, maybe you're right. We'll
get to the bottom of this. But you must help us. After all, yours isn't a
criminal but a Party case, an ideological case. You must demonstrate
that you have condemned in your own heart all those mistakes you
committed in your youth. You know what I'm talking about?—that
Trotskyist business. No holding anything back, now! The more reso-
lutely you condemn your past sins, the more trustworthy you will be in
regard to your present actions. All right, Vinogradov, why don't you
cut it short? You can see he's not well, needs some rest. Well, see you
later. Here, have some more tobacco.'

He left the room together with Barinov. And Vinogradov put the
question that became crucial to my whole case.

'Tell me, when did you first join the struggle against the Party and
the Soviet government?'

'What do you mean? I joined no such struggle!'

'I'm talking about your Trotskyist past. Either you really condemn
that past and are prepared to give it the proper political evaluation, to
expose the roots, or you're not prepared to evaluate it, and, therefore,
you do not bare yourself ideologically before the Party.'

With that piece of sophistry he outwitted me. Yes, I thought, I
certainly couldn't take exception to that. Not only my illness, but the
whole process—the unexpected interrogation, then the threats, then
the friendly concern (a routine technique, I later learned), and finally
the crude but internalized logic of the question, combined that night
to make me reply, 'In February 1929.'

## 12

I WAS sixteen, in Kharkov, and looking for work. The juvenile labor exchange didn't have much to offer, and I spent most of my days reading: Marx, Engels, Plekhanov, Lenin, Kautsky, Bukharin, Trotsky, Lunacharsky, Zinoviev, Stalin, Preobrazhensky; minutes of Party congresses; the memoirs of Clemenceau, Noske and Denikin; various magazines—all this and more used to be published in those days. Politically, I was one of the 'unorganized.' At the age of fourteen I had been thrown out of the Pioneers for smoking, drinking vodka and keeping company with 'bourgeois' girls who smoked, painted their lips and wore high-heeled shoes. And in the technical school where I studied electrical engineering, my application for membership in the Komsomol was rejected because of my past sins, compounded by new offenses: I had taken part in a fistfight with pupils of another school, and, at a Komsomol meeting, I had spoken up against the Comintern line in China, condemning the alliance with the Kuomintang. With a repetition of the fistfight, I was expelled from the school.

Now and then the labor exchange would find me work unloading trucks or delivering messages or selling subscriptions, and I would spend the money on cigarettes, movies and beer. Evenings I liked to spend at the debates and poetry readings at the local writers' club. My friends and I would also meet there to read each other our verses, some of which would be published on the literary page of *The Kharkov Proletarian*.

One morning in February 1929 my cousin Mark Polyak came to see me. Looking mysterious, he said he had been waiting out in the street for my parents to leave for work and for my brother to leave for school. Taking two large packages wrapped in newspaper and tied with string out of his briefcase, he said, 'Hide this. They may search my place. And not a word to anyone.'

Mark was seven years older than I was, and his family considered him a genius. He had graduated with a degree in biology, had published a pamphlet called 'Dreams and Death,' and gave lectures in various clubs on such topics as 'What Is Life?' and 'The Beginnings of Man.' I looked up to him as a scholar and the possessor of a fabulous library—the entire half of a large bookcase. His desk was always piled high with books and brochures: philosophy, biology, history, political science (but no literature). He scoffed at my literary pretensions and attempts at poetry. 'Read Kant and Hegel, Plekhanov, Lenin, Freud. Verses are romantic piffle—nineteenth century—good for girls' albums, nothing else. And a smart, modern girl will prefer science, philosophy and serious political writing. To waste time on some tail-wagger, some silly goose with an album, is even more stupid than to write verses. Don't tell me you can be attracted to even a pretty girl if all she can talk about is, "Do you believe in love? Whom do you like better, Pushkin or Nadson? Ah, Lermontov—how lovely!" Better practice onanism—it's less harmful than killing time that way.'

He gibed at me but wasn't offended when, snapping back, I would call him a withered husk, a bookworm, a Laputan, a wart. And he gave me wonderful books to read.

One morning he told me confidentially that he was an active member of an underground group of 'Bolshevik-Leninists'—the political opposition, which the Stalinist bureaucracy had stigmatized as Trotskyist and Zinovievist. He let me read pamphlets about Trotsky's exile, the platform of the 'united Leninist opposition' of 1927, the 'Notes of a conversation between Bukharin and Kamenev in August 1928,' etc. Even before that, I had pored over the records of the 14th and 15th Party congresses, the Party conferences, the plenary meetings of the Comintern executive committee, and Pravda's 'discussion papers.' Reading all this often had an unsettling effect on me. The speeches and articles of the oppositionists had a compelling revolutionary logic and ardor: they spoke out against the NEPmen,* the kulaks, the bureaucrats; against deals with the international bourgeoisie; for a world proletarian revolution. Yet I knew that they had been rejected by the Party majority, and, for a Bolshevik, the will of the majority was the highest law. Besides, with the country a besieged fortress, it was no time for schisms.

Mark contradicted me on that score. He reminded me that Lenin too had opposed the majority when it came to issues of principle, funda-

*NEP: Lenin's New Economic Policy of 1921–28, a partial concession to private enterprise.

mentals and the fate of the Revolution—when he split with the majority over the Brest-Litovsk peace treaty, for instance, or over his introduction of NEP. And the situation then had been much more difficult than now. He had me meet 'Comrade Volodya,' our contact with 'the Center' —the opposition leadership. This was Ema Kazakevich, who was later to win the Stalin Prize for literature. As far as I know, this role of his in the 1920s was known throughout his life only to a few of his closest friends. One day Mark took me along 'on business'—we took a droshky and brought home a trunk containing a small hand printing press, dubbed *Amerikanka*. Several times later I had to disassemble it and hide it, piece by piece, with my friends.

Mark was arrested in March, leaving me with two packages, which he had said were 'part of the Center's archives, particularly conspiratorial in nature.' I gave them to Vanya Kalyanik to hide. Vanya's father was a factory director and a staunch Stalinist, but Vanya was for the opposition, though he was more interested in poetry. Yet his was the home they searched. Apparently one of our crowd was an informer. Vanya behaved splendidly—didn't divulge a single name. The father was stunned when a cache of opposition literature, including texts of political appeals, reports, resolutions, planned announcements, figures, lists of political prisoners, and so on, was found in the space between the top of the Dutch stove and the ceiling. Vanya insisted that he had had no idea how this terrible material had gotten there—that he didn't even remember who had been to his house, since he had been blind drunk all week. His father, to his credit, didn't volunteer any information, although he knew of our political sentiments, having often argued with us.

Vanya was ordered to report to the GPU the next day. Naturally, I decided to go with him and confess. Being sure that I would be arrested, I said good-bye to the girl I was then in love with, wrote a farewell note to my parents (which she was to deliver if I did not return), and took along a supply of cigarettes. At the GPU, I said that I had hidden the packages in Vanya's house without telling him or anyone else and without knowing what was in them (which, strictly speaking, was true). I also declared that as a convinced Communist-Bolshevik-Leninist, even though not a member of the Komsomol, I was duty-bound not to reveal who had asked me to hide the packages, since I believed that the GPU in this case was following an incorrect line, persecuting genuine Leninists.

The interrogator at first twitted me: 'Some conspirator! When did you stop playing cops and robbers?' Then they let Vanya go, and two of them proceeded to 'educate' me. I, in turn, sought to indoctrinate them, quoting Lenin and Trotsky, citing facts, pointing out that before adopting the policy of 'building Socialism in one country'—the U.S.S.R. —Stalin himself had written in the first edition of *Problems of Leninism* that to believe in that goal was to believe in utopia. They let me go, making me sign a promise not to leave town. I was almost disappointed: The good-bye scene had been so moving; she had kissed me for the first time; I had felt like a gallant revolutionary, heir to the Old Bolsheviks and the People's Will movement, and here they had sent me out of the room like a naughty schoolboy!

At the labor exchange they had a whole week's work for me, collecting subscriptions for newspapers and magazines. In the process I took to distributing opposition leaflets. I even pasted some of them up in a locomotive factory, and I couldn't resist boasting about it to the very friend I had earlier told about the packages. The next night I was arrested.

It was curious, after my imprisonment in 1945, to recall the ten days I spent in Kharkov's House of Corrective Labor (the word 'prison' had been relegated to the vocabulary of the old regime). A clean cell, for three people; a sunny window; the voices of other inmates, arrested for ordinary crimes, raised in cheerful bickering or in their hoarse, underworld songs. They let us keep several rubles in cash, and with this money we could buy newspapers and magazines and complement our tasteless but plentiful meals (meat, noodles, gruel) with bread, sausage, cheese and candy. We could even order books from a woman librarian who came around every other day. The guards addressed us as 'comrades.'

They released me on April 9, my seventeenth birthday. My father was made responsible for my good behavior. Still true to my convictions, I attended several underground meetings and read and passed on a number of pamphlets. But by May of 1929, with the 'unmasking' of Bukharin, Rykov and Tomsky, the opposition movement began to disintegrate. There were letters in the newspapers by people announcing that they were leaving the opposition; one such letter, signed by Preobrazhensky, Radek and Smilga*—all three highly respected figures and longtime friends of Trotsky's—had a particularly strong effect. A secret underground meeting was held in a wood outside the city; a certain 'Comrade Alexander' from Moscow delivered a report on 'the

*Evgény Preobrazhensky, economic theoretician; Karl Radek, writer; Jan Smilga, political figure—all associated with the Trotskyist opposition within the Soviet Communist Party in the 1920s.

Zabashtansky standing *center* (marked with X)

Kopelev, *left*, with General von Seydlitz-Kurzbach, Stalingrad prisoner and vice-president of the *Freies Deutschland* Committee

Kopelev, *second from left*, in 1944 with German Generals Traut and Hoffmeister

Kopelev, 'Interlude' January–
February 1947

Dr. Nikolai Telyantz

Kopelev in prison, 1949–50

A sketch of Lev Kopelev in prison, 1948

current situation and the problems of the Leninist opposition.' He explained that the Party's Central Committee had, in effect, adopted the opposition's program of industrialization; that the danger of a kulak comeback was over; that Stalin himself had destroyed the sociological and theoretical base of his usurped power by appropriating the concepts and proposals of Preobrazhensky, Piatakov, Zinoviev, Kamenev, Rakovsky, Zalutsky and the other Leninists.

There were questions from the audience; debates sprang up; I found myself among those who argued against the need for any further opposition. The rightists had been exposed; an era of construction was beginning; the Party's general line was basically sound—why continue with the underground struggle against the Central Committee? To argue about who had appropriated whose thoughts—this was petty squabbling. The main thing now was to build factories and electric power plants, strengthen the Red Army. Let Trotsky in exile take care of the world revolution—we at home had to work with the Party and the working class, instead of widening the split and undermining the authority of the Central Committee and the Soviet government.

Soon after this meeting, Mark returned from 'political isolation' in the Urals; he too had left the opposition. Won over by newspaper articles, by the example of people like Mark, and, most of all, by Nadia, whom I had by then met and fallen deeply in love with (we registered as man and wife a year later), I went to the Komsomol and announced my resignation from the opposition.

The joyous welcome for the prodigal son that I had half-imagined when I wrote out my long declaration did not take place. A sharp-faced fellow who was chairman of the control commission met me with a dry and businesslike air.

'Hmm. Finally realized your comrades are full of bull, huh? Better late than never. Here. Here's a piece of paper. Write down all their names—everyone you knew. Which of them were Trotskyists, which were Zinovievists, and so on. If you don't remember the surname, write down the first name or the nickname—who, where from, where you met. What do you mean—why? Are you baring yourself before the Party and the Komsomol or just throwing dust in our eyes?'

I sat down and made a rather long list. I wanted to be frank; I believed that nothing should be kept hidden from the Party and the Komsomol. All the same, I held back a dozen or so names—people who had never been arrested or expelled from the Komsomol and who weren't in any kind of trouble. Sitting there under the portraits of

Lenin, Dzerzhinsky, Chubar, Petrovsky,* I was embarrassed to know that I was deceiving them. But I knew full well that if I added the names of Tanya A., Zina I., Kima R., Zoya B., Ilya B., Kolya P. and some others, I would be identifying people whom I myself had drawn into the opposition, who now thought differently (as I did), and who could never be enemies of the Party or do anything to damage Soviet interests. I would feel more ashamed naming even one of them than I did in holding back the whole list. And yet, if they found me out? Then I would say that I had forgotten these names, that I attached no importance to them—I'd think of something. But now I wouldn't write them down.

The official looked over my list. 'Fine. You didn't forget anyone? Sure? Good. That means you're baring yourself before the Party. Now, about you—what are you doing? Well, the labor exchange isn't for you. You're not a country boy; you're an educated sort. So educated that you got mixed up with the opposition. You've been using your education against us. Now you must try to use it to help us. The whole country is caught up in this liquidation of illiteracy business. The construction of Socialism requires literate cadres. You go to your labor exchange and tell them you want to be sent where you can combat illiteracy. Show what you can do—then apply to the Komsomol. Words—let them be as pretty as you like, as revolutionary as you like—are still only words. With the Party and the Komsomol what counts is deeds.'

They sent me to a railroad depot in a nearby village, where I was made director, no less, of a night school for semi-illiterates. A year later, in 1930, I was working for the newspaper of the local locomotive factory. Renewing my application for Komsomol membership, I gave a detailed account of my past 'Trotskyist connections,' exaggerating them, if anything. How exciting for an eighteen-year-old to see himself as a man 'with a past.'

They took their time with my application. The secretary of the Komsomol committee at the factory, a tall, thin fellow with a tubercular flush, would say to me, 'You seem to think you're a pretty deserving comrade—all those books and Party documents you read, all those discussions you had with the Trotskyists. Maybe you think we ought to say "Thank you" and bring you a Komsomol card on a tray, with musical accompaniment? Well, we're not saying thank you. Because I don't get the feeling that you've thought it all through. I don't seem to feel you know the reasons, the class reasons, for all your deviations. Here's

*Vlas Chubar and Grigori Petrovsky, then members of the Central Committee of the Ukrainian Communist Party.

Pashka—he's about your age. Pashka, did you ever sympathize with the opposition? No, he says, And you, Nikola, did you ever speak up for Trotsky or Bukharin at any meetings? Never—you were more interested in soccer. And you, Anya, did you always agree with the Central Committee? Always.

'You see—these are working lads, proletarians like their fathers and grandfathers. They laugh at your waverings and your doubts, your twists and turns. There's real class instinct for you! So you go think about it. Go on the production line. Show what you can do as a shock worker. And then we'll say, "Welcome to the Komsomol."'

For almost a year, I worked at a lathe during the day and for our newspaper at night. We took turns writing, editing and proofreading, and I didn't get more than three or four hours' sleep before day shift on the production line. After I became a full-fledged member of the Komsomol, they put me in charge of a paper at a tank shop. Leaving my lathe, I worked at my new job virtually around the clock, sleeping on piles of newsprint. The GPU representative at the factory, a stern but good-natured veteran of the Cheka, would often visit us in the evenings, asking us to take note of the workers' attitudes, keep an eye out for kulak propaganda and expose any remnants of Trotskyist and Bukharinist thoughts. I wrote several reports on conditions at the plant, although there was little I told him that I had not already said at meetings or written in our paper. My editorial colleagues did the same. The GPU man would chide us for our frankness in public. 'Don't you see, now they'll hide things from you—they'll give you a wide berth. No, fellows, you've got to learn Chekist tactics.' These words didn't jar us. To be a Chekist in those days seemed worthy of the highest respect, and to cooperate secretly with the Cheka was only doing what had to be done in the struggle against a crafty foe.

How could there be anything to be ashamed of in that? Yet I found it more than trying, because of my makeup. I was an enthusiast, I was hot-tempered, I lacked self-control, and I didn't know how to pretend or hide things from my friends (of which I had quite a number). The GPU representatives (another one came on the scene soon after) had to keep impressing me with the need for secrecy. It was a problem for them: They had some full-fledged undercover agents working for them at the factory, whom they saw only at special meeting places, but they were also dependent on more or less open cooperation with Party and Komsomol activists like us.

In the winter of 1932–33, our editorial brigade took part in forced collection of grain in the countryside. The GPU representative, in full uniform, with a Mauser in a wooden holster, accompanied us to meetings with the peasantry and in our search for buried grain. We saw him as a true comrade and helped him compile the reports that led to the arrest and exile of 'malicious hoarders.'

In 1933 I enrolled in a history course at the local university and wrote him several reports on political conditions at the school. When Kirov was assassinated, Mark was arrested again (this time to perish in a labor camp several years later), and a week after he was picked up I was expelled from the Komsomol and the university for 'maintaining relations with a Trotskyist relative,' though I had not seen Mark for quite a while. With the GPU man's help, I obtained a character reference from the factory which said: 'He did not hide his family ties, or the gross political mistakes he had committed before joining the Komsomol. . . . At the factory he proved himself as a worker . . . and he struggled actively against Trotskyism and other forms of hostile ideology.' A month later I was reinstated in the Komsomol, with a reprimand for a 'lapse in vigilance,' inasmuch as I had not known about my cousin's arrest.

In 1936—by then I was in Moscow, studying at the Institute of Foreign Languages—I was called in for a number of interviews with some serious-looking men, who explained that the class struggle was becoming more acute than ever and that there was no telling how many enemies of the people were still in hiding in the very bosom of the Party, spying, wrecking and hatching plots. They told me to join an Esperanto study group and find out who its members were and what mail it received from abroad. They also wanted reports on some of the teachers and foreign students. I wrote only what I knew to be true. For instance, when one of the instructors, Fritz Platten, was arrested, I wrote that he was a considerate and demanding pedagogue, a good athlete and an excellent raconteur, fascinating in his account of how he had accompanied Lenin in the sealed car of the famous train from Switzerland, and a man who spoke of Lenin with fondness and admiration.

My interrogators were often dissatisfied with me: 'You ought to be a lawyer. You're too trusting. If it turns out that you have given a clean bill of health to an enemy, it will be a blot on your record.' But I was sure that in telling the truth and only the truth, I was doing my duty as a Komsomol patriot.

Today I realize that a truthful police report on someone is still a police report. Today I don't see any substantial moral difference between an informer who invents and an informer who sticks to the facts. And it is

painful and humiliating for me to recall those assignments I had carried
out and my rationalizations of them. As Pushkin wrote,

> I read my life, the painful sum of years;
>   I shudder and I curse—but nay:
> For all my grief, for all my bitter tears,
>   No wretched line is washed away.

# 13

'STILL,' THE interrogator asked, 'what was it that attracted you to the Trotskyists in the first place?'

I had told him everything in detail. I was glad that I remembered all the dates. It was comforting to know that the character reference that had won me reinstatement in the Komsomol was on file in the Komsomol central committee. And at the end of that long first night's session, what did Major Vinogradov do but rephrase his original question, as though he hadn't understood a word I said.

My answer was held over for the following night. My sinus headache and nausea no better, I contested his definitions of my political past, demanding that he take note of my testimony regarding the character reference, which proved that I had struggled against Trotskyism after leaving the opposition.

Vinogradov put me off irritably. 'You'll have time to bring that up at the trial.'

'No, I want to bring it up now! If you get all the facts, you'll have to let me go *without* a trial!'

Major Vinogradov was sly, boorish, choleric and something of a coward. His deep-set eyes glowered darkly under a heavy forehead topped by sparse gray hair; his yellow cheeks sagged on either side of a thin mouth. He limped about the room with the help of a cane; whatever his disability, there was no battlefront insignia on his uniform. He had a convoluted, bureaucratic way of expressing himself, while falling into lapses of grammar and pronunciation, and he wrote down what I said in a large curlicued script. When we were alone, he could be polite. But there often were others present—Rossiisky, animated and loquacious, threatening and fatherly by turns; Barinov, silent, contemptuous, but without his rubber truncheon; the prosecutor himself, a short, swarthy man who did his best to hide a gutteral Jewish accent. And at such times Vinogradov was particularly harsh.

As the interrogations continued, I began to notice that many of Vinogradov's questions betrayed echoes of my sometime arguments with Nina, the woman who had seen me off to the hospital from which I was transferred to the field prison, and with her husband, Georgi. He sought out my opinion of Ilya Ehrenburg, the Versailles peace treaty, Poland's historic claims on Pomerania, and other issues that had come up during those arguments.

One day I was taken into his office, and there was Nina. She was doubly flustered to see me sick, flushed with fever and with a growth of beard, and her eyes widened with fear and pity.

To the first question—how would I describe my relations with the witness—I replied that I thought they were good. True, we had had our arguments, but I regarded her as my friend.

She gave a little sob and said, 'Yes, we argued, but in a friendly way, and we were friends.'

'Nina,' I said, 'I beg you, tell the whole truth. You know that Zabashtansky made Belyaev write a deposition against me. You know that Zabashtansky hates me.'

She looked beseechingly from me to the investigator. 'Yes, it's true. Colonel Zabashtansky did—'

Vinogradov interrupted, shouting. 'Don't exert pressure on the witness! Don't terrorize her! We're going to send you to a prison camp —they'll teach you there how to—'

'To a prison camp? You mean this is not an investigation? I'm on trial?'

He brought his fist down on his desk. 'Again your Trotskyist demagoguery! Who said this was a trial? I'm merely expressing my opinion, as a Communist, that your place is in a prison camp. Don't think you can impress us with your glibness!'

Under his questioning Nina squirmed, trying to find good things to say about me. Vinogradov grew more and more testy and finally asked her, 'Do you confirm the evidence placed in the hands of the investigating authorities that he spoke in defense of the Germans, criticized the Soviet high command, abused the Soviet press and the writer Ehrenburg, and condemned the actions of the Soviet armies on the territory of East Prussia?'

And I realized then that Nina had been reporting on our arguments to counterintelligence.

Nina gave me an agonized look. 'No, he never said that. He spoke against the looting, the breaches of discipline. He's hot-blooded; he gets carried away. I told him, "Some comrades could misunderstand what you're saying; they could think you're defending the Germans."'

Vinogradov listened with a sour look on his face but continued to take down what she said. Finally, as required by law, he read out loud the record of her testimony:

'He made damaging remarks to the effect that our armies allegedly engaged in looting. Together with other comrades, I called on him not to defend the Germans and to stop making these damaging statements.'

I stood up, outraged. 'But that's not what she said! It's exactly the opposite!'

He snatched a pistol out of a desk drawer and screamed, 'Sit down! This minute! Sit down!'

Nina's eyes seemed about to jump out of her head.

I sat down. 'You can stop playing with your pistol. You're only scaring the witness. I'm not signing that record. It's not true.'

He put down the pistol but continued to scream. 'There—that's what I mean! To listen to you, everybody's a liar; only *you* tell the truth! But let me tell you, your little game is over!'

Nina wept quietly. When he gave her the record to sign, she whimpered, 'But I . . . it says here . . . it isn't exactly what I . . .'

'What? Are you declaring your solidarity with him?'

She signed.

Vinogradov turned to me, smiling. 'Well,' he said amicably, 'this page that you don't agree with, you don't have to sign it. But these other pages that don't have anything you object to, read them, please, and sign them.'

The procedure was for the detainee to sign each page. I read all the pages, and, rejecting one of them as doubtful, I signed the rest. The interrogator was satisfied. He knew—as I was to find out later—that no one would bother to see if every page was signed.

The day before the field prison was moved from its old location in Poland, the door of our cell opened and in stepped an unprepossessing type with a fat, pimply face and a fur hat rakishly askew. Pausing an instant for effect, he executed a little jig and intoned in a nasal twang:

'Oh, give me change for ten million
And buy me a ticket to Rostov . . .'

His name was Mishka Zalkind. He claimed that he was an army scout and proceeded to regale us with his military exploits—clearly a pack of lies. He said that he had been arrested because he had struck his commanding officer while in his cups. At roll call, however, it developed that he had been charged under Article 175—i.e., for banditry. Mishka was a common thief, with wide experience of many jails and prison camps in the Soviet Union.

His tales of his adventures as the best scout in his division, as the best burglar to have worked the international-class cars of the Soviet train system, and as the indefatigable lover of a succession of adoring women continued in our new cell with a sameness that was deadening. The women were generally actresses or wives of doctors, prosecutors or generals (lower than colonels' wives he would not stoop); they were nearly all beautiful; and they all wanted to give him their silks and diamonds, leave their husbands, fathers and careers, and follow him in his life of crime. He loved them in luxurious bedrooms or the suites of the best hotels and left them nobly and sadly, taking only a ring or a clasp for a keepsake—'which I wouldn't sell, not for a thousand rubles,' but which he would always lose, under even more romantic circumstances, leaping from train to train, or reconnoitering some German staff headquarters, or attaining the embrace of yet another 'highly cultured' beauty.

His monotonous bragging got on our nerves, and one day Tadeusz and I told him to shut up. Mishka grew ugly. 'What's the matter?' He bared his teeth at Tadeusz. 'A Soviet warrior not good enough for you, you Pilsudski Fascist?'

I was filled with disgust and let him have it.

Mishka yelped. 'And what's the matter with *you*? Article Fifty-eight, that's what you are—an enemy of the people, a Fascist, and sticking up for another Fascist. Maybe I'm a thief, but I'm a *Soviet* thief, a patriot, and I think all Fascists should be strung up!'

Crazed with fury, I was ready to attack him when a guard flung open the door. 'Stop this noise!'

The incident rankled, and two days later, requesting, and getting, a piece of paper and a pencil, I wrote out a request for a transfer to some other cell. 'I am an officer of the Red Army,' I wrote, 'and I do not want to be in the same cell with thieves, spies and the like. This is an insult not only to me but to the army whose uniform I wear. Therefore, unless I am transferred, I will refuse to accept food.'

Half an hour later I was called before the prison commander, who said wearily, 'Now why are you making trouble again? Didn't I tell you I haven't got room to put everyone where he wants to be? Where am I going to move you?'

'In Tuchel I was in a cell with Yugoslav officers.'

'Which ones?'

I gave him their names. An hour later I was told to take my things and was led along a corridor, past empty rooms with smashed cupboards and wild boars' heads on the walls, and into a tiny chamber with a narrow window giving onto a garden and a piece of sky. There, stretched out on the floor, on a pile of clean straw, were three of my Yugoslavs, including Ivan Ivanovich.

There was a joyous reunion; but when I told them how quickly I had been moved after threatening a hunger strike, their manner changed. They were obviously afraid that I had been placed in their cell to report on what they said. Yet I couldn't very well say, 'No, my dear friends, I have not been planted here to spy on you.' All I could do was avoid asking personal questions.

My chagrin paled before an unexpected pleasure. The Yugoslavs' prison status permitted them daily airings—not in the courtyard, where we had been taken twice a day to a malodorous trench, but in a real garden—and I was allowed to go with them. The fresh green of bushes and young oak leaves glowed against the hardier blue-green of fir trees. Scattered puffs of white drifted across a lofty blue sky, and a breeze blew warm and soft, as from afar. My head spun; I felt weak and sat down on the ground. Never in my life had the smell of the grass, the damp earth, the warm spring breeze been so delicious, and I thought: these bushes, this earth, this grass are much more important than everything that infects my life right now—the prison, the interrogations, the petty angers and small joys, all these things that have come together in one tight, painful knot in my head.

And soon I found another source of happiness—books. Led one night to be interrogated, I noticed a bookcase against the wall just before we came to a sharp turn of the dimly lit corridor. On the way back to the cell, with my sleepy guard walking behind me, I put on speed just before turning the corner and, without stopping, scooped up as many books as I could, hiding them under my overcoat. The guard shouted, 'Where are you running? Homesick for your cell?' I shot back, 'Got to pee.'

The books were a collection of stories from the lives of the Prussian knights; a German translation of an American novel about cowboys, outlaws and gold prospectors; a nineteenth-century schoolbook with the fables of Lessing and the ballads of Schiller; a high-society novel; some fairy tales. The following night I had a younger guard, who saw me taking the books and snapped, 'Put them back.' I began to wheedle.

'Aw, come on. I've got to have something to wipe myself with. Besides, they're all in German.' He made me put some of them back, but I got away with an illustrated book on the genealogy of the Counts of Knebel-Deberis, whose family castle this apparently was; informative calendars of the years 1902 and 1903; and a statistical source book on Pomerania.

I could read during the day. They had not gotten around to making a peephole in the door of our cell, and by the time the guard would turn the key in the lock and slide open the bolt, I would have the book I was reading buried in the straw, where the other books were hidden. The Yugoslavs became less distrustful of me. Two of them could not read, since their eyeglasses had been taken away, and the third was weak in German. I would give them a summation of what I read. We all liked the American novel best.

One sunny morning they brought in someone new. A Soviet cavalry coat thrown across his heavy shoulders, he gazed sullenly around the room from under the visor of a blue-ribboned cap, not bothering to respond to our greetings. Then he turned around and began pounding on the door.

The guard outside yelled, 'What do you want?'

'Open up!'

The door opened, and we could hear him muttering about 'the procurator,' 'the front,' and 'the army.' The duty officer brought him a fresh pile of straw, which he spread on the other side of the room from us, keeping himself apart.

We asked him who he was.

'What's it to you? If I tell you I'm a cavalry officer, will it make you feel any better?'

His singsong tone, his manner of replying to a question with another question, placed him for me. 'You're from Odessa, aren't you?'

'And what if I am?'

But gradually he thawed out. His name was Pyotr Alexandrovich Balakshev; he used to be a prosecutor in Odessa; prior to his arrest, he was the prosecutor of a cavalry division. He had bleached eyebrows, peppery eyes and a pinched, rosy face; his olive-drab jacket, blue trousers and well-polished boots were all of the highest quality.

'They stuck as many charges on me as flies on flypaper,' he growled. 'More than a hundred German women, and a certain number of Polish women—that's how many I was supposed to have raped. You know what that would have worked out to? Several women a day. Now

I'm a man in my prime, haven't had any complaints yet, but several a day—that's absurd! Even at the Party commission they had to laugh— "What did you want to do, sample the whole female population?" I'll tell you what it was: false witness, paying back old scores, and all because of my sense of justice—because I always tell the truth. So when they went through all the accusations, what were they left with? Two women, both Polish. And even there, let me tell you, no sound juridical basis at all!

'Rape comes under Article One Fifty-three, and what does it say? There must be a charge brought by the victim or by her parents, and where is this victim? Are they going to look for her all over Prussia or all over Poland? All they have are two so-called witnesses—my chauffeur and a Pole in whose house we were staying. And this chauffeur charges that I committed a crime against the person by bonking him on the nose, though he admits he was drunk at the time. What does that mean? It means he has a personal grudge against me, so as a witness he isn't worth a kopeck. So what do we have left? No real witnesses, no plaintiffs, yet they frame two charges of rape and throw in corruption of a minor. Why? Because that comes under a different article, that's more serious. It can get you ten years, and with aggravating circumstances you can even end up with the ultimate penalty, though, of course, only in peacetime.'

He proved a loquacious companion, and, on learning that Ivan Ivanovich was a military judge, he tackled him on the legal aspects of various 'theoretical' cases. But it seemed to me that he was worrying about one particular case, his own, and that it did not involve rape but a crime against the person, a clash with someone in the army. For his part, he regarded me suspiciously at first and thought that I was lying about my case; but then he came to believe me and took an interest in me, while grumbling that I 'didn't know which way was up.'

On May 8 we were moved to Stettin. Once again, loaded on trucks, we passed villages and towns with many undamaged houses, red brick roofs and abundant foliage. Once again we were overtaken by columns of soldiers shouting, 'Where are you taking them? Hang 'em on the spot!'

Stettin was a real city. We drove past fire-blackened walls and shoots of green peeking from rows of blasted trees. At the outskirts we stopped before a tall brick wall with iron gates. The guards were unexpectedly friendly. Many of them were soldiers, with insignia for war wounds. Getting out of the trucks, we heard the news.

'It's over. . . . It's over. . . . You'll all be going home.'

The war was over!

Crossing the inner courtyard together with the hapless Prosecutor, Balakshev, I stepped on something. 'Hey!' I shouted. 'Tobacco!' It was a box filled with thick cuts of the stuff. Several prisoners crowded around us. The guards taxed us casually, 'Come on, come on, get going,' and I understood: the tobacco was a victory present from them.

Balakshev, on his knees, stuffing tobacco into his pockets, was disgusted. 'Idiot,' he whispered. 'What did you want to shout for? We could have had it all for ourselves.'

All around me there was a happy hum. The war was over. The sky was blue. The sun was warm. Even our new prison, a house of light-colored brick, looked cheerful.

'Come, Prosecutor,' I said expansively, 'let us not be greedy. Let the others share.'

'Don't call me prosecutor,' he hissed. 'They'll hear—all these criminals. Then we'll be in transit somewhere, and they'll kill me.'

He and I were placed in the same cell; the Yugoslavs were put elsewhere. Our only cell mate was a lieutenant who had shot his sergeant in a drunken brawl. The room was small but sunny, with a wooden floor, a tiled stove and luxurious sanitation—a metal bucket with a tight-fitting lid which could be flushed with water through a hole in the bottom. For dinner that evening there were two cans apiece of marvelous potato gruel. The guard gave us a whole box of matches. We smoked, stretched out on cotton mattresses. I was sure that there would be an amnesty. The prosecutor from Odessa explained how an amnesty would work in various theoretical cases. In my own case, he noted, the effect would be doubly beneficial, since those who had accused me falsely could admit their mistakes without having to fear indictment for perjury.

# 14

THE LIEUTENANT was tried several days later and sentenced to ten years, and Balakshev and I had the cell to ourselves. Each day we would be taken out for a walk in a garden which had a lawn speckled with dandelions. The lilac bushes were bursting into flower.

Balakshev would stride up and down furiously. 'Come on, come on! Get into training! They'll march us off—your legs will give out; you'll be done for!'

Back in the cell, he was irritated by my untalkativeness. 'Why don't you say something? Let's talk. About anything. About women.'

But my memories of Moscow's theaters, my explanations of our propaganda work with the Germans at the front, bored him. 'Forgive me, but you're a fool. That's why you're here. You've read too many books. Damaged your eyes, and your head as well. These Fritzes—they were laughing at you! Who were you to them? A Red, a commissar, and a Jew to boot. They would have drowned you as soon as say good morning. But they were prisoners, you represented authority, so they pretended: *"Genosse, Genosse, Hitler kaputt."*'

Sometimes we would quarrel, and I would call him a rearguard operator and advise him not to entertain any front-line troops with his reminiscences of his women and his horses, his tailors and his cooks, or he might be surprised by a punch in the mouth. Then he would fly into a rage: no wonder I got hit with Article 58—I was a demagogue, I reasoned like an anarchist, I didn't know a damn thing about Marxism or about life. For an hour or two we wouldn't speak to each other. He'd sit in his corner, whistling melancholy tunes. Then he'd demand loftily, 'Why are you sitting there, sour as yogurt? All right—I got a little excited. Who started it?'

I learned not to argue with him—just listen—but he liked that even less. 'What are you turning away for? I'm turning my soul inside out for you, and you . . . zero attention.'

Sometimes he would wonder about the future. 'No, this business of being a prosecutor—never again. Not for all the money in the world. Not even if they find me innocent on all counts. I'll become a lawyer. I have the education, the experience, God knows. You know how much lawyers make? Thousands! And with my kindheartedness, it'll be easier to defend than to accuse.'

One morning, out in the yard, I saw our neighbors—two foreign-looking middle-aged men. The next time I met one of them, on a staircase, I slipped a piece of paper into his pocket. On it I had written the Latin alphabet and our prison code for communicating between cells. That same day they began tapping on the wall, in German. One of them had been the Spanish consul in Danzig. He was full of questions. What did I think would be the fate of Spain? Would Poland be Sovietized at once? Would Russia go to war with Japan? Would they be executed?

Balakshev would grow impatient. 'Why do you bother with him? Send him to hell, the Fascist.'

Other times he would sit manicuring his nails for hours with bits of wood and glass.

Yet he was not a bad man at heart. He wanted above all to be admired. Sometimes he could even rise to philosophizing.

'I'm a materialist—naturally. But you've got to admit, there is such a thing as the soul. Take Comrade Lenin. Who was he? An aristocrat. And Comrades Marx and Engels? Bourgeois. And yet they went against their own economic and class interests. Why? Conscience, you will say. Yes, conscience plays a decisive role. But we Marxists know that conscience is created by the environment, and not vice versa. And their environment was bourgeois, aristocratic. Then how do you explain it? I'll tell you how. We're dealing here with a certain fact—the fact of the soul, a fact that our Marxist science is only beginning to become aware of.'

He gave me one piece of useful advice. He explained that at the end of my interrogation I had a right under Article 206 of the Criminal Code to see everything in my dossier, in the presence of the prosecutor; and that I also had a right to ask that additional witnesses be called and additional material be added to the record.

One day, while we were walking in the garden, Balakshev was ordered to appear at once before the tribunal. He was so unnerved that he didn't say good-bye. After the trial, in accordance with regulations, he was taken to a different cell.

About two weeks later, while out in the garden, I saw him at a distance; he was one of a group of prisoners being led from the bathhouse. He waved to me; then he held up one hand, the fingers spread apart. Five years.

That same day, a guard brought me a present—a handful of tobacco and some matches wrapped in a piece of paper. 'From the major who was in here with you.'

Vinogradov and the prosecutor, Zabolotsky, were unpleasantly surprised when I said, 'I'm not going to sign anything until I see the entire dossier.'

The prosecutor reddened. 'What? You don't trust the investigating authorities?'

'I put my trust in Soviet law. You have just told me you are proceeding under Article Two hundred and six. I demand that this article be applied in full.'

Vinogradov whispered to him, 'He was in the same cell with that—'

Zabolotsky looked threatening. 'Who taught you to start with this demagoguery, this formalism? You'd better tell us, or—'

'It's not demagoguery or formalism but the letter and the spirit of Soviet law. Who taught me? You and the interrogator. You have often said that the law must be strictly observed. I am asking you to observe it.'

Zabolotsky fumed, but said, 'Let him see it,' and left the room.

Vinogradov handed me the file. On the dull-green cardboard folder, I saw the words, stamped in black: 'To Be Preserved Forever.'

*Forever!*

'Why forever?'

'That's the law. So that no enemy of the people can cover his tracks after serving his sentence. And so that if there's a mistake, it can be corrected.'

The first page of the dossier came as a surprise. It was a letter from an army political instructor, Captain Boris Kublanov, to the newspaper *Red Star*. Written in 1943, it drew attention to some articles I had written for the paper that year and named me as 'one of the active leaders of the Trotskyist underground in Kharkov during the years 1921 to 1929, and the collaborator of a number of well-known enemies of the people.' There followed a list of names, most of them unknown to me or known only by hearsay, and a collection of completely outlandish 'facts.'

I remembered Boris Kublanov well. He was a cocky loudmouth, a power in the local Komsomol, who could never forgive me for skipping from the first-year philosophy course at the Kharkov university to the third-year course, while he was bringing up the rear 'due to the pressures of political work.' His antagonism hardened when, at one of our seminars, I allowed myself to show up his lack of grounding in Marx and Lenin, the decisions of Party congresses, and the whole history of the period. On top of that, there was a nonpolitical conflict over a certain curly-haired, blue-eyed literature student named Galya. When, after my cousin Mark's arrest in 1935, I was expelled from the Komsomol and the university and was then reinstated in the Komsomol, Kublanov succeeded in preventing my reinstatement at the university. Two and a half years later, when I was studying in the Institute of Foreign Languages in Moscow, he sent them a long letter denouncing me as a Trotskyist and alleging that I had been taken back into the Komsomol 'due to the patronage of enemies of the people who have since been exposed.' His letter to *Red Star*, containing the same twice-refuted charges, had been forwarded to the army's Central Political Administration, which had sent it onto counterintelligence. And now it formed the opening exhibit of my dossier, with its official stamp: 'To Be Preserved Forever.'

For about two weeks I was alone in my cell. The cell next to me was empty. I exercised several times a day; recalled the lines of my favorite poetry and the words of popular songs; began composing a long poem on the face of chill eternity before which man strives to find meaning for his works; and dashed off other, shorter and more cheerful verses. One of them I scratched on the door.

> Let them slander, let them curse
> The truth and honesty you sought.
> Remember, as you face the worst,
> There is no jail for dreams or thought.

The ordinary soldiers who were our guards in Stettin were an easy-going lot, and they let me out for airings in the back yard, where there were always some of the prisoners who worked in the kitchen and on other tasks, and where I could loiter in the sun without attracting attention.

One day I saw a girl in the uniform of a tribunal secretary standing in a gateway that led to another part of the building. As I walked past her, she seemed to give me a friendly nod. This was most unusual. I hesitated and whispered, 'Do you know me?'

She nodded again and smiled.

I walked on but circled and walked past her again. 'Excuse me, but . . . do you know about my case?'

'Yes. The tribunal set aside your case. There isn't enough to it.' She spoke under her breath.

I didn't dare stop, but soon I was abreast of her once more. 'Thank you! Oh, thank you! But . . . what will happen to me now?'

'They could go on with the investigation. But they're hardly likely to find new material. Most likely they'll drop the case.'

Before I could circle back a third time, they led out a defendant and she left together with him.

I was able to launder my underclothes in the boiler room in the basement. There was a lot of rubbish on the floor. One day I noticed a book lying there—or, as I saw, a set of pages torn out of a Roman Catholic prayer book, in Latin and in German. There was no lamp in my cell, but it was the end of May; still light enough in the evenings to read by; and before falling asleep, I would read and reread the Pater Noster, the Ave Maria and the Credo.

The words that had been spoken for almost two thousand years—in Roman catacombs, in slaves' quarters and monastic cells and kingly castles—the words that had been carried across the world by crusader and conquistador and priest—I, an atheist, a Bolshevik and a Stalinist officer, muttered to myself in my prison cell. It was strange, and strangely attractive, to think of it that way. I wrapped the remains of the prayer book carefully in some paper I fished out of the rubbish; I kept it under the head of my mattress at night, and during the day I kept it in the pocket of my coat. I explained my interest in the prayer book by my sense of respect for those powers of the human spirit that had found their way into those beautifully simple and immortal words. I told myself that the spell the words had cast over me (even though I had known them before) was understandable in purely rational terms: I was in jail, without any other book, undergoing an incredible investigation, and filled with new hope. Yet, waking up each morning, I would repeat the Lord's Prayer in Latin, in Russian and in German, and would be very much upset if I forgot any of the words, and very happy if I remembered them all without a slip. 'Lead us not into temptation,' I would repeat over and over again, 'but deliver us from evil.' In Russian we would say 'from the sly one,' and I wondered why the Latin *malum* and the German *Boese*—evil—were rendered in our language by the concept of 'slyness.' I thought of various social and historical explanations for this and mused about the kind of book that could be written on concepts peculiar to Russian moral philosophical development. Out of these prison-cell meditations over a Catholic prayer book, a novel perception emerged many years later in my mind—that conscience possesses not only a moral quality but an esthetic one as well. Still later this insight served to show me why the German Catholic writer Heinrich Böll is so close to Russian readers and to the dominant traditions of Russian literature.

All of a sudden I was moved to another cell, smaller and darker, but with an actual cot. The walls preserved the barely discernible scratchings of previous inmates: a star, with a hammer and sickle; a fist with the words 'Rot Front!'; and, in two columns of minute German script, the titles of Shakespeare's plays.

I soon acquired a cell mate. Young, with a pale, nervous face, wearing an officer's blouse with a row of darker spots indicating the decorations of which he had been stripped. First Lieutenant Sasha Nikolaiev, battalion commander, native of Gorky, arrested for killing a sergeant who had been about to rape a teenage girl. The sergeant, a holder of the Glory Medal, was drunk; when Sasha ordered him to leave the girl alone, he became obstreperous. Sasha fired a warning shot into the air; then a second shot. The sergeant went for his submachine gun, and Sasha shot him in the heart. It turned out that the sergeant was the best scout in his regiment and had been recommended for a second Glory award.

'Granted,' Sasha conceded, telling me about it, 'if I had gone by the rules, I should have shouted for my men and had him disarmed.' From time to time he was called in for interrogations, mostly about details: who stood where, how many shots were fired, and at what intervals. The interrogator kept trying to make out that Sasha had first shot the sergeant and only then had fired into the air.

By an extraordinary coincidence the prison commander turned out to be a townsman of Sasha's; they had lived on the same street. He brought us several packages of cigarettes, some tobacco and cigarette paper, and matches. And we were shortly moved to another part of the prison. From our two ample windows we had a view of a yard with plump trees, lilac bushes and untrampled grass. We had beds with metal bedsprings, even a table. From the nearby kitchen came the indescribably delicious aroma of cooking.

June 8 was a very special day.

In the morning my friends the Yugoslavs were all released. I had managed to speak to one of them in the corridor and to give him my

Moscow address. Now we saw them out in the yard, putting on their shoulder pieces and leather straps and belts. We shouted, 'Good luck!' and waved.

In the evening the duty officer took us to a shed that served as the soldiers' mess. The soldiers had already eaten.

'The commander's orders. The men who left this morning—we had provisions for them until the end of the month. So you can have it instead.'

The cook, a young, red-faced soldier, placed before us a soup bowl filled with a thick, fragrant mixture of noodles, meat, potatoes and onions, and a loaf of bread. He looked on sternly as we dug in, grinning incredulously at each other and slipping pieces of bread into our pockets. The cook said, in an undertone, 'Don't worry. There'll be fresh bread tomorrow.'

The soup bowls scraped clean, we leaned back, perspiring and tired, and lit up.

'Wait,' the cook said. 'The second course.'

Another wonder sprang up before our eyes: a golden mound of fried potatoes with a brown aureole of fried meat.

Sasha gave a little sob. 'Why didn't you tell us? We're crammed. We'll burst if we have any more.'

'Take your time. Go take a little walk. You've got a whole hour before lights out.'

We took his advice and consumed most of the second course, though we couldn't eat it all. Our stomachs bulged, and we were drunk with repletion. The cook poured a generous portion of makhorka on a sheet of newspaper. 'Pure stuff, this. Homemade.'

We couldn't sleep all night. Sasha was racked by stomach pains and, by morning, so was I. When we were taken to the mess hall again, we could hardly stand.

The cook nodded knowledgeably. 'Your stomachs are rebelling. Not used to it. Drink plenty of hot liquid. That'll clean out your insides.'

We drank inordinate quantities of a weak but hot brew he called coffee and gradually got used to three square meals a day.

For two weeks Sasha and I were in heaven. The door of our cell was often open all day long, and we spent most of our time in the yard or playing cards (a present from the cook). One of the guards told me in a whisper that there were a lot of books in the rooms directly above us. 'But there's plenty of brass around, so keep your eyes peeled.'

What happiness! Going through the piles of books spread over the floor, I found several pocket-book editions of Goethe, two books by

Ludwig on Goethe, a pocket Bible. My days were now filled. I would spend hours reading in my cell or outside behind the bushes. Or, sometimes, just staring at a page and imagining how I would be called in, how they would give me back my shoulder boards, my medals and my suitcase; how I would be on the way to Moscow. In the past, whenever I thought of freedom, my daydreams would immediately take the form of two sizzling fried eggs, surrounded by a helping of golden-brown potatoes. I would be cross with myself and start anew, but the image would return. I would enter my home; there would be Nadia and the girls; Mama, bathed in tears, would place on the table an outsize frying pan with two fried eggs and a heap of golden-brown, thinly cut potatoes, crisp at the edges and soft inside. Now, no longer constantly hungry, I saw my return in the form of reunions with family and friends. But when? Our soldier-guards kept assuring us that the amnesty would not be long in coming, that we would all go home.

June 22, 1945, was the fifth anniversary of the outbreak of the war. That morning I was called in and asked for the second time to sign the record of the interrogation. Some of my demands had been granted. They had taken the testimony of my friend Ivan Rozhansky and of Galya Khromushina, my plucky woman assistant at Graudenz. Reading the transcript, I smiled to see how both of them had resisted Vinogradov's efforts to make them speak badly of me, how staunchly they had stood up for the truth. But my request for testimony from two other witnesses—Yuri Maslov, a Moscow friend whom I had written in detail of Zabashtansky's campaign against me, and Arnold Goldstein, who had been present when, according to Zabashtansky, I had vilified the Soviet high command and the Soviet government—this request had been denied.

Insisting on the vital importance of their testimony, I renewed my petition, in writing. Vinogradov looked bored. Zabolotsky, the prosecutor, lost his temper.

After the midday meal Sasha and I were ordered, with surprising severity, to go out into the yard; soon after, we were ordered back to our cell. There had been a surprise search, ordered and led by Zabolotsky himself. My books and Sasha's playing cards were gone.

The next day we were all taken to the railroad station and placed in freight cars. The train headed east.

Back in Bydgoszcz. The jail was ancient. Sasha and I were placed in a cell whose only window gave onto a brick wall.

We had improvidently smoked all our cigarettes. By the second day we were scratching out our pockets for grains of tobacco. After the prodigality at Stettin, the daily fare of balanda,* musty bread and tiny portions of soggy sugar was a depressing sight, but the craving for tobacco was worse. When we were taken outdoors, we kept our eyes on the ground; the sight of a cigarette butt would send shivers up the spine. Sometimes the prisoners who worked in the kitchen passed by with their guards. We would plead with them. 'Please . . . something to smoke. Just a tiny bit of tobacco . . . just a puff . . .'

During our stay in Bydgosczc, Vinogradov called me in only once.

'It is my duty to inform you that your new petition under Article Two hundred and six has been rejected by the prosecutor and the investigating authorities as lacking in grounds. The investigation of your case has been concluded, and your case is being turned over to the courts. Do you understand?'

He was smoking a fat cigarette. A blue ribbon of smoke ascended to the ceiling. My head swam.

'Give me a cigarette,' I said. 'Please.'

'I asked you a question. Do you understand?'

'I understand, I understand. Give me what's left of your cigarette. Let me finish it. I beg you.'

He studied me with distaste and with a certain satisfaction. He took another puff, spat on the floor and placed the remains of his cigarette, with its wet, chewed hollow tip, on the desk in front of me.

I tore off the tip and inhaled greedily. I saw his look of contempt. But there were still two or three drags left. And there wouldn't be any more interrogations.

'Thank you! Let me have another one—please! To take with me. I've been a week without cigarettes. I'm going out of my mind.'

He leaned back with a triumphant, supercilious stare. 'It isn't my responsibility to keep you supplied with tobacco. Get out.'

I was barely able to keep myself from pleading with him.

On the way back to my cell I picked up a butt of makhorka. Sasha had two matches left. As we shared my find, I daydreamed out loud of how I would meet Vinogradov again, someday, somewhere. I wouldn't hit him, but I would give him a bad scare, and I would spit in his face. I would smoke one cigarette after another and spit the wet, chewed butts in his frightened, greenish face.

*Derisory camp slang for the gruel that was the staple of the prison diet.

# 15

I WAS called at dawn and told to take my things with me. That meant the tribunal. Sasha and I embraced, exchanging our addresses.

Downstairs in the waiting room several hundred prisoners in uniforms and civilian dress were lined up against the walls. The orderly, looking up my name in a thick file, said, 'Your case has been referred to the Special Commission* of the Ministry of Internal Affairs of the U.S.S.R.'

They gave me my suitcase; the books and pencils inside had been confiscated, but they had left me my notes and verses. We were marched off in a long column to the railroad station, under the curious stares of the women, children and soldiers in the streets; there, we were loaded aboard freight cars. Our train moved east. Several days later we arrived in Brest. We waited for hours at the station under the baking sun, then were marched through hot, dusty streets.

Pleading voices rose from the column. 'Water . . . water . . .'

At last we gained the shade of a prison yard. Shaved heads appeared in the windows. 'Look at them—warriors!' 'Not enough to eat, so they bring in more of 'em!' 'Hey! When's the amnesty?'

The prison guards searched us and gave us receipts for our belongings. (But I never saw my suitcase again.) There were some common thieves among us, and I could hear one of them negotiating with a guard. 'Let me rot in jail if I'm lying. Feel it. Real wool—American— Boston. Just give me some bread, some tobacco. And some pork fat, some eggs . . .'

Our group was herded into a cell with nothing in it but an iron

*A Special Commission of the security police empowered to impose summary judgments in cases involving 'socially dangerous' acts, abolished in 1956.

bucket. 'When it's full, take it out,' an orderly said. 'You're in quarantine. Who'll be cell boss?'

'The major!'

The orderly looked me over. 'Major of what army?'

'The Red Army.'

'Then you're cell boss. See you keep order.'

They brought us gruel but no bread. They said they'd been out of bread for three days.

Shouts reached us from the other cells. 'Bread! We want *brea-a-ad*!'

And from the courtyard: 'Get away from the window, or I'll fire, fuck your mother!'

A shot, then another.

One of our thieves clambered up to the window. 'Bread, you sons of bitches!' A burst clattered against the wall. The thief jumped down.

I remembered that I was cell boss. 'No climbing up to the window! If you don't get yourself shot, you'll get the rest of us punished.'

A chorus of voices rose in my support.

The thief turned from troublemaker into clown. 'Citizens, brothers, peasants, warriors! Our distinguished major is right! What do we have here? An absence of bread, on top of considerable congestion in our living standards. Also a collection of nervous horses' asses firing blindly right and left. But these, comrades, are only temporary inconveniences on the periphery of history, petty problems of logistics, which must be, and will be, tackled at the root. And meanwhile, under these prevailing conditions, we must ask all of you to keep calm and save wear and tear on your nerves, so as not to undermine your precious health—or, as they say in medical circles, not to croak before your time. Because that would be regarded as pure sabotage. For if your country awards you a legal term of confinement, it is your duty to serve it to the full, straining every muscle, for the common good of Socialism. He who does not preserve his health and croaks before his time is a saboteur and an enemy of the people and must be punished with the utmost severity.'

The cell rocked with laughter.

It was unbearably hot and stuffy. We sat on the floor in our underpants. We were all thirsty. The bucket could be carried out only when it was full to the brim. There was no shortage of volunteers for the malodorous task: they could stop a minute by a water faucet outside. One of the prisoners winked at me: 'You'd better leave it to these thieves. They're the go-betweens.' Between us and the guards. That, it seemed, was the system.

The next morning there was still no bread. Again, shouts from the other windows: 'Bread! *Brea-a-ad*!'

The thieves had their own corner. Once again they scorned the prison balanda and feasted on their own supply of bread and sugar. The others in the cell stared hungrily or looked the other way.

On the third day there was still no bread. The shouts and wails were louder than ever and the reports of automatic rifle fire more frequent.

'Shot three of them today,' said one of the guards who brought us the midday meal. He explained that there was no bread because the bakery had burned down, and they were waiting for bread from another bakery.

That night a prison searchlight stabbed convulsively at the darkness of our cell. In its lavender glare the heaps of men sprawled in the weirdest positions seemed twisted and broken, like toys. Some slept quietly; others snored or moaned or cried out in their sleep. 'Ahhhh! I won't any more ... ahhh ... don't kill me!' 'Stop or I'll shoot!' 'Ma-a-ama!'

It was barely dawn when the door clanked open and a voice called, 'Cell boss! Come out here. Bread.'

Everyone seemed to wake up at once. 'Bread! Bread! Bread!' Pandemonium. From the thieves' corner came a shrill whistle. 'Go on, boss—take some help with you.'

I stumbled to the door, stepping on bodies.

'Keep your eyes peeled, Major!' came from another corner. 'These thieves—'

'Anyone who grabs an extra ration—death on the spot!'

The thieves joined in. 'Sure! We'll drown him in the bucket!'

'Major, don't let that scum get near the bread!'

The guards held the door barely ajar. I squeezed through. The wonderful sour smell of freshly baked bread. Two carts filled with small loaves stood in the corridor. The head guard handed me two loaves, and two more to someone who had squeezed through behind me.

'No!' I said. 'I won't accept the bread! Not like this!'

'Are you out of your mind?'

With all my might, over the howling and cursing that poured out of the cell, I shouted in his face: 'Don't you hear what's going on in there? Do you want ten more corpses? They're starving—they're out of their minds—they'll kill each other for a loaf of bread!'

The guards exchanged worried looks. 'We can't go into that darkness handing out bread,' agreed the man behind me.

'Look,' I said. 'Let's get them all out of the cell. Line them up in the corridor. Then let them go back, one by one. Each one gets his ration at the door.'

The guards whispered to each other. 'All right,' the head guard said. 'But if anything goes wrong, it'll be your neck.'

I opened the door and bellowed, 'Attention!' They fell silent. I explained the procedure. There were shouts of approval. Then an objection: 'There's an old man here—he can't walk. And there's a sick man there—he can't walk either.'

Half-naked, barefoot, they poured out into the corridor. The guards struggled against the melee. 'Quiet, or we'll turn the fire hose on you! Where are you running? Stand here!'

'Attention!' I shouted again. 'We'll begin. Look—I'm taking two rations. That's for the two men still inside.'

Suddenly, utter stillness. I groped in the darkness to what seemed like someone propped up against the far wall of the cell. Two hands snatched at the bread. The same with another form in the center of the room.

The racket in the corridor resumed, louder than before. Hurrying out, I saw that one of the thieves had turned on the fire hydrant. A jet of water was playing on the floor. Everyone was scrambling to drink, to drench his face and head in the cooling stream. The same young jokester who had clambered up to the window was sitting in a pool of water, laughing happily: 'Gentlemen! Gentlemen! Welcome to the baths! Try our seawater—restore your health!'

'Shut off the hydrant!' the guards were yelling, but half-laughing, too, and suddenly I saw them for what they were—peasants' sons, who knew what hunger was, and what thirst was; calloused and brutalized farm boys whose deadened or indifferent eyes had lit up with brief humanity at this unexpected celebration of bread and water in the darkness of dawn.

After that the rationing went quietly and easily and was quickly done.

Our homeward journey was resumed in September. Our train had windows, reinforced with wire netting, only on one side; the compartments converted into cells on the other side of the passageway were windowless. We lost our thieves but picked up four more in Orel, where we were imprisoned for ten days. One of them, Fedya, a sociable

❖ 134 ❖

fellow of about forty, told us how he had escaped from a prison camp in far-eastern Siberia in 1937. He and two others had wandered in the taiga for three weeks.

'We were famished. We came upon a young Korean. We sliced him up and fried him. Wasn't so bad.'

Another thief, Alik, a sullen stalwart of about twenty, was a 'substitute.' He had been sentenced to one year but had swapped names with another thief who had been sentenced to ten years. In the prison camp where he was going, he would have to keep up his pretense for one year —until the other went free. Then he could confess. The worst he would get was another year, as party to a fraud.

Fedya explained this to me aboard the train after we left Orel. That, he said, was the law of the underworld.

We weren't long out of Orel before Alik and his sidekick, a grimy youngster named Kolya, began to 'inspect' their cell mates' belongings. It surprised me to see the others—men like the broad-shouldered Gerasim, whose years of military service went back to Czarist days; the quarrelsome mechanic Ivashyuk, forever protesting that he 'wasn't afraid of anything or anybody'; the young Stas, a policeman under the Germans, said to have 'shot two Jews and one Russian war prisoner' —to see these and other tough-looking specimens in our compartment submitting docilely as the two thieves, hardly more than adolescents, appropriated whatever clothes took their fancy.

The old veteran Gerasim did begin in a frightened whisper when they pulled out a hidden bundle, 'That's my—what are you—'

Alik's hand swung sharply down against his Adam's apple, and the old man choked, wheezing and coughing.

Fedya warned me, 'Major, don't interfere. Believe me, if you want to stay alive, think only of yourself.'

Kolya spoke to the cell at large. 'Listen, peasants, and understand. That's how it's done. What good will this stuff do you? They'll confiscate it anyway in the camps. But this way you'll get something in exchange—something to eat, something to smoke. You'll see. We won't let you down.'

Old Gerasim yelped, 'No, no, Alik! Please—the doctor ordered it— I'll die otherwise—'

His bundle had revealed a secret cache of pork fat, sugar and stale bread.

Alik pushed him away. 'You pigface! Where do you think you're going—on a military campaign?'

The thieves, true to their word, shared part of the haul. Fedya, with the airs of a hotelier, presented me with a slab of pork fat. The sight and smell of it brought on hunger pains. I bit into the hard, salty lard. I was ashamed of myself; so, I could see, were the others who got a share; but we all ate whatever was given us.

Gerasim's gray, stubbly face was damp with sweat and tears. 'Kind people, let me have a little of my pork fat—just a little piece—'

I tore off a piece with my teeth and gave it to him, regretting my action immediately. So did someone else.

Gerasim mumbled his thanks, chewing and glaring at us with hatred.

The fourth thief in our compartment was an urchin of about twelve. All four would sometimes be moved to another cell. There they would 'inspect' other suitcases and would return with trousers, jackets and underclothes. These would disappear on their next foray, and they would return with bread and makhorka. Or new prisoners would be moved into our cell, to undergo 'inspection.'

The train commander, a rosy-cheeked lieutenant, liked to pace the passageway in his squeaky boots. He took pleasure in the sound of his self-confident baritone; his favorite witticism was, 'I'll teach you to love freedom!'

At one of our stops two of the nearby compartments were filled with women prisoners. When the thieves among them began their 'inspection,' the women let out a caterwaul of piercing shrieks.

'Robbery! Guards! Get away, bitch! I'll kill you!'

The guards rushed in, and the shrieks turned to squeals. 'Captain honey! . . . It wasn't me, sweetie. . . . Don't hit me, don't hit me!'

We could hear the commander's sonorous voice. 'I'll teach you to love freedom!' And a boy's cry: 'Why me, why me? Comrade commander, I didn't do anything!'

An outburst of rage flared from our cell, and from other cells up and down the car. 'Stop beating women and children!' 'Executioners!' 'Robbery—that's what it is—legalized robbery!' 'We'll write to Stalin!'

The guards ran up and down the passageway. 'Silence, fuck your mothers! Or we'll put you in irons!'

Our train stopped somewhere near Moscow, then in one of the Moscow stations. But we weren't taken off. Then we moved on—east.

A hundred and fifty kilometers east of Moscow—Gorky.

'Out! At once! One step out of line, and we'll fire without warning!'

We pour out of the car.

'No talking! Sit down! *Down*!'

We sit on the ground, between our train and the parallel track.

'Heads down! No looking up!'

We are in a station. We hear voices—women's voices, children's voices, laughter.

Our new guards, soldiers in shabby-looking rear-guard uniforms, are standing to one side, with some police dogs. The station platform rears up ten feet away. Little boys in shorts can be seen running up and down, playing. Two drunks look down on us reflectively. One of them breaks into song: 'In Siberia's distant land . . .'

A guard climbs onto the platform. 'Citizen, on your way.'

'And who are you?' the drunk blusters. 'I fought for the Motherland.'

From a bench behind him women in dusty kerchiefs look on. A one-legged man with medals on his soiled army blouse hobbles up on crutches. 'Vlasovites, eh? We spilled our blood, and you, you rats, you worked for the Fritzes. To the gallows—all of you.'

'On your way, citizen.'

Two young women appear. One of them is tall; she wears a brightly colored dress, stockings rolled down to her calves, a battered pair of men's shoes. The other is shorter, blonder, big-breasted under her cheap blouse; she has sunburned legs without stockings. The tall one calls out: 'Boys, any front-liners there?'

'Some.' 'A few.'

I, and a captain next to me, respond louder than the others. We two stand out anyhow in our officers' coats. Even seated, we are taller than the rest.

Two guards advance on the women. 'On your way, citizens, on your way. Not allowed.'

The women leave. But they are back almost at once, their arms full. 'Hey, boys, front-liners—catch! You—the dark one—catch!'

Something flies from their hands and lands in mine—a cucumber. Something else—a roll.

'And you—the blond—' Something for the captain.

'Back!' the guards shout, alarmed. 'Back—stop it—not allowed—'

The hateful voice of the train commander: 'What's this? You can be tried for this! You can be shot for this!'

And the reedy treble of the lieutenant at the head of our new contingent: 'Guards! Attention! Clear the platform!'

The two women throw the rest of the food into the swarm of prisoners. The taller of the two remonstrates in a husky voice, 'What's it to you, comrade officers! It doesn't come out of *your* pockets!'

And the shorter one, practically in tears: 'They're from the *front*!

Whom did *you* ever fight? Wait till *you're* in prison—*you'll* be glad for a crust of bread!'

The two drunks turn on the guards. 'Who're you going to fire at—women? And for what—for showing a little mercy? Who are you—Germans?'

The one-legged veteran who had consigned us to the gallows sides with the women. 'Go ahead, shoot *me*, riffraff, if you dare! I'll flatten you with this crutch! I captured Warsaw, fuck your mother!'

The little boys drop their game to crowd around. Passersby stop. A small crowd collects. Our new guards press against it. 'Citizens, citizens—' Whistles. The police dogs bark excitedly.

I devour my cucumber and the sweetish roll. How marvelous these women are! Never will I forget them! Something sticks in my throat—whether a lump of dough or tears of gratitude I'm not sure. The dogs bark angrily. The guards next to us are in a state. 'Squeeze in, squeeze in closer! Heads down! No talking!'

Overlooking the platform, under the roof, there is a big, weathered placard. A painted garland of branches cradles the faded fragments of a massive portrait—a mighty mustache, heroic shoulder boards, medals across the chest. Underneath, I can make out the discolored words: 'Our thanks to the great Stalin for our happy life!'

# 16

IS THERE anyone who has not felt the magnetic attraction of unseen cities, train whistles, the rhythmic chant of wheels on the railway tracks stretching behind you, where you came from, and before you, where you're headed—who knows to what chance encounters and fresh hopes? Wonder about faraway places is born in us in childhood; and, with me, it never dimmed. How bright and fresh, as though washed in rain and painted by sunshine, did Kiev look to me when I was five! Kharkov, to my thirteen-year-old eyes, seemed less festive—wintry-white, brick-red, yet alluring, with the mysterious lure of the new and the unknown. At twenty I saw Moscow, and my eyes and ears were filled with a many-voiced and multicolored chaos, and my heart with love at first sight. And now, marched from the railway station in Gorky, we came to a bridge over the river Oka—and there, off to one side, was the gleaming expanse of the Volga. How sad that I should see it for the first time like this! And yet it was beautiful; to see the Volga was wonderful; and I was almost happy, taking delight in the open air, the sun, the physical pleasure of walking.

A crenelated wall (Gorky's ancient kremlin); a steep street; a tram. People crowding the sidewalk. A boy belonging to one of the women prisoners sent a paper plane—a note—winging toward a group of youngsters standing on a corner. I saw one of them cover it with his foot.

'Who threw that?' the guards shouted. 'Who picked it up?'

The lieutenant was brandishing a pistol. But the boys on the corner pressed close together and laughed.

Several more notes floated from the column of prisoners. A guard recovered one of them. The others disappeared.

But someone reported the boy. One night, in the prison in Gorky, where we were confined for two weeks, we heard his heartrending cries.

Three or four hours out of Gorky, the trucks stopped and we got out —some sixty of us, under the care of three guards, a new batch. We were on a dirt road leading through a forest.

'All right, you all know the rules—one step out of line, etcetera, etcetera,' said the head guard, conversationally. 'No need to strain ourselves—it's only four kilometers from here. No lagging behind. And breathe deeply—this is real forest air.'

The command post of the labor-camp complex known by the acronym Unzhlag was surrounded on three sides by pine trees rising like a wall several hundred meters from the barbed wire. The lieutenant in command of the post had polished boots and battle ribbons on his uniform.

'Any front-liners?'

There were two of us—the blond captain (sentenced for the murder of his mistress) and I. He was made overseer of the disciplinary cell, and I was put in charge of a potato-picking brigade. The next morning, at dawn, I was in the fields.

The Unzhlag complex consisted of twenty-seven or twenty-eight camp posts, including three hospitals, two woodworking factories and two sewing establishments. The camp had its own railway line, 150 kilometers long. There were close to twenty-five thousand prisoners and several thousand guards, and about two thousand day laborers were hired from outside the zone. (The forested region east of the Volga was thickly settled by people of different ethnic origins.) Spread out among the camp posts were villages, collective farms and state farms, as well as camps of another kind—one for war prisoners, for instance, and two for women from the German ethnic settlements, mobilized into labor battalions. At night the darkness was cleaved by searchlights. Night and day the freight trains poked about, loaded with lumber and planks, stocks for rifles and submachine guns, furniture, toys, mattresses, coats, quilted jackets, trousers, felt goods, overalls, underclothes, dressing gowns—all the products of prison-camp labor.

Compared to what lay behind me, the camp, at first, seemed like paradise. The forest all around, the bracing air, the smell of moss, mushrooms, resin . . . We could buy our own makhorka, soap and bread over and above our rations; I sold my army overcoat and ate a kilogram of bread at a sitting. We could write to our relatives and receive

Lev Kopelev, *left*, with Friedrich Dürrenmatt at the Moscow Theater in 1964

Alexander Galich, a poet, *left*, with Kopelev at Moscow Airport

Kopelev and Countess Marion Dönhoff

Kopelev, *standing right*, with Victor Nekrasov, the novelist, *standing left*; *in front*, Andrei Sakharov and his wife, Elena

letters and parcels. There was a club. There were newspapers. There were women. The older hands said that although camp 'marriages' were punishable offenses, anyone who was bold enough and clever enough . . .

This euphoria soon evaporated before the persistent hunger and stupefying meaninglessness of a slave existence. Everything around us was hostile—the gigantic pines resisting our axes and saws, the gluey mud clutching at our feet. My potato brigade was disbanded after only a few days. We had managed to roast some of our crop over an open fire, the guards looking the other way, and most of us came down with diarrhea from eating half-cooked potatoes.

The infirmary was under the charge of a young woman doctor, Nina T. She had thick black eyebrows, big, dark blue eyes and a wide, generous mouth, and to me she seemed a real beauty. In my unsightly nakedness—slack, wasted, muddy from work in the fields, and covered with boils—I stood shamefaced before her while she ordered me matter-of-factly to raise my arms, turn around, bend over, and gave instructions to her male assistant.

'You see those hollows? Complete emaciation. Why wasn't it marked on his card? Write it down: "Light work only."'

She asked me what my profession was, whether I had been at the front, whether I had been taken prisoner. 'Stop scrunching up,' she said. 'I've seen worse. You can get dressed. I'm an army doctor. I was taken prisoner on the Izium-Barvenkovsky front, when Timoshenko* made a present of two armies to the Germans. I was wounded, slightly. Then some of us escaped and joined the partisans. Then we linked up with our troops. All the same, they gave me ten years. At first, I felt so bad about it I wanted to hang myself. Now I've gotten used to it. They need doctors everywhere. For a philologist like you, it's harder. Especially in the shape you're in. Any infection you get now is going to stick. Your organism has no resistance at all. Go back to the barracks. I'm prescribing three days of rest. Tell the dining room orderly Doctor Nina wants you to be fed out of the infirmary supplies.'

That evening I sat in a partitioned-off part of the dining room and was served a powdered-egg omelet, baked potatoes and kippered herring. How long since I had seen such food! I tried not to look at the men on the other side of the partition, their gazes fastened on my plate,

*General S. K. Timoshenko, one of the generation of Civil War heroes whose disastrous showing against the Nazi armies led to their replacement by a new class of Soviet generals.

or to hear their soft sighs: 'Listen, Uncle . . . listen, buddy . . . a tiny bit . . . at least let me smell it. . . .'

October was wet and cold. In the evenings I had the chills; during the night, according to my bunkmates, I shouted and swore in my sleep. My headaches became incessant.

One morning, burning with fever, I was back in the infirmary. Doctor Nina examined me again. 'You've got a whole collection of illnesses this time—pellagra, bowel infection, a bad cold—enough for a carload. I'm sending you to the hospital. There's a group leaving tomorrow. The SPI will look after you there. The Society for the Preservation of the Intelligentsia. That's what one of the prisoners called us camp doctors.'

We formed up in the evening, thirty-five of us. It was sleeting. The commanding officer ordered: 'All property belonging to the camp to be returned.'

Whereupon all suitcases, bags and sacks were searched and their contents flung out, right onto the mud. The guards said we could take extra clothes with us only if they were our own. Frightened protests rose all around me.

'But these clothes *are* mine, comrade commander! This jacket and these trousers—my wife sent them to me!'

The guards bellowed and cursed. 'Silence! They'll give you all the clothes you need in the hospital.'

There were moans and cries.

'What are you doing? Oh, my God, they're taking my last things away from me!'

'That's *my* shirt! It's Polish, don't you see? You don't have shirts like this here—'

A woman's wail: 'No! It's mine!'

A gaunt old man, his face and head bundled in a piece of cloth, had apparently not heard or not understood the orders. Two guards ripped his knapsack off him. He mumbled, alarmed, 'Why? What did I do?'

I burst out: 'Where is the post commander? I demand to see the post commander! This is mockery of Soviet law! This is not an inspection; it's robbery!'

The man behind me whispered, 'Don't start anything . . .'

A sturdy fellow with a submachine gun across his chest bounded up. 'Shut up, fuck your mother, or I'll show you the law!'

The commanding officer came up. 'Someone agitating about his rights? Someone insulting the camp authorities?' He stood before me. 'You calling for the lieutenant?'

I grew frightened—frightened of being beaten, but even more of being left behind, of not getting to my heavenly, longed-for hospital.

'Lost your voice, son of a bitch, enemy of the people? You want us to cure you, right on the spot?'

I remembered stories of prisoners being killed in transit 'while attempting to escape.'

'Keep your eye on this joker,' the commanding officer said, moving away.

My little sack contained some leftover bread, two onions, a wooden spoon and the tattered remains of my army underwear. They didn't bother with it.

The 'inspection' completed, we were linked by a length of rope—one arm tied to the arm of the man behind, the other to the arm of the man in front—and were marched off at a stiff pace. My feet sank in the mud. 'Closer together!' the guards commanded. 'No lagging! Faster!'

In the darkness ahead of me someone stumbled and fell. There was a crush of bodies and more shouting. 'Anybody who holds us up will be shot!'

We slogged through deep, icy puddles. I tripped up and felt one of my galoshes come off.

'One minute, comrades, please . . . I lost my shoe. . . .' I bent down, searching blindly.

A guard's voice: 'Who's lying down there? It's you again!'

I heard a rifle bolt click next to my head. Terror! Will he shoot? The men before and behind me pulled desperately on the rope, trying to get further away from me.

'Up!'

He isn't going to shoot! I lunged forward.

'Faster!'

In the sleety murk splotched orange by the flashlights, we came at last upon a waiting train.

'Come on, come on! Move!'

We crowded together before a freight car, the guards yelling, the dogs growling. I helped the old man up into the car, then the woman. There was a whistle from the locomotive, and someone pushed me aside, clambering up, moaning in panic. I grabbed the metal door-slide and tried to pull myself up after him, but didn't have the strength. All I could do was hang on with one elbow, my legs dangling helplessly.

The car gave a jerk. Oh, horrible! The train would start. I would fall under the wheels.

'Save me!' I cried.

Someone above me grabbed me by the scruff of the neck. Someone below butted me. My jacket strangled me; I worked my legs desperately. Then, suddenly, I was aboard.

In blissful half-sleep, I sat in a bright, clean hospital room, on a bunk covered with an unbelievably clean sheet. I could barely recall arriving the previous night and falling asleep on a warm wooden floor, next to a warm friendly wall.

The doctor was a small, round-faced man, whose gray mustache and thick eyeglasses added to his air of kindness and concern. 'In Moscow,' he asked, 'did you know a literary critic named Motylyova?'

'Tamara Lazarevna Motylyova? Of course!'

'She's my niece.'

Uncle Borya, as I came to know him, looked at the thermometer. 'Oho! Have him washed,' he told his assistant. 'Have his clothes boiled. Get him into bed.'

The next time I woke up, I saw six pieces of bread on a stool next to my pillow. Three pieces of black bread and—miraculous sight!—three pieces of white bread. I ate them greedily, my eyes filling with tears.

It was the beginning of my regime of intensive nourishment, the cure for pellagra. Lentils or oatmeal for breakfast; potato soup, turnips, carrots and a piece of herring for lunch; lentils or oatmeal again for dinner; five hundred grams of black and white bread a day; yeast and mustard to spread on the bread; and cupfuls of a brew made of pine needles. Then I received a parcel and some money from home and was able to buy boiled potatoes, milk and makhorka. I also began receiving newspapers and books, and, even more important, letters—letters from relatives and friends, all trying to cheer me up, all assuring me that soon, very soon now, my case would be reexamined and would be seen for the 'terrible misunderstanding' that it was.

Unzhlag's hospitals were famous for their doctors. Uncle Borya was one of the best. In 1937, as an amateur stamp collector in Yaroslavl, he was invited to a philatelic congress in Sweden and sought the advice of the authorities. He was thereupon arrested and beaten. Trying to get him to 'confess,' the security police broke two of his ribs and one of his fingers, and pulled out one of his fingernails. After Ezhov was removed as head of the NKVD, Boris was freed. But a year later he was arrested again for telling the doctors who treated him for his injuries how he had come to receive them. Without much further ado, he was sentenced to eight years. In the camp Uncle Borya continued to collect stamps, but only those of prerevolutionary Russia and the Soviet Union.

Unzhlag, one of the oldest camps in the entire Gulag system, was also known as a soft berth for actors. The camp commandant was a lover of the arts, and actors were generally kept in the hospitals as 'convalescents' or as orderlies, so that they would be in better shape for the theatrical performances. One evening, as I grew stronger, I slipped out of the ward without permission to see the camp's 'Central Troupe' put on Tolstoy's play *The Power of Darkness* in the hospital dining hall. There was a small stage; the curtain was made of old sacks of different colors, with the factory markings stenciled on them, and the effect was nostalgically reminiscent of the little theaters of the 1920s. The room was packed; the noisy, quarrelsome spectators sat on the benches, on the floor, on tables moved against the back wall.

Ah, to hear Tolstoy's words again, spoken from the stage! If only the audience were quieter! Most of the prisoners listened attentively, but a row of women, young, loud-mouthed and plainly of criminal background, addressed a running commentary to the characters of the play.

'Ekh, you little fool. Can't you see—he wilted you and jilted you.'

'What are you sorry for him for? Bash him between the eyes—that's all they understand.'

'Ah, stop moaning. So you're knocked up—you'll get an extra ration.'

Each sally was accompanied by a gale of laughter.

A man who turned around to shush them got a broadside. 'You keep your eyes on the stage, you ninny, or we'll unscrew your head for you and stick it up your backside and say that's how it came!'

And the commentary continued. 'Stop blubbering, you slut. . . . He's lying, and she believes him!'

'Go ahead, you liar. Bamboozle her—that's all she deserves.'

And another explosion of laughter.

Howling over the tragedy of a young pregnant woman abandoned to a dark fate, they were mocking themselves and their own disfigured lives.

On the first anniversary of the end of the war—by this time I had recovered and had been put to work making boots out of woody fiber (bast)—there was a solemn meeting at which the camp commandant gave out prizes to the best woodcutters, the best workers in the woodworking and sewing shops, the best technical workers, and the best nurses and doctors. One of the recipients was the head of a woodcutters' brigade named Assan. He had served several years for robbery and had earned release ahead of time by his incredible production records. Now he lived outside the zone but continued to work inside it as a hired laborer. An orchestra of two guitars, several balalaikas and a mandolin sounded a fanfare, and Assan, called onto the stage, was presented with a pocket watch, complete with chain.

Pushing aside the officer who had made the award, Assan strode up to the table in the center of the stage and placed the watch before the commandant.

'Take the watch, Comrade Colonel,' he said. 'Take it. I thank you. "Prize"—that's a fine-sounding word. But I *have* a watch. I have three watches—no, four. I don't need any more.'

'You're right, Assan,' said the commandant. 'I don't know what clown picks your prizes. But now I want you to tell me. What do you want? Your clothes aren't very fancy. How about a suit, a fine wool overcoat?'

'I don't need a suit, boss. I don't need an overcoat. I have three suits. I have two overcoats. I ask you for another prize, a real prize.'

'What?'

'Take me back into the zone.'

'Are you crazy? You're a free citizen.'

'I want to be back in the zone, you understand? When I was a zek,* I had a clean room—clean bed, clean sheets, clean pillow. I ate good food—hot dinners, enough bread to fill my belly. If I wanted to drink, there was drink. If I wanted women—there were women. Money in my pocket. Never had to count it. And now what?

'Food? Got to have ration cards. No one to cook it. So I go to the restaurant. Stand in line. And get shit. Wages? Stand in line. And they take the tax. Nothing left. Women? All whores—no shame. I had one move in with me. Took all my things in a suitcase—disappeared. Now I sleep on a sack. In the zone I didn't know what lice were. Now I'm covered with lice—here, see for yourself.

'Take me back into the zone, commander. I'll do the work of five. Take me back, please, like a good fellow, or I'll go nuts, kill someone, and they'll give me a long sentence and put me in some other camp.'

*Derived from ZK, which is the way prisoners (*zaklyuchyonnyi*) were referred to in camp announcements and records. Zek became the camp term for prisoner.

Assan did not get his wish. But an economist imprisoned in Unzhlag since 1937 explained to me, when I told him the story, that the wood-cutters who worked for wages in the prison-camp areas lived worse, as a general rule, than the camp inmates. By the same token, he said, production costs inside the camps were one and a half times higher than outside, or even twice as high.

'Take a normal lumber enterprise—what are your expenses? Equipment, pay, workers' benefits. But in a camp, for every hundred able-bodied laborers you have another hundred convicts working as trusties or in other capacities, and even more sick and invalided. Then the money spent on the guards, the camp authorities, the hired laborers from outside the zone. Your convict gets no pay, but how much do you think is spent on him, to feed him, clothe him, guard him, doctor him, transport him from place to place? Much more than any pay would be. Of course, he's lucky if he gets a quarter of what he's supposed to get— too many sticky fingers down the line. And all this goes into the cost of every cubic meter of wood product. Then there's the falsifying. On paper, the camp has delivered one and a half times the norm. But count the stuff, and if you end up with half the norm, you're lucky. In short, production costs in a prison camp are so high that it would be cheaper for us to buy the lumber from Canada.'

It was my first lesson in the economics of our 'Socialist' slave labor.

# 17

IN PRISON we used to be afraid of informers and talked about them in whispers. Here in the camp we spoke of them out loud. The lowest of all the minions of the mighty state, as helpless and humiliated as the rest of us, and often as falsely accused and as unfairly sentenced, they were nevertheless the indispensable cogs of the cruel punitive machine. They served for the sake of the little handouts the machine threw their way, and they served out of fear.

An informer talking: 'I'll tell you, as one front-liner to another, even in a camp a man can make out. A camp has its own laws. All you have to do is follow them.'

I listen. I like to find out what made them sink so low.

'They'll tell you I'm a stool pigeon, and maybe you'll think that I'm a rat, that there's nothing I wouldn't stoop to. Well, don't you believe it.

'True, I have some business with the Oper*—you know, the one they call the godfather. Of course I do—I'm a patriot, I used to belong to the Komsomol. And who is he? The representative of the Cheka, and this camp is full of enemies of the people.† Of course, there's also the other kind, like you and me. I can tell about people. I was educated. And life taught me plenty. I've been in the Crimea, in Rome, Germany,

---

*The Oper was the Operational Representative of the security police, responsible for law and order and disposing of a network of informers among the inmates. Each camp had at least one Oper. He would also be referred to by the prisoners as *koum*, the Russian word for godfather (and, in popular usage, friend).

†The year 1946 was when the NKVD was renamed the MGB. This informer's reference to it as the Cheka is a sly aping of a lingering habit among some idealistic Bolsheviks who associated the earlier designation with an earlier and more idealistic concept of the role of the secret police.

and in France. As a prisoner of the Germans, of course. "*Boche cochon, Russe très bien. Vive la France, vive la Russie!*" You understand? Of course you do. You're educated, too—I could tell about you at once. If the Oper asks me about you, I'll say, "He's one of us, law-abiding, a patriot."'

Then, without stopping for breath, without a change of tone: 'You have any buddies? Only one? Which one? Oh. What does he do? Was he in the Party? Was he taken prisoner? Oh. And you believe him? I'll tell you, as one front-liner to another, don't believe what you hear. One buddy—that's all right. But if anyone else tries to get friendly, you come to me—I'll tell you what he's after. The cook, for instance. He's a stoolie—hates everyone like you who's here under Article Fifty-eight. Be careful of him.

'Have some tobacco—first-class quality, this. You want to go to the bathhouse before you turn in—come to me. You want some under-clothes, some soap—'

He goes on and on, endlessly. Why the confession? Some particu-larly subtle game? Or some human need to reveal himself or to play the big shot?

Another informer: 'Ah, you've got some books. I can see you're a cultured man. I also love books. Gorky, Kuprin, Ehrenburg . . . And do you get newspapers, too? What do you think of this Churchill? He was our ally, our buddy, and now, did you see what he said about us?'

On another day, mysteriously: 'I want to talk to you privately. I know you're a good guy, but . . . Just by chance I found out—some-body squealed—that you and this nurse are, as they say . . . Well, I want to tell you as a friend: tonight, be careful. There's going to be an inspection. I found out by accident. I hope that as a cultured man, you won't tell anyone I told you. . . .'

Uncle Nechipor and young Iosip were Baptists. The older man had been nursed back to relative health, but they kept him on in our ward while putting him to work tending the heating system. Iosip, recover-ing from an operation for a chronic ear infection, was pale and thin and the youngest in our fourteen-man ward. When anyone spoke to him, he smiled sweetly. 'As the Lord wills,' he would say, and 'God bless you.'

Nechipor, polite and companionable, would tell us of miracles performed through faith—of the fatally ill cured by the power of prayer, of bums, thieves and errant husbands reformed by Holy Scripture. But in the evenings he would often take Iosip out into the corridor so they would not hear our 'worldly' conversations. Sometimes we would hear them singing softly in harmony.

> 'The feast is spread, the guests rejoice,
> And Jesus calls you to his side.
> Why do you not hear his voice?
> Why does your timid spirit hide?'

My new buddy, Seryozha, was a raw kid sentenced to ten years for having contemplated deserting to the Germans when his front-line unit was surrounded in the summer of '42—even though the plan, put to him by others, had never been carried out. He would receive parcels from his working-class family in Moscow; my parcels kept arriving every two weeks or so; and both of us would share our bounty with the others in the ward—most particularly with poor, sick, uncomplaining Iosip.

One day Nechipor received a parcel of cereal, cheese, pork fat and homegrown tobacco (the last to be realized into cash, since, as a Baptist, he did not smoke). Nechipor cooked some gruel, thickened it with lard, and brought in four platefuls—for Seryozha, me, and two others in our ward.

As we ate, Iosip looked on sadly, meekly, unable to avert his eyes. We went into the kitchen and said, 'Uncle Nechipor, thank you, but aren't you forgetting Iosip? He is hungrier than we are.'

'You gave me to eat,' Nechipor replied in his cheerful, self-assured way, 'and now I am giving you to eat. As the Bible says, "Give, and it shall be given unto you. Repay good with good." I love Brother Iosip with my soul, but I love all men and I do not have enough to give to all.'

'But Iosip needs it more than anyone. He's so thin he's practically transparent!'

'That is the cross he has been given to bear. Whom the Lord loves He burdens with tests. Brother Iosip bears his cross humbly and gains virtue in the sight of God.'

This was too much for Seryozha. 'You—you kulak, you lousy bloodsucker!' He let loose a string of blasphemous oaths.

Nechipor turned away. After that he held himself at a distance and avoided looking at us. If we happened to meet in the morning, he would say hello with a soft, sad voice. He forgave his enemies.

The director of our hospital was a young woman who had graduated as surgeon before the war and had served at the front, with the rank of captain. She now wore the uniform of the Ministry of Internal Affairs,* but she retained some of the decisiveness and informality of front-line doctors and treated the two men under her as colleagues, though both were convicts, in the camp since 1938. One was Boris Liebenson (Uncle Borya), who was in charge of our section. The other was Nikolai Telyantz, chief surgeon for the entire hospital.

Telyantz was an Armenian, a son of the craggy Caucasus, who took great pride in the history of his ancient, brave and wise people. He had been Deputy People's Commissar for Public Health in the Tadzhik Soviet Socialist Republic and had been arrested and tried together with the entire Tadzhik government. He never talked about that, but liked to discuss philosophy, literature and history. He was demanding and hot-tempered—even the hospital director was a little afraid of his sharp tongue—and he made no secret of his hatred of informers.

As winter wore into spring and I began to study to become a male nurse, while working in the boot shop, Telyantz and the other doctors warned me that one of our orderlies, Stepan, was an informer. Stepan was another of those unfortunates who had been sentenced for falling prisoner to the Germans. Silent, slack-jawed and melancholy, he always seemed to be present when any of us were talking about anything out of the ordinary.

We became conscious of it only when we found out that he was an informer. Pan Leon, a former fur dresser from Belorussia, whose case, like mine, was still before the courts, would challenge him loudly. 'Why are you hanging around us, Stepan? Is there something you want? What is it? Tell us; don't be shy.'

Stepan would grin uncomfortably. 'I'm just ... I'm only ...' He would flush and perspire. 'What's the matter; can't I stand where I want to? What are you afraid of—that I'll wear a hole in the floor?'

Some of the others in our company made their feelings even plainer. One of them, a young village tough named Vasya, once 'accidentally' dug his elbow into Stepan's midriff, so forcefully that Stepan gasped for breath. Another time, seeing Stepan standing in the doorway, he charged out to the toilet, knocking Stepan violently aside. 'Out of the way, you lump of carrion—can't you see I'm in a hurry?'

Vasya liked to tell stories in Stepan's presence of how they had disposed of 'Judas-informers' in his former prison barracks. 'We took this stool pigeon by the arms and legs and swung him up—high, high. Then we brought him down on the floor, right on his ass. Again, and

*The ministry had overall responsibility for the Gulag system.

again, and again. You couldn't see any marks on him. But the next day he was spitting blood. A week later he was dead. His kidneys were gone.'

Stepan listened with seeming unconcern, a drop collecting at the end of his nose.

Stepan's assignment from the Oper was no sinecure. He had to haul sacks of bread, buckets of balanda and other supplies from the distributing center to our kitchen, where the food was warmed before serving; he had to serve the meals, keep the place clean, lead those who could walk to the bathhouse, help carry the bedridden on stretchers to the X-ray room, get the linen to the laundry and back, and do a variety of other odd jobs. Trying to ingratiate himself with us, he would get us additional food whenever he could. 'Got this little extra for our gang,' he would confide in a stage whisper. 'Pull is stronger than Council of People's Commisars.'

He was at his most zealous when the blood was handed out. Sometimes, in addition to the usual gruel for dinner, we were given rations of coagulated blood, said to be very good for pellagra. Many of us refused to touch it, hungry as we were; it stank too much of carrion. So a lot of it was left over. Bringing in a trayful of dark-brown clots, Stepan would sing out: 'If you're delicate, light up; if you're a blood drinker, set to! Lots for everyone!' He became lively and talkative, feeling more than ever the benefactor.

Pan Leon and Vasya were in awe of medicine; besides, Pan Leon never gave and never turned down anything and Vasya never got food parcels. So, unlike Seryozha and me, they gobbled up the dried blood and took a kindlier view of Stepan.

Aunt Dusya, our housekeeper, was a small, prematurely withered woman with big, gray, youngish eyes smiling out of a wrinkled face. Her voice was hurried, eager, with a musical lilt. Never did a bitter or unseemly word come from her mouth: a reproachful 'Now, dearie,' or a resigned '*Ekh*, you cabbage head' was the closest I heard her come to anger. She had spent more years in labor camps than anyone else I had met—since 1932. I liked to listen to her peasant speech.

'I'm a village girl, dearie, born on a bed of straw. Tended geese when I was just a little tyke. What time was there for school, when Papa was taken off to be a soldier, and me the oldest of eight children? Ten years old I was then, and what we didn't have to do—milk the cows, and feed the pigs and chickens, and grow the vegetables, and plant the field, and harvest the grain. Two classes of school was all I had when the war came to our door—the Reds and the Whites and the Greens,* and the taxes and the levies. Then Papa came back from soldiering. He was wounded, and he limped and he coughed, and he wouldn't do any work but was always in the village arguing with the other men and drinking vodka. Froze to death one night when he was drunk, may the Lord have mercy on his soul.

'But I was taken to wife for love. I was sixteen then. His father was a rich man and had a farm near Kaluga. In my family we were poor, and slept on gunnysacks or on the stove, and ate from one bowl. At my father-in-law's they slept on sheets in their own beds and ate from plates. And I did not even bring a dowry. But I came pure of body and soul, and I sang in the church choir and knew all the prayers, and I liked to work and laugh and dance and sing. My father-in-law would say to his own daughters, "Dusya doesn't have a lead kopeck, but she has a golden mind, and you have gold earrings and heads of lead."'

When Lenin adopted the New Economic Policy, the father-in-law became one of the 'Red merchants.' He would send Dusya and one of his daughters, Nastya, to Moscow with supplies of butter, cottage cheese and yogurt, which found ready buyers in the food stores. With the end of the NEP period, such 'speculation' became a crime again. But the father-in-law continued with his arrangement, only now the two young women disposed of their products through secret middlemen.

They were spending the night at the home of one of these 'partners' when the place was raided.

'I had time to tell Nastya: "Remember, you don't know who I am—you met me on the train; you came to Moscow to buy clothes for your dowry." They believed her and let her go. And me—I had the goods and the money. What could I say?'

At the interrogation she feigned idiocy. 'I cried, and I prayed. "Let me go," I begged. "Where I'm from I won't tell you. Whose money this is I won't tell you. I swore to God I would not tell anyone. Let me go, in the name of Christ."

'Two months I kept it up. Then they brought in one of our partners. They had broken him, poor soul, and he had told them everything. So they gave me five years for speculation. Then, in camp, they gave me ten more years for conversation and agitation. And this happened through one old woman who told them that I was saying all kinds of things about the collective farms and about the government.'

*The anarchist peasant bands of Nestor Makhno and other guerrilla leaders of similar persuasion.

Her father-in-law, warned by Nastya, had meanwhile left Kaluga with his family and escaped arrest. Her husband was with the army engineers and had sent her a parcel from Germany. Her two children, a boy and a girl, had been told that she was dead.

'It's for the best. They are being raised by my sisters-in-law. They go to school; they have their lives ahead of them. Better to be an orphan, dearie, than to have a convict for a mother.'

Aunt Dusya's room was next to the kitchen. It was in the kitchen, where I could read and smoke after lights out in the wards, and which also served as the duty room for the night nurse, that my liaison with the nurse Edith began. Edith, who was from one of the ethnic-German areas, was serving the last two years of a ten-year sentence.

In April of that year Aunt Dusya invited us to a secret observance of Easter. One of the inmates tending the stoves was a priest, two of the laundresses were nuns, one of the cooks was an expert in religious services, and the four of them, together with Aunt Dusya, had made one of the women's barracks into an improvised chapel, greasing palms wherever necessary to keep it quiet.

Seryozha was invited as well.

'So what if you are unbelievers?' Aunt Dusya said. 'You and Seryozha stand up for people, and whoever stands up for people stands up for God. Your Nechipor, the Baptist, is always talking about God, and I don't believe him. But you and Seryozha, and your Edith, you are people with soul. I see right into you, and what I see is good, and I pray for you as for one of my own.'

The service was held in the evening. The beds were placed alongside the walls. There was a fragrant smell of incense. A little table covered by a blanket was the altar. Several homemade candles cast their glow on an icon. The priest, wearing vestments made of sheets, held up an iron cross.

The candles flickered in the dark. We could hardly see the faces of the others in the room, but I felt sure that we were not the only unbelievers present. The priest chanted the service in an old man's quaver. Several women in white kerchiefs joined in softly, their voices ardent and pure. A choir gave harmonious responses, softly, softly, in order not to be heard outside.

There, outside, ten steps from the barracks walls, was the barbed wire, with its watchtowers, its sentries in sheepskin coats; and, further on, the houses of the guards and the camp officials; and beyond them, all around us, the dense and ancient forest; and beyond the forest, the west, the Volga, and a string of villages, gray and hungry; and finally, hundreds of kilometers away, Moscow. The ruby stars in the Kremlin towers. An old, peeling house. A narrow room, where my daughters were asleep. And beyond Moscow, toward the west, a trail of ruins, ashes and freshly dug graves . . .

The next day, Easter Sunday, some of us were invited to Aunt Dusya's room. Each of us had tried to contribute something, and she had prepared a festive spread. There were hard-boiled eggs, painted according to Easter custom, and meat and baked potatoes; there were American canned beef and sausage, and biscuits and sweets—the yield of parcels from home. The doctors had contributed some alcohol, which Aunt Dusya had mixed with a bottle of liquid vitamins for color and taste. She had even managed to bake a kulich* and to adorn it with colored paper flowers. We exchanged the traditional Easter toast— 'Christ is risen!' 'Truly risen!'—and Aunt Dusya took two plates of food and two glasses of the improvised vodka to Uncle Borya and Dr. Telyantz, who lived in the doctors' house.

Aunt Dusya also insisted that we invite the informer Stepan.

'Dearie,' she argued, 'with his poor, lost, dark, sinful soul, where will he find a ray of light if we don't show it to him? Let him see that even here, in prison, the light of Christ still shines and there is pity even for such as he. We didn't tell him about the church service, because others would be held responsible if it became known. We invited only those we could be sure of. But here in my little room I am mistress. Around this little table we are all equal, believers and unbelievers, and for all of us this is a bright holiday, and there is only good here.

'And there is another reason. Oh, dearie, don't think I haven't learned. I'm a crafty one, I am. Just think—everybody who drops in for a bite and a drink—don't you think Stepan will smell the alcohol on their breath? You'll take a little food to your friends in your ward— don't you think he'll ask: from where? His eyes, his ears, his nose are always on the job, and so he'll have to squeal on us. But if we invite him and treat him and exchange toasts with him, in Christ's holy name —for Jesus taught us to love and pity our enemies—he will see things differently, and he will not be able to repay good with evil.'

Aunt Dusya did as she proposed. She called Stepan, and poured a drink for him, and exchanged the Easter toast with him. And Stepan drank and ate and beamed. 'Thank you—thank you.' He even winked, as though to say that he understood and that there was no need to worry.

*Traditional Russian Easter cake.

We were all in a tender mood and smiled and said kind things to each other. Someone made a speech about this being a holiday not only for Christians but for all men of goodwill. I argued compellingly that a good Christian and a good Communist not only shouldn't, but couldn't, be enemies.

Two days later, Aunt Dusya, her face stained with tears, told us that Stepan had squealed. She had her own intelligence network and usually knew what was going on. She had learned that Stepan had reported the reception to the Oper. The Oper wanted to conduct an investigation, but Uncle Borya and Dr. Telyantz opposed the idea, and the hospital director sided with her convict-doctors. Instead, as a compromise measure, Aunt Dusya was to be transferred to a harder post in a sewing shop.

There were more tears, particularly among the younger nurses, the day she left. Stepan was replaced as orderly and transferred to an adjoining barracks. If we ran into him after that, we pretended not to see him; when he spoke, we pretended not to hear. For us, he ceased to exist. But Seryozha swore he'd kill him; it was only a question of finding a way.

I told the whole story to Dr. Telyantz.

'Don't do anything,' he said. 'Tell your friend to lay off. Leave it to me.'

About a week later, I reminded him of his words.

'I haven't forgotten.'

One evening in May I was having dinner in the kitchen with Edith when an orderly came in. 'The doctor wants you to play chess with him.'

I went to his room. Dr. Telyantz sat before a chess board.

'Some of our convalescents are well enough to go back to work. There's a batch of them leaving for Post Number Eighteen tonight. I've added that snake of yours to the list. Have the telephone operator call Post Number Eighteen and give them his name. Just a hint will be enough.'

Dr. Telyantz spoke absently, as though concentrating on the chess problem before him. Then he looked up. 'Have a seat. We'll play a game. You will also observe a little scene. Only no commentaries, if you please.'

Post Number 18 was located in the thick of a swampy forest and had one of the heaviest labor regimes in the whole camp. Where you were sent after you regained your health depended partly on luck, partly on the wishes of the hospital authorities, who could hold up your transfer until there was a transport for one of the softer work posts or who could wait until a transport for one of the hard-labor posts came by. Those authorized to decide were the hospital director, her deputy, and the chief surgeon, Dr. Telyantz. On this particular day the director and her deputy were both away on a trip to Gorky, and Dr. Telyantz was in charge.

We had hardly made the opening moves when there was a knock on the door. A woman secretary entered. 'Doctor, here's this list. Here's a zek named—' Noticing me, she faltered. 'Well, the Operational Representative says this zek shouldn't be sent with the others.'

'Which zek?' Dr. Telyantz looked at her list. 'Ah, that one. He has recovered. Fully. I ordered him sent off. So there's no reason for the citizen Operational Representative to be concerned. Understood?'

'Understood . . .'

The secretary lingered, disconcerted. She was a free citizen, attached to the camp administration; he was an inmate. But he was the 'wild doctor,' a legend to the whole camp. He had operated on the camp commandant's daughter and saved her life when she was dying of peritonitis. He even had NKVD officers for patients; they came all the way from Gorky to see him. He was afraid of no one.

'If you understand, what are you waiting for?'

The secretary left.

'So.' Dr. Telyantz returned to the game. 'I see you're playing by the rules tonight—'

Soon there was another knock on the door. The secretary was back, in a state of frightened agitation, with the same list.

'Doctor, the Representative says that he forbids you to send this man, that you must cross out this name or else you must go to see him personally at once. . . . That's what he said.'

Dr. Telyantz got up. His swarthy, sharply etched face, with its thick black eyebrows under a shock of black hair, wore a look of such fury that the woman fell back a step. He spoke to her softly, slowly, with exaggerated precision.

'Please tell the citizen Operational Representative that, as far as I am aware, I am still the chief surgeon of this hospital and, hence, am responsible for the hospital's patients. I have issued my instructions, and I don't propose to change them. I also don't propose to go to see him. I have an operation scheduled for an hour from now, and I am resting before the operation by playing a game of chess. That is my way of preparing myself. And for that reason I request that I be spared further interruptions. Is that understood?

'And another thing. If the citizen Operational Representative cancels my instructions, it will mean that he has become the chief surgeon in my place. In that event I shall stop working immediately, and the citizen Operational Representative can perform the operation himself—a case of appendicitis. And then an operation for hernia. One of his colleagues, by the way—the Operational Representative in Post Number Nine.'

He looked at his watch and continued. 'In half an hour, I want to be informed if the transport has left. You don't have to come back yourself—send one of the orderlies. But don't forget to let me know. Otherwise the citizen Operational Representative will have a few operations on his hands. Is *that* understood? Now, good night.'

He sat down and studied the chess board. 'You're not paying attention. You've lost your knight.'

The transport left on time. Later that night our telephone operator spoke with the operator at Post Number 18—both men were zeks—and expressed particular interest in the health of one of the men in the new batch, hinting at his role.

A month passed. By then I was working as a male nurse. One evening, when I was on duty, Edith came in.

'Do you remember Stepan—the one who got Aunt Dusya transferred? They just brought him in. Fractures of both legs and spinal column. A tree fell on him.'

Was it an accident or the outcome of the telephone call? I never knew.

# 18

THE HAPPIEST day of my life? I'd be hard put to answer that question now, but there was a day in early August of 1946—the fourth of the month, I believe—when I would have replied unhesitatingly: Today.

After a train journey from Unzhlag in which something like twenty or thirty of us prisoners were packed into compartments meant for six or seven passengers, after days of gasping in the heat and stench while the train moved and stopped and waited and moved again, I was in Moscow, in what was regarded as a model prison, and about to be called for a new judicial hearing. My case, I had been officially informed in July, was being 'reexamined.'

Cell Number 96 of the Butyrki prison* was high-ceilinged and roomy, with no more than a score of inmates, and I was lucky enough to land a place near the window, away from the latrine bucket. The breeze from the street was pleasantly cooling. The chirping of city sparrows on the other side of the iron bars was like a promise of deliverance. I stretched out on the mattress and fell blissfully asleep.

I had not one but three interrogators; they worked in shifts. All three took down everything I said, and none of them threatened me or tried to catch me in a falsehood. They seemed impartial in their attitude toward me—favorably disposed, if anything—and by the time the interrogation was at an end in October, I had reason to hope that the ridiculousness of this whole affair had become clear to them and that I would be set free—all the more so as some of the accusations brought against me had become laughably anachronistic. For instance, in the spring of '45 I was charged with 'slandering our allies' because I had argued that Churchill would never stop being an enemy of the Soviet

*A major prison, named for a district of Moscow, built in Czarist times.

regime, that we would have to compete with the Americans and the English for the friendship of the German people, and that we needed the German workers as allies against the Anglo-American capitalists. I was also charged with 'slander against the Soviet press and the Soviet writer Ehrenburg' because I had disagreed with his wholesale condemnation of the 'criminal' German race. But since then, there had been Churchill's speech at Fulton, the outbreak of the cold war, and the appearance of Alexandrov's article attacking Ehrenburg for the very reasons I had criticized him.* In fact, I was soon to learn that all reference to the Ehrenburg matter had been removed from my file.

But when I was called in again, it was to be told by the senior interrogator, 'In accordance with Article Two Hundred and Six of the Criminal Code, you must now sign the record of this interrogation.'

I was stunned. 'I had counted on the case being dismissed.'

'Only the prosecutor can do that. And the prosecutor's office is placing your case before the tribunal.'

'But why? It's all perfectly obvious—absurd accusations, patent calumny—'

'The tribunal will decide about that. We've got different kinds of evidence here—some favorable, some unfavorable. You see how much paper—enough to fill two tomes. The tribunal will sort it out from an objective standpoint. Now go ahead and sign this.'

I said that I wanted to read the contents of the two files first.

The interrogator was provoked. I insisted, citing the spirit and the letter of the law. He grew all the more annoyed, accusing me of bureaucratism and formalism. In the end he let me go through the second—and more recent—file, hurrying me along as I read.

There was new written testimony from people acquainted with my case. General Burtsev, he of the Central Political Administration, had made a particularly nasty deposition, starting, as though in an objective vein, with my qualities, erudition and achievements, and moving quickly to the nub: 'He was always known as an oppositionist. He was always at odds with his immediate superiors . . . morally unstable in his private life . . . got involved with women in military service and in civilian ranks . . . made serious political errors, which interfered with the work of the Political Department. . . .' The other senior political officers gave me a better character, one of them commencing with my faults (hot-tempered, brusque, self-opinioned to the point of insubordination) and expanding at greater length on a variety of virtues.

*Georgi Alexandrov, the then head of Agitprop, the Party's central propaganda department.

The dossier, which I read all the way through despite the interrogator's grumbling, cheered me up. I was almost sure that the tribunal would free me even if the prosecutors didn't.

Two or three days later I was called out again—with my 'belongings.' As I stuffed my collection of odds and ends into a sack, my heart pounded and my thoughts raced: Was I about to be released? I gave away what I had in the way of food, and I said good-bye to my cell mates, hardly able to make out their faces or to hear what they were saying. Someone was asking me to telephone his wife and kept repeating her number. She was to send him seven boxes of matches; that would tell them that I was free.

Outside the cell door, the guard said, 'Your case has been handed over to the tribunal of the Moscow Military District.' Feeling as winded as though I had run a long-distance race, I dragged my mattress and my things down the corridor, and then a second corridor, to Cell Number 105, the 'tribunal cell,' identical to Number 96, but with half the number of inmates.

The next day I was led down a staircase and into a room where a man sat at a plain wooden table. With his full gray beard, he was the image of a nineteenth-century intellectual.

'I am your lawyer, Alexander Vladimirovich Kh————,' he announced. 'I was retained by your family.' In an undertone, he added hurriedly, 'Your mother asked me to tell you that everyone is well. They all send you their love.' Then, his voice rising emotionally, 'But I want to tell you that I have been a Party member for more than a quarter of a century, and that I will defend the truth and nothing but the truth, and only in the interests of the Party and the government!' More matter-of-factly: 'Now, then, do you have any particular wishes to express? Whom would you like the tribunal to call as witnesses?'

We talked for half an hour. He made notes but did not listen very attentively. I named witnesses and told him of the falsehoods and contradictions in the evidence against me.

'All right, all right. You can tell that to the court. First, let me familiarize myself with your case. I'll do what I can to lighten your lot.'

'What do you mean—lighten my lot? I am a Communist, completely loyal to the Party. I am not guilty of anything. I demand full exoneration and the exposure of those who have defamed me.'

He looked at me quizzically. 'I've told you: I intend to conduct your case in conformity with the interests of the Party. You can understand that, can't you, if you're really a Communist? The charges are serious ones. In wartime, in a case like this, you could be shot. As it is, the Criminal Code provides for up to ten years. So get hold of yourself. Exercise restraint and common sense. It seems to me that you have already done yourself enough harm by your unbridled behavior.'

He went on like this, in smooth, rolling sentences. But, saying good-bye, he held out his hand, smiled encouragingly, and, I thought, gave me a wink.

That evening, after inspection, the guard took me to his own little room. There, amid the piles of mattresses and stacks of aluminum mugs and bowls, he let me read the official indictment, typed double-space on three pages of thin, flimsy paper. All the familiar accusations: 'undermining the morale and political consciousness of the Soviet troops,' 'slander,' 'discrediting the Soviet command,' 'disrupting military operations,' 'propaganda in favor of the enemy,' with quotations from the testimony of Zabashtansky, Belyaev and Nina. I noticed that while this testimony still spoke of my 'pity for the Germans,' that accusation had been dropped from the indictment, and there was no mention anywhere of my 'slandering our allies.' In the list of witnesses to be called, I saw the names of my friends Abram Belkin, Arnold Goldstein, Yuri Maslov, Ivan Rozhansky and Galina Khromushina.

On October 15, the birthday of my younger daughter, Lyena, four in our cell—two Chechens* who had been captured by the Germans, a Vlasovite and I—were called out, 'together with your things,' and marched off into a courtyard and then into a police wagon. We were driven for only a few minutes and found ourselves in another courtyard, then in a cellar—a small, square room without windows, with blinding electric light and with illegible writing showing through the fresh paint on the walls. We waited for half an hour. I was the first to be called.

Two guards, propping me up gingerly by the elbows—'like leading a condemned man to his death,' I thought—led me up the back stairs to a broad corridor. Men in uniform and in civilian dress. The clicking of women's high-heeled shoes. A spacious office. Someone in uniform seated behind a long desk. My attorney's gray head at a narrow table placed against the desk like the stem of a T. Officers and civilians seated along the walls; some of them nod to me and smile; two of them are women. I am seated on a chair facing the desk. Metal buttons, gilded shoulder boards, women's stockings glisten in the morning sun. After

*Members of the Chechen ethnic minority of the northern Caucasus.

the wan grayness of prison life, there is a feeling of dazzling luxury. I gape around me, hardly hearing what is being said. I recognize my friend Ivan Rozhansky. The woman in the blue dress must be Galina, so much older looking than the eager kid who was always ready to rush into danger at Graudenz. The woman in the military jacket must be Nina.

The presiding judge, a lean-looking colonel with eyeglasses, speaks in a scratchy voice. The guard standing behind me touches me on the shoulder. I hear my attorney whisper urgently, 'Stand up, stand up!'

Standing before them, I can see myself through their eyes: shaved head, unshaven face, wrinkled gray jacket, quilted pants and enormous ginger-colored American boots. By prison camp standards, a dandy.

Any objections, the judge asks, to the composition of the tribunal? No. . . .

'In view of the nonappearance of the witnesses Zabashtansky and Belyaev, it has been moved that the session be postponed. What does the defense say? Then you agree. Accused?'

I am crushed by a sense of anticlimax. 'And what if they don't appear the next time either? They lied at the interrogations, and now they can avoid—'

'We're not asking you about that. What we do next time we'll decide next time.'

My two guards lead me out, again propping me up by the elbows. Over my shoulder, I see someone's raised fist: 'Hang on.'

That year the Butyrki prison was being rapidly filled up. We estimated that a score or so of prisoners arrived each day. By the end of 1946 there were perhaps twenty-five thousand inmates in the prison. A few of them I remember to this day.

Alexei was a pilot. His slow-moving early-model bomber was shot down at the beginning of the war. Injured and taken prisoner, he escaped with several other fliers and tank men and joined a partisan group in Belorussia. In the winter of 1940 he slipped through the German lines, back to our side, and rejoined his squadron. In the autumn of 1942 his fighter-bomber was hit and set ablaze over German territory, but he managed to drop his bombs on target and crash-land behind the Soviet lines. Lame in one leg after a long hospitalization, he chose not to be demobilized but stayed on as a technician. He married a pilot of a women's flying detachment, and they had a daughter.

In 1944 Alexei was sent to the rear on an engineering assignment. At the railway station in Moscow he was placed under arrest. The interrogator said that his wife had flown over to the Germans, and this meant that he had returned from captivity on a German mission. The interrogator called him a Fascist; Alexei brought a chair down on his head. They tied him up and beat him, and kept him in solitary for twenty days. By August 1946 he had been imprisoned for two years without being interrogated again.

A self-possessed man with a soft, deep voice and the physical grace of an athlete, Alexei spent most of his days stretched out on his mattress.

'Conserve your strength,' he advised me. 'Not many proteins in that gruel. No use wasting your energy on idle chatter either.'

Once a month each of us was given a sheet of paper on which we could write out a complaint or petition. Each time he made the same request: that his case be brought to a speedy conclusion. Every three months he received a reply: His case was before the prosecutor of the Moscow Military District.

Another Alexei I remember was a red-bearded young stalwart who had been an adjutant to the Cossack general Krasnov.*

Alexei spoke well of the general. 'He was a kind old man, a dreamer. Outdated ideology, of course—"For God, Czar and Country"—but a just man, and sincere and bighearted. Not like that Shkuro,† who was a boor, a drunkard, a fool and a German puppet. Krasnov had arguments with the Germans. He wanted to conduct his own independent Cossack policy.'

Toward the end of the war, Alexei recounted, most of the anti-Soviet Cossack units were in Yugoslavia, active mainly in exchanging their arms for food and slivovitz. Then they fell farther back and surrendered to the English, who housed them in barracks in western Austria, letting them keep their arms. Krasnov and Shkuro asked the English officers to tell their government that the Cossack units were prepared to serve in the British army, fight the Japanese, do garrison duty or serve as engineer battalions in India or Africa. After two months the Cossack officers were invited to a conference in a nearby British camp. When their vehicles passed through the gates, the Cossacks found themselves covered by British machine guns. An

*General Pyotr Krasnov, a Don Cossack leader who left Russia in 1919 and headed a German-sponsored anti-Soviet Cossack force during the Second World War.

†Another dissident Cossack general.

◇ 164 ◇

English captain announced through a translator: 'In agreement with the allied Soviet government, the British command has decided to intern all Cossacks who served under the Germans. You are requested to surrender your arms.'

'There was yelling and swearing, but Krasnov said, "Gentlemen, we must submit and place our faith in God. We have been tricked, but we will comport ourselves with dignity." Three of the officers shot themselves; the others yielded. For dinner the English served excellent meat, a sweet pudding, and whisky. Then they showed a movie. And we began to take heart. We'll live like this for a while, we told ourselves, then, probably, we'll be recruited one by one into the British colonial army, or the Foreign Legion, or some work force.

'The next morning the English commandant announced the order of the day: Breakfast, then lunch, then the handing over of the inmates to the Soviet command.

'Two more officers shot themselves—they had hidden their pistols—and three or four hanged themselves. Krasnov made the rounds of the barracks: "Calm, gentlemen; put your faith in God." In the afternoon we were put aboard trucks. When we were crossing a river, two of our Cossacks jumped out. The English shot them in the water like ducks in a shooting gallery.

'Then, straight into the arms of our beloved countrymen. You never heard such swearing. The enlisted men had already been handed over. The cattle cars were there, waiting.'

In 1942 Captain Yakovlev was invalided out with a pension, having sustained serious head and chest wounds commanding an artillery unit near Mozhaisk. At the beginning of 1945 he was arrested as a traitor and 'Vlasovite agitator.' The story was an incredible one.

Several men of his division had been captured by the Germans, then liberated and placed in processing camps, where it was demanded of them that they name as many traitors and collaborators as possible. They agreed among themselves to start by naming the dead. Among these, they thought, was Captain Yakovlev. They had seen him lying in a pool of blood with a bullet hole in his head and they were sure that he had been killed. Hence, they accused him of having recruited for General Vlasov in the German prison camp, and the captain, living in retirement, found himself under arrest.

His alibi was not hard to verify: the hospitals where he had been treated for his wounds were all near Moscow or in the capital itself; and at the time when he was supposed to be recruiting in the German camp, he had actually been employed in a government economic bureau in Moscow. Yet, when I met him, the investigation had been under way for more than a year. He was still being confronted with his accusers, some of whom were brought in from distant labor camps, and all of whom were thrown into fear and confusion on seeing him.

Captain Yakovlev sadly wondered why the interrogators did not take the simplest and easiest course of confirming the record of his hospitalizations and his employment but persisted in questioning him, getting angry and shouting—though, of late, their ire was directed more at the unfortunates who had not counted on seeing him among the living.

Alexander Nikolaievich, a Moscow architect, was arrested with his wife because their daughter and son-in-law had defected from one of our embassies abroad.

'Now the interrogator says it's five years in prison camp for us—at least,' he told me. 'Unless we officially disown our daughter—you know, in the newspapers; unless we condemn and denounce her. Otherwise, he says, you are accomplices and must be held accountable under the statutes on betrayal of the Motherland. But that's unthinkable—to deny your own child, no matter how much she has erred, and to do it on official orders. . . . And this interrogator—he's a brash young man with shoulder boards—he wants me to name all my daughter's friends as well. Do you know why? So he can make more arrests—overfulfill his quota.

'No, I'm too old to learn how to do mischief, how to denounce my own daughter and send innocent people to jail. I'd rather stay in prison myself. After all, people go on living in those camps. Maybe they'll let me work at building something. I'm just worried about my wife. She's not in the best of health, you know—her heart. . . . But her spirit is as hard and bright as a diamond. If I weakened because of my worries about her and gave in, she wouldn't understand; she would never forgive me. Oh, in the Christian sense she would forgive me, but as a mother, as a wife—never. Thirty years we've been together. Six children she has borne me—three of them died when they were little, and now our eldest son was killed in Stalingrad. As for our daughter, how my wife used to argue with her and her husband. Even more furiously than me. But she loves her daughter unconditionally and will never disown her. She'll accept any punishment, but she'll never give in. All the more reason, then, why I can't give in either.'

.    .    .    .    .    .

Many Vlasovites and *hiwi* passed through. Their stories were all alike: encirclement, despair, hunger—weeks and months of hunger, destroying all ability to think; then capture, recruitment, the irresistible temptations of food and tobacco, the sudden hope of cheating death. Then Vlasovite barracks, or work in German military bases, transport columns, military factories, bakeries, depots. Then the road home— some through the processing camps; some after service in our penal or regular units, often in battle, often wounded, decorated and demobilized. And at the end, all of them—all who had served in Vlasov's army or had joined the Germans as *hiwi* or had worked for the Germans as ordinary, hungry, defenseless prisoners of war—all were charged under Article 58, Section 1, with 'betrayal of the Motherland while in military service,' or, if they were lucky, under Article 58, Section 2, with 'collaboration with the world bourgeoisie.'

The three Chechens kept to themselves. The oldest, Akhmet, looked like a swarthy, dark-haired Czar Nicholas II. Taciturn and reserved, he rarely spoke even to his countrymen. The second was younger—tall, pale, with a pinched face that came to a point in his big, sharp nose. The third was small and frail, with a black stubble that reached all the way up to his eyes. One day, one of the other prisoners swore at Big Nose while the balanda was being handed out, and the Chechen threw himself at the man with an enraged cry, pushing aside those in his way with unexpected strength. But Akhmet spoke one or two words in a voice barely above the normal, and the other stopped, went back to his bunk, and sat with his back to us, face to the wall.

The Chechens would pray several times a day, mumbling softly, staring at the wall. There were several others in the cell who prayed. I don't remember anyone's sneering at them or censuring this 'religious opium'. In prison, anyway, freedom of conscience was sacrosanct.

When I got parcels from home, I would share them first, as was the custom, with those who came from distant places or did not get any parcels of their own. The first time I offered the Chechens some onions, cookies and sugar, Akhmet was surprised and inspected them distrustfully. Then he nodded and let the other two take them, thanking me with unflinching dignity but not touching anything himself. The next day he spoke to me: Where was I from? Father, mother still living? Brother? Any children? Fought in the war? Taken prisoner? What did I do before the war? Was I ever in the Caucasus?

Akhmet would never address me when I was reading, or playing chess or dominoes, or talking with others, or had something on my mind. But when he saw that I was looking at him, he would give a barely perceptible smile and make some polite remark—'You were reading a book today, yes?' or, 'The professor spoke beautifully today. I didn't understand everything he said, but I listened, and he speaks beautifully: a learned man!' Only when he felt that his bid was welcome did he strike up a conversation.

Responding to my questions, he spoke willingly about his life. 'We live well. We live properly, by the law. You have people who steal. We don't. With us, he who steals will not live. His own father will cut his throat.'

'But how about your "baranta"?' I asked diffidently. He himself had told me proudly how, as a boy, he had taken part in the Chechen baranta, or rustling, chasing cattle off the pastures of the Ingush people.

'Baranta isn't stealing,' he said. 'Baranta is worthy of a man. Your dzhigit* rides out to the baranta, and the dzhigit is a brave man; your thief is a coward. The new law—the Soviet law—says a man must have only one wife. That is a good law for Russians. It is a good law for the Ossets and the Georgians. It is a good law for him who is poor, who has little to eat, and a small house. But for him who has a big house and money and property of all kinds—for him there is another good law, the old law of the shariat†: two wives, if you want; three, if you want— but in accordance with the law, in all honor, everything in proper order. One wife—her own place to live, her own food. A second wife— also her own place, her own food. Russians drink vodka and swear ugly on their mother.‡ Why? Because the Russian woman doesn't know order, goes wherever she wants. And the men don't know order. The law says: one wife—one husband; but no one listens. The husband goes with another man's wife, or with a girl. The wife goes with another woman's husband. With us, such things cannot be. Take me—I have three wives, under the law. I give each one her own room, her own food. I was a head man in a sovkhoz.§ I had a house, I had a garden, I had sheep—I had everything. We have a school; we have a club—they show moving pictures once every week. Who goes? Women, girls and young boys, and whoever else is told to. Why is he told to? Because

*Dzhigit: the horseman of the Caucasus.

†Shariat: the code of the Moslem peoples of the Caucasus.

‡A reference to the oath, blunted by casual usage, consigning the addressee to sexual relations with his mother.

§A state-owned farm paying wages to the workers.

women cannot go alone. I tell my younger brother, or my nephew, or the neighbor's son: Go with my wives, see that everything is in order.

'What order? Well, if a man speaks to my wife, my brother, or whoever is with her, will cut his throat. And if my wife speaks to a man, laughs like a Russian woman, my brother, or my nephew, or my friend, will cut her throat. If he doesn't cut their throats, I will cut his throat. No, this does not happen often, but only because everyone knows that if it has to be done, it will be done.

'Two years before the war one of the men in our village—a good dzhigit—learned to drive a truck, drove all over, all the way to Russia. He had a wife. She was beautiful, and young, and he thought she was good. He comes back when they don't expect him and sees a strange man. His wife screams: "Give me a divorce. I don't want to love you; I want to love this man!" The man yells: "The new law permits divorce; give her a divorce; I will give you money, I will give you sheep." The dzhigit took out his dagger and cut the man's throat, and cut his wife's throat. Their son was small—two or three years old. He wanted to cut his son's throat also, but could not—took pity. He thought: the boy has his mother's blood, bad blood; but he has my blood, too. He thought for a long time, and wept, but he did not cut his son's throat.

'Then there was a trial, and the prosecutor shouted, "He must be shot." But our whole village went to the city where the trial was held. All the men went, and the old men went to the judge and to the police and to the city authorities, and everywhere they said: "Your new law is good, and our old law is also good. All laws should be respected. If he is shot, the judge will certainly have his throat cut, because it is not right for this dzhigit to be shot: He lived by the law. If it is bad for him in the court and in the prison, then it will be bad for the judge and for the police. All the Chechens will feel offended. You must respect our law."

'The judge was a wise man. He talked for a long time; the trial took a long time. And he sentenced the dzhigit to three years for lack of culture and suspended the sentence.'

Almost two months passed before I was ordered out of the cell again. The day was December 16. I found myself in a dimly lit hallway. My wife, Nadia, and my parents were out in the corridor. They were nodding encouragingly and smiling. Then I was in a long, narrow room, seated on a chair in front of a long desk, behind which sat the three judges of the military tribunal. My attorney sat at a little table to my left. Behind him the witnesses sat along the wall: Ivan Rozhansky, Galya, Nina, as well as others I had recognized at the previous session. And Zabashtansky. And Belyaev.

The presiding judge, a dour colonel, opened the proceedings in an even, matter-of-fact voice, saying that the prosecution would not take part in the trial and reminding the witnesses that they were under an obligation to tell the truth—failing which they would be held accountable under the appropriate statutes. He then asked them to wait outside the courtroom; they would be called in one by one.

The secretary of the tribunal read the indictment. The judge asked me to stand up: how did I plead?

Not guilty, I said; the charges were based on malice and lies; the interrogation had been prejudiced against me from the start.

'Sit down, please.' The presiding judge was duly polite. 'The trial will begin.'

# 19

THE FIRST to testify was Zabashtansky.

Heavier than I remembered him, stuffed into a military jacket with three rows of service ribbons, he planted himself before the judges, very much at ease, his soft, slow voice resonant with those tones of plainspoken sincerity and country-bred judiciousness that I had once found so attractive. He repeated essentially what he had said at the Party meeting in Poland and in the course of the subsequent interrogations, but with certain accommodations to the political changes that had occurred in the meantime. Instead of speaking of my attitude toward 'the Germans,' he used the words 'German-Fascist civilians,' and he glossed over my alleged sins of 'pity' and 'bourgeois humanism.' But he brought even more distress to his account of my 'defeatist attitudes' and my 'altercations with the commanding officers and enlisted men, leading to the disruption of an important military-political mission.'

My attorney had a question. How, in general, would the witness characterize the work performed by his front-line comrade and subordinate, who, while at the front, was accepted into the Party, was given responsible assignments and was decorated for action in battle?

'Well, of course, while we still had reason to trust him, while we still thought all this was just the hangover of his petit bourgeois past ... There's no denying, he's an educated man, very educated. Wore out the seat of his pants reading books while others like us spent their lives working and fulfilling five-year plans and fighting the kulaks and enemies of the people. He can speak German and Polish, and a couple of other languages as well. Knows how to put his best foot forward, how to throw dust in your eyes. Sure, he worked well when he wanted to.

And we trusted him and rewarded him, until he revealed his defeatism and his petit bourgeois essence, and began slandering the high command and speaking up against the decisions of the Government Defense Committee, which were signed personally by Comrade Stalin, and disrupting our military mission.'

'Defendant,' said the presiding judge, 'do you have any questions for the witness?'

'Let him tell the court when and where I spoke up against the decisions of the Defense Committee? Who heard me?'

'Why,' Zabashtansky said, 'this disgraceful occurrence was discussed at the meeting of the Party members of the Political Department. Why, that was the reason he was thrown out of the Party.'

'The whole thing is a lie, a barefaced lie! Two of the witnesses to the conversation in question, Klyuev and Mulin, failed to confirm that I had said what I was charged with. And the third witness, Goldstein, denied that I had said it.'

'Defendant,' said the judge, 'sit down. You are not to jump up. You are not to make statements without the court's permission. Do you have any more questions?'

'He did not answer my first question: When and where was I supposed to have said this, and who were the witnesses?'

Zabashtansky gave a small, condescending smile. 'That's how he always tries to wriggle out of things. This Goldstein is his crony— under his influence—got a reprimand from the Party because of it. And the whole question was examined at a Party meeting. This thing has to be seen in its proper light. There we were, more than a hundred front-line officers, in the middle of a war, of mortal combat, gathered together—and for what reason? Because of one army major who was undermining the morale of our fighting men. They had waded through blood all the way from Stalingrad. Their fathers and mothers had perished at the hands of the Fascists. Their breasts were filled with the sacred fire of revenge. And what did we have here but some overeducated major giving them little sermons about humanism! It's like'—his voice vibrated with repressed emotion—'spitting into their very souls! Resulting in altercations and disruption of the military mission.'

'Defendant, sit still. Do you have any further questions?'

'So I was to blame for the disruption of a mission, was I? What mission?'

'A mission,' said Zabashtansky, 'assigned by me personally, to explore the military-political situation in East Prussia at the time when our

Jean-Paul Sartre in Moscow with Kopelev, *left*

Moscow, 1969, Heinrich
Böll and Kopelev, *left*

Kopelev in Moscow in the early 1970s

troops were entering that country. To assess the feelings of the civilian population and the size of the Fascist underground. And instead, all he could talk about when he got back was how badly our men were behaving. It seems he was so displeased by our heroic fighting men that he forgot all about his instructions. I had to go there myself and do the job he had failed to do.'

'That's a lie!'

'Defendant, sit down! Stop jumping up! You are before a military tribunal, not at a political meeting. Conduct yourself properly, or I will have to punish you. What else do you want to ask?'

'It's true that the mission to East Prussia was carried out badly, but not through any fault of mine. And Zabashtansky didn't know anything about it. He left our base before we got back.'

'I told you not to comment on the witness's testimony. Do you have any more *questions?*'

'The mission to East Prussia was headed by Major Belyaev. I was his second in command. What reprimand did Belyaev receive for bungling the job?'

'Not true!' Zabashtansky exclaimed. 'The mission was headed by Major Kopelev. Major Belyaev was given his own separate assignment recruiting German war prisoners and civilians for our anti-Fascist school. Of course, Belyaev tried to prevail on him'—a glint of venom broke through Zabashtansky's mask of contemptuous indifference toward me—'to persuade him, like a comrade, like a friend. But there's no talking to him. Why, even here he's jumping up and down, and in those days—oh, how high and mighty he used to be, as though only he knew anything and all the rest of us were dunces, the great unlettered rabble.'

'I ask,' I said, 'that the court take note of his statements that *I* was the senior officer of the mission and that *he* had to go to East Prussia to make up for my failings.'

'Defendant, who is conducting these proceedings—you or I?'

'May I make a request of the court?'

'You may.'

'I request that you compare this testimony of his with what he said at the preliminary interrogation and at the Party meeting—'

'Be good enough to stop instructing the court. Don't compel me to punish you.'

My attorney asked Zabashtansky how he would evaluate my work in Graudenz, for which I had been commended by the military authorities.

'He didn't do badly—and no wonder. He was in trouble with the

Party, and he was trying to make up for it. Of course, he didn't do as well as before, because of his defeatist attitudes. We had to prod him and keep him on course.'

'Who was senior officer at Graudenz?' I asked. 'Who was in command of the group?'

'I—personally.'

Now he wouldn't look at me at all.

'Then let the witness tell us when the battle of Graudenz began and when it ended.'

'It was in March. I don't have to remember the exact dates.'

'How long was our group there? Approximately. How many days or weeks?'

'Maybe ten days, maybe less.'

'And how many days did the witness spend with the group, since he says he was directing it personally?'

Zabashtansky gave the judge a look of weary condolence, as though to say: how tired you must be of this drivel. But the judge said, 'Comrade Lieutenant Colonel, would you answer the question?'

'What kind of a question is that? Of course I wasn't parked there every day. As head of a front-line Political Department I had more than this one major to worry about. This was just one local operation, and we were advancing all along the front; the Germans were operating behind our lines—'

'Still, how many times,' I appealed to the judge, 'did he visit our group at Graudenz?'

'Enough,' the judge said. 'Sit down. All this is irrelevant. Anything else?'

'I earnestly request that the following be made part of the record: The attack on Graudenz began on February 13, and the last German units capitulated on March 6. Major Belyaev commanded our group on February 15 and 16. Then he left, and I was in command from then on. During those three weeks Zabashtansky visited us only twice. The first time he got as far as regimental headquarters and saw me only in passing, since he was in a hurry. He heard my report, but he did not give me any instructions. The second time he got only as far as corps headquarters, several kilometers from the city, and he ordered me by telephone to turn in our sound truck, which put a crimp in our work. Fortunately, we were able to get our hands on a film truck and adapt it to our needs. These are facts known to all the members of my group.'

'That will be enough. Sit down. Comrade Lieutenant Colonel,

would you be good enough to remain in this room? The court now calls the next witness—Major Belyaev.'

Zabashtansky blinked in confusion. Now he wouldn't be able to forewarn Belyaev!

Belyaev was in dress uniform, with all his ribbons and medals. He looked past me, straight at the presiding judge. He answered the judge's questions quickly and succinctly, confirming his earlier testimony that I had defended the Germans and had busied myself protecting German civilians and their property.

'He also spoke harshly of our soldiers and officers and argued against taking vengeance on the enemy. He even cried with pity for the Germans.'

What was that mission to East Prussia, the judge asked; and was the mission accomplished?

'The mission was to investigate and report on the general situation— the political mood and morale of the population, and the activity of the Fascist underground. And the mission was, of course, accomplished. Well, *essentially* accomplished, insofar as there were certain shortcomings, for which the defendant was wholly responsible—'

'What shortcomings?'

'He kept interfering. Kept stepping out of line, to save German lives, to get into all kinds of squabbles.'

'And who was in command of the group?'

'I was.'

The judge looked up. 'A question for Lieutenant Colonel Zabashtansky: you testified that the mission to East Prussia was disrupted and that the group was commanded by Major Kopelev. Do you still adhere to your testimony?'

Zabashtansky stood his ground. 'I do! The mission was disrupted as a result of his defeatist, anti-Party activities.'

'And he was senior officer?'

'I appointed him senior officer.'

'Major Belyaev,' the judge said, 'was the mission accomplished or not?'

Belyaev squirmed. 'Insofar, of course, as there were certain mistakes made . . . Still, all in all . . .' He glanced over his shoulder at Zabashtansky, who was standing behind him.

'And who,' the judge asked, 'was senior officer?'

'I was.'

'A question for the witness Zabashtansky: who was senior officer Major Belyaev or Major Kopelev?'

'I appointed Kopelev. What they arranged among themselves they didn't tell me.'

'A question for the witness Belyaev: which of you two was senior officer?'

Belyaev, discomposed, opened his mouth several times soundlessly. Finally, he muttered, 'I can't recall. . . . Of course, I do remember I was senior—at least, that's how it was written down in the orders. . . .'

The judge turned Belyaev over to my lawyer.

This anti-Fascist school, my attorney began— he was in charge of it? Yes. . . . Did he give lectures there? Oh? He didn't know the language well enough? Lieutenant Rozhansky directed that part of it? Oh. And what did Lieutenant Rozhansky think of Major Kopelev's lectures at the school? He thought very highly of them? Oh. And who arranged the curriculum? You left that to Rozhansky? You mean you didn't know what was being taught at a school placed in your charge?

My attorney questioned him politely but with withering contempt. Belyaev grew red in the face, perspired, wiped himself with his handkerchief. Hearing the presiding judge say, 'Defendant, do you have any questions for the witness?' he gave me a frightened look.

'Does the witness remember how long our trip to East Prussia lasted?'

'Five—no, six days.'

'And how many times did I act to save German lives?'

'Two or three times . . . In Neidenburg, and then in Allenstein.'

'And how long did this take, each time?'

'I don't remember. One hour . . . two hours . . . three . . .'

'And how many times did I argue with our soldiers and officers about our attitude toward German civilians?'

'I didn't count.'

The judge interrupted. 'Why these statistics?'

'It was this witness who wrote the report about my conduct in East Prussia which started this whole case against me. Let him remember—approximately—how often did I argue? Once? Twice? A hundred times?'

Belyaev answered dully, 'Well, three . . . maybe four . . . maybe five.'

'And how much time was taken up by these arguments—approximately?'

'Some half an hour. Some one hour.'

'Let's say two hours. That means these arguments took up no more than eight or ten hours, and saving German lives didn't take up more than six or eight hours—all told, no more than eighteen hours out of a total of six days. And does the witness remember how much time was spent transporting booty out of Neidenburg and Allenstein?'

'And I suppose *you* didn't take anything? You carted off a whole library! After all, I didn't do it for myself but for our comrades.'

'May I request the court—as many as ten or twelve tons of booty were hauled back: tapestries, a piano, a grandfather clock—all kinds of stuff. And it's true, I did argue with the commander of our group, Belyaev, against all this lawlessness, rape, pillage; and against his attempts to justify this robbery and murder as some sort of holy vengeance. And I did remonstrate against his being so carried away by the looting that we hardly had any time left for our mission. And one more question. Does Major Belyaev remember: When we got back from East Prussia, whom did we report to—Colonel Zabashtansky?'

'No. The Colonel had left for Prussia. We reported to General Okorokov.'

'May the court take note: Zabashtansky said he had been forced to go to East Prussia himself *after* our return, when he saw that we had failed to do the job.'

Pale and slim in her blue dress and high heels, Galina Khromushina answered the presiding judge's questions calmly and concisely. She confirmed that at Graudenz I had been the senior officer; she didn't remember seeing Zabashtansky there at all. As for that earlier mission to East Prussia, she and Zabashtansky had not waited for Belyaev and me to return before setting out on their own trip across the Prussian border. And their trip had nothing to do with any failure of any mission.

Then came Nina. Nina wore a tunic with a row of service ribbons, and she was questioned on the same points: who was in command in East Prussia; who was in charge in Graudenz. She answered truthfully. Asked about my behavior generally, she gave me a kindly look.

'He was considered a good worker, a very good worker. He speaks German well—knows their psychology. A cultured man, but hot-tempered, unrestrained—even rude. He allowed himself criticisms of the high command. He expressed pity for the Germans. Because he wanted to sound original, I thought. And because he's softheaded.'

Nina's husband, Georgi, a colonel in the Political Department, was a handsome, brave and vain Cossack, and a fervent Stalinist. My friendship with him went back almost as far as with Nina; but, unlike her, he never let personal feelings interfere with his disapproval of me when I got into trouble. Called as the next witness, he said that we had been on friendly terms but began to have political differences when I betrayed signs of serious ideological instability—underestimation of the need for complete destruction of German imperialism, overestimation of German bourgeois culture, and unhealthy humanistic tendencies, such as pity for civilians of the German-Fascist state. Tall and foppish, with a becoming streak of gray in his black hair, Georgi testified with easy-going self-confidence and was greatly surprised when the judge asked me if I had any questions.

I asked him if he remembered when we began to argue on ideological grounds. In the late summer and fall of 1944, he said, when we had reached the German border. I asked him if he remembered recommending me for promotion from candidate-member to full member of the Party—*in January 1945.*

Georgi looked at me openmouthed, like a startled child.

'And what if I did? What are you getting at? Subsequently, I withdrew my recommendation. The Party explained to me that I had been unduly trusting.'

But how, I persisted, if he had really regarded my attitude as unhealthy and politically dangerous—how could he have recommended me for full Party membership? Georgi plunged into an emotional explanation: that he had underestimated . . . that it was only later that he had realized . . .

The judge cut him short. 'Comrade Lieutenant Colonel: You recommended your comrade; then you found out that he had been arrested on serious political charges. The war was on; you were at the front. But now almost two years have gone by. You have had time to think. Is it your view now that he was an enemy of the Party and of the Soviet Army? Is it your view now that his conduct at the front was hostile and harmful?'

Georgi's grand manner had quite collapsed; he fidgeted worriedly. 'Of course I've thought about it; I've thought about it a lot—I've even suffered over it. After all, we were comrades—even, you might say, friends. . . . No, speaking personally, I can't say that he wanted—that he consciously intended—to go against the Party or the high command. No, I didn't think so then, and I don't think so now. But from an objective viewpoint, from the viewpoint of the military situation at the time, he made mistakes, he gave way to unpardonable vacillation, and —uh . . . Of course, you understand, all this wasn't what you'd call counterrevolution, but still—'

The judge excused him—rather abruptly, I thought. The atmosphere of the trial, it seemed to me, had changed. The judges seemed to be regarding me not with distasteful curiosity, as before, but thoughtfully, almost sympathetically.

Ivan Rozhansky in court was no different from the way he always was —wearing a slight frown, as though intent on his own unhurried thoughts, with now and then a look of bright comprehension in his deep-set eyes. He spoke of our work together in the anti-Fascist school; of our friendship; of our long, frank discussions. He said he knew for a fact that Zabashtansky's and Belyaev's charges against me were unjustified; I had never held the views or made the statements imputed to me. He said that we had often talked about Zabashtansky's ill will toward me and of my unpleasantnesses with our section chief.

Ivan also revealed that he had wanted to speak up for me at that Party meeting but had been ordered by Belyaev, in Zabashtansky's name, not to do so; and that he had been forbidden by Belyaev to vote against excluding me from the Party. Subsequently, he was told by Belyaev that they were dissatisfied by what he told the interrogator in my case and that this could make for difficulties for him unless he 'corrected' his testimony.

Questioned by the judge, Belyaev mumbled that, yes, he had said something to Rozhansky at the Party meeting; but, of course, he had not *forbidden* him but had merely *advised* him, in order to save him from possible unpleasantness; that, yes, he had relayed the fact that the interrogator had told Zabashtansky that the witness Rozhansky was protecting the defendant and trying to hide something, but that he, Belyaev, hadn't meant to put pressure on Rozhansky—he had just wanted to help him, as a friend.

'A question to the witness Zabashtansky,' said the judge. 'You have heard the testimony of Captain Rozhansky and Major Belyaev. What can you tell the court about these matters?'

'I object. I object categorically.' Zabashtansky's face darkened, but he clung to that soft, sincere, heartfelt way of speaking. 'These comrades here have apparently forgotten what the situation was like. The front. War. The days of final, decisive battle. In those days at the front, defeatist sentiments of this kind were no better than treason! You could have been shot for talking like that! Now, of course, it's all peace and a happy life, won for us by those heroes who were not to the liking of this —this defendant, because he called them looters; he laughed at them, glorying in his own education. And today those comrades who were indignant at him at the Party meeting and who condemned him— today they have either forgotten or they want to forget, because they're sorry for him, and were his friends, and they talk about things that never happened. I categorically object. I still remember what happened, and I still have my Party conscience.'

The judge regarded him reflectively. 'Then you deny that the interrogator was dissatisfied with Captain Rozhansky's testimony and asked you to influence him so that he would alter his testimony?'

'What the interrogator told Rozhansky I don't know—I wasn't there —and I never passed anything on to him, and didn't try to influence him, and had no intention of influencing him.'

Abram Belkin was an old friend. Before the war both of us had worked in the Institute of Philosophy, Literature and History in Moscow. Now he stood before the judges as though on parade. After a while he relaxed, and his words flowed as easily as though we were at one of our literary seminars. He praised me and he reproached me, but his reproaches were better than praise.

'He's hotheaded, you see. Storm and Stress, as they say. When he left for the front—he went off half-cocked to volunteer the first day of the war, you know, to be the first to parachute into Berlin—I was very worried about him. Not so much about his being killed—that's a tragic but noble fate in wartime—but about how he'd take to military discipline. Then I heard from friends that he had taken to it well enough. Still, I heard, there was that same lack of self-control, hotheadedness, Storm and Stress. You know, there have always been people who have this—this intolerance to lies, to hypocrisy, to meanness, like some people who can't stand the sound of chalk on a blackboard. And so he flares up and often does himself harm, sometimes very serious harm. Because it can be unpleasant—even dangerous, with some superiors. Not all, of course. Vladimir Ilyich,* for instance, put a high value on just this inconvenient trait in people, this passion—irascibility even—in standing up for the truth. The poet Mayakovsky wrote, "Let ignominious prudence never be my guide." Gorky celebrated "the folly of the brave."

'Yes, I have been told that the defendant had his disagreements with some comrades during the last months of the war; that he objected to some of Ehrenburg's articles—my wife and I, by the way, argued with him about Ehrenburg when he came home on visits, the last time in January of forty-four. Later, when we read Alexandrov's article in *Pravda*, I said to her, "That's just what Lyova† was saying, isn't it? He

*Vladimir Ilyich Lenin.
†Diminutive for Lev.

❖ 180 ❖

must be crowing, now that he's been proved right." We didn't know he was under arrest—and partly because he had been right too soon. When we did find out, we were stunned. No one who knew him will believe that he could have done or said anything against the Party. We knew him inside out—he never learned how to hide his feelings.'

Responding to my attorney's questions, Belkin lavished praise on my 'political maturity' and 'profound erudition,' as evidenced by my lectures and articles, etc., etc. He defended me like a thesis in a dissertation.

The final witness was another prewar friend, Victor Rozenzveig, a member of the All-Union Society for Cultural Relations with Foreign Countries. Victor told the court that I was held in high regard by the German proletarian writers Bredel* and Weinert. He testified to what he called my well-rounded Marxist-Leninist-Stalinist outlook. All this was well-known to him, he said, from our work together at the Institute of Philosophy, Literature and History and from our many frank and friendly talks.

The day was done, the windows were dark, by the time my attorney began his summing-up. He said that he had familiarized himself with this case, which he considered highly unusual; there had never been one like it in his practice. He enumerated the obvious contradictions in the testimony of the prosecution witnesses. Then his voice rose, and he began to speak with affected emotionalism and theatrical flourishes, embarrassing me with his stilted phrases about my 'delicate nervous constitution,' the 'impressionableness of the artistic personality,' and my 'elevated spiritual level as Communist-intellectual.' Holding up old copies of *The Teacher's Gazette* and *Red Star* with my articles in them, he exclaimed: 'Here are his brilliant, clearly reasoned writings in the pages of *Pravda*, the central organ of our Party!' Tossing back his gray locks, he expatiated on the sorrows of a family with one son killed in battle and the other, their hopes and pride, in prison on the most serious and discreditable charges, and all because of the calumny of semiliterate know-nothings. He passed in silence over Zabashtansky for some reason, but tore into Belyaev and even more roughly into Georgi—perhaps because those two seemed to have made the worst impression on the judges. Georgi took umbrage and shouted something from his seat, earning a dressing down from the court.

And now the time came for the defendant to have the last word. How often had I composed this speech and rehearsed it in my head! I spoke for a long time, and I could see—I could feel—the judges paying close

*Willi Bredel, a German Socialist writer.

attention. The president of the tribunal sat with head bent, his eye-glasses flashing occasionally in the lamplight. The other two leaned back, regarding me steadily throughout. I tried to look deep into their eyes—to drive my truth and my anguish into their very brain.

'My conscience is clear. I bear not even a shadow of guilt before my country and the Party—not in word, not in deed, not in my innermost thought. I ask not for mercy but for justice. Only justice.'

I stopped.

The judges needed time to deliberate. Everyone else left the room. I was taken down into the cellar. My mother and my wife were still standing in the corridor. They smiled and nodded encouragingly as before.

After an hour and a half, they brought me back. All the witnesses were back too. The judges were standing behind the long desk. Everyone remained standing.

'In the name of the Union of Soviet Socialist Republics . . .'

The presiding judge read from the verdict. I heard favorable things said about me. Then I heard the words:

'. . . is acquitted in the absence of a finding of any criminal act and is to be released from detention.'

And more: Zabashtansky and Belyaev are found guilty of slander, though not subject to judicial action owing to the amnesty of 1945—a finding, however, that 'is to be brought to the attention of their Party organizations.'

Everything dissolved in a shimmery orange mist.

## 20

I sat in the corridor. The guards barricaded me off by a long bench. My friends and family stood at a distance, calling out words of congratulation. Mama kept instructing me in a loud voice: 'Your suit and overcoat are at Elena's. Her new address is Novoslobodskaya Forty-eight, Apartment Forty-seven. Go there first. Remember!' She asked the guards to pass on a bar of chocolate, but they wouldn't do it, no matter how much she pleaded. 'Not allowed. Parcels accepted only at the prison.'

After a while I was led out of the building and placed in a police wagon. I did not allow myself to hope for an early release. I knew that acquittals under Article 58 were always reviewed, and were often referred to the Special Commission* and reversed. Still, what a decision! What an acquittal!

Then I was back in Butyrki prison and was placed in a windowless room with eight other men, all with their belongings. Four of them, I learned, had served their sentences; two had been acquitted; another—a general's son arrested for carrying his father's pistol and demonstrating it to friends—had been told that he would be freed that night.

We were called out one by one by a guard with a collection of thick prison dossiers. My spirits soared each time the door opened and sank each time he called someone else. At length there were only I and the general's son; the guard entered with one remaining file in his hand—and called the boy. Seeing my woebegone expression, he said, 'You'll have to wait a while. Your papers aren't ready.'

An hour or two passed. I dozed fitfully, stretched out on the cold floor, waking to the sound of footsteps—then the clanking of keys. It was morning. Inspection.

*See footnote on page 131.

'How long will I have to wait?'

'Your papers aren't ready.'

Later that day I was moved into a smaller room, also without a window. Then it was evening. A janitor who took me to the toilet said that they usually released people before dawn. I took heart and got in a few hours of restful sleep.

The door opened. 'Let's go. Take your things with you.'

But it wasn't a guard with my dossier—just another janitor. A trip to the washroom. Regulations.

So nothing had changed. I took my time under the shower. If you closed your eyes and put your hands over your ears, you could imagine yourself standing in the warm summer rain.

Then, to another part of the prison. A small, square cell; a cot; a table; a window, with the usual bars. In the morning they brought me bread and hot water. I asked for books. The guard waved me aside.

I measured the cell: ten steps from one corner to the one diagonally across. I paced up and down three times a day, a thousand paces at a time.

That night I was sure that I heard someone outside my door muttering, 'Let him go.' Morning again. I demanded books to read.

'Not allowed.'

'Why was it allowed when I was an accused prisoner, but not now, when I have been acquitted of all charges? I declare a hunger strike.'

'Go ahead. All the worse for you.'

I went without food for two days. The guards were mildly remonstrative. One fat old fellow reasoned with me. 'You may be here another week, for all you know. So what happens if you get all weak from hunger? They'll have to put you in the hospital. Can't let a sick man out, can we? So that will hold you up again.'

On the fourth day they brought a parcel from home. I wouldn't accept it. 'I'm on a hunger strike until they give me books to read. I am an officer. I have been acquitted.'

The guard was a small, slit-eyed fellow with a crooked mouth and discolored teeth. 'Oh—an officer! Used to giving orders! Well, you can't give orders here!'

Soon after, I received a visit from a harassed-looking young lieutenant. 'What are you making a row for? What do you want? All right—you're an officer. All right—you've been acquitted. Try to understand. There are twenty-five thousand prisoners here, and there's only one of me.'

That's when I first heard the figure: twenty-five thousand prisoners in the Butyrki prison! I agreed to accept the parcel if he gave me his word as an officer—he looked surprised on hearing those words—that I would have books to read.

'All right,' he said with a half smile. 'You'll get them today. Just sign for the parcel. They must be worrying about you—your wife, your family. You must think of them too, you know.'

They brought me *Rob Roy* by Walter Scott, something by Alexander Kuprin, and a couple of other books. Ten days later I got Stendhal's *Charterhouse of Parma* and the memoirs of Panaieva.* During the day I read, paced the cell, slept. The nights were sleepless.

One day I heard a metallic tapping. The sound came from the steam pipe. Two taps, then five. Four taps, then three. Three taps, then four. Then all over again. The prisoners' code. 'Who are you? Who are you?'

Putting my ear to the pipe, which doubtless connected a row of cells, I tapped out an answer. Then I heard a woman's voice, faintly but distinctly.

I had learned that you could converse with prisoners in other cells by placing the bottom of a metal cup against a steam pipe and talking into the cup, then listening by holding your open mouth over the cup. I did this now. 'I hear you,' I said. 'Get a cup. Talk through the cup. Listen with your mouth. Find the best spot on the pipe.'

After a while we talked with no trouble. She was three cells away. There didn't seem to be anyone in the cells between us: no one joined in.

She introduced herself: Antonina—Tonya, for short. She was in with three other women, all awaiting trial.

'I'm 163–1–G, but that's silly. Theft of state property, with accomplices. There was this boy—he was going around with my girl friend, and they said he robbed a store or a savings bank or something, but what's it to me? I was studying to be a seamstress or a hairdresser. I live with my mama. I'm twenty-six. And you?'

She made me promise, after I told her about myself, to see her mama after I was released and to tell her to go to Uncle Vasya and ask him to get a good lawyer for the trial. In the following days she kept making sure that I had her mother's right address.

'Tell her, next time she sends me a parcel, to include four onions and three heads of garlic. Then I'll know you've seen her and she understands.'

As December drew to a close, I accepted the thought that they had refused to confirm my acquittal and had handed my case back to the

*Avdotia Panaieva, a nineteenth-century Russian writer.

Special Commission, which would mean camp again. I comforted myself: They couldn't give me more than five years, and I had served two already. I had lived through the war; I would survive the camps. Or maybe they just didn't want to exonerate me completely; they'll give me three years and suspend the sentence, exile me from Moscow, and bar me from any further ideological work. Well, I could go back to studying medicine, seriously this time. I could write. I could volunteer for work in the far-northern or far-eastern regions; there I'd prove myself. . . .

The guards got used to me. The good-natured fatty, announcing lights-out, would joke: 'Get to sleep now. You know your wife won't give you much time for sleep when you get home.'

But the ugly-looking runt who was on duty when I was agitating for books had it in for me. 'Wash out the toilets,' he ordered me one night.

I was the last to be taken to the lavatory that night, and I assumed that it was my turn. Armed with mop and bucket, I spent an hour at the malodorous task. In addition to cleaning out the bowls, I had to scrub down the walls and wash the filthy floor.

Two nights later I was again the last to be taken by him to the lavatory.

'Wash out the toilets!'

'I won't. I washed them out two days ago.'

'Then you know how to. Or don't you want to soil your dainty officer's hands?'

He bared his teeth with such spite that I could see it was no use pleading with him.

'I will *not* wash out the toilets. It's not my turn.'

'Then spend the night in this shithouse, officer!'

The iron door slammed on my face. I beat against it with the mop handle and shouted for the head guard. The peephole opened and the runt said, 'Go on making a noise and we'll tie you up. And tomorrow you can complain to the Supreme Soviet, if you like.'

I set to work.

An hour or an hour and a half later, he was back. 'Everything clean?'

'See for yourself.'

I walked back to my cell ahead of him as required by the prison rules, with my hands clasped behind my back. At the door of the cell I stopped and fixed him with what I hoped was an inquisitive and pitying look.

'Who you staring at? Into the cell with you.'

'I can see that you are dangerously ill.'

'Who's ill? What are you—a doctor? You're an officer!'

'If you look in my file, you'll see I've had medical training and experience. In the camp I worked in the hospital. And I can see that you're a very sick man. Your color, your eyes—they're signs of cancer of the stomach or liver.'

I spoke with deliberate gentleness.

'All right, all right ... Some doctor ... No talking after lights-out. ...'

The next time he was on duty he seemed almost civil. Again I was the last man in the lavatory. He smiled triumphantly. 'All right, doctor. Wash the toilets.'

I boiled with fury. An hour later, walking back to the cell, I murmured, 'I'm sorry for you, citizen. You'll have a very difficult death. You'll be in terrible agony.'

'No talking!'

Locking me up for the night, he exclaimed in a hoarse, scared whisper, 'You'll croak before me, fuck your mother!'

On New Year's Eve I received a particularly generous parcel—fried chicken, pies, chocolate, cigarettes. The feast before my eyes saddened me: apparently they knew at home that I'd be in for a long while.

I resigned myself to transfer to a camp, and, for the first time since my trial, I slept soundly that night—and the following night as well. I redoubled my pacing, did pushups and shadowboxing, and strengthened the edge of my right hand by banging it against the frame of the iron cot—all this in case I got into a fight with other prisoners during transit.

On the third night of the year 1947 I woke up with a start. Someone was in the doorway. 'Come. Off we go,' he said softly.

It didn't take me a minute to throw my things into my sack. I still didn't dare to hope. I'm being transferred, I told myself—nothing more.

'Go on ahead,' the man ordered. 'Don't look to the right or to the left, or you'll have dreams about this place.'

Could he be joking so lightly, this good, kind, cheerful stranger, if he were merely taking me to another cell?

We turned off into another corridor. Several men with sacks stood facing the wall, their hands behind their backs. A chill went through me: We were being transferred.

'Stand here.'

I was the last. We were marched off into another room. Then we were called out, one by one.

'Name, birthplace?' I was asked when my turn came.

They checked my answers against their records. Then they returned me my belt, shoelaces, pencils and money. They took my fingerprints and compared them with the ones in their file—only this time they gave me soap and a brush and told me to scrub the ink off my hands.

A sleepy lieutenant colonel in the prison office handed me a certificate of release. 'No complaints? Sign here: your promise not to divulge information about the internal regime. You understand? No talking to anyone about the prison or about the investigation—not even to your wife or mother. If you break your promise, you will be held fully responsible. Here is your pass.'

I wanted to say something solemn, something significant, but nothing came to mind. So I clicked my heels and rapped out: 'Happy New Year, Comrade Lieutenant Colonel!'

He looked up with surprise. 'The same to you.'

With my sack over my shoulder I walked through the great prison gates, out into a snow-covered yard.

'Pass?' said a sentry. He examined the certificate. 'Go, and don't look back.'

A morose guard shivering in a black overcoat led me through the yard to the outer office, where they questioned me again. Name? Date of birth? Birthplace? Wife's address?

A rosy-faced wit in a thick jacket said, 'Maybe you'd like to wait a while? It's cold out there, and it's still dark. And it's nice and warm in here.'

Everyone guffawed, and I laughed with them. I wished them all a Happy New Year.

'Go, and don't look back.'

I walked through the outer gates. It was six o'clock. A freezing wind blew snow like white dust along the wide, empty street.

The houses were dark. As I walked, a window glimmered yellow. Then another. And another. Now and then a truck rolled by.

I walked on, unhurriedly. In the gathering light I could make out white placards on the walls. An election of some kind. I read the biography of one of the candidates and thought: splendid fellow.

I saw my first pedestrians. I thought: I am walking along a Moscow street; I can go wherever I want. I slipped and almost fell, and grew alarmed: I could have broken my leg! What a new beginning that would have been! I stepped more cautiously on the ice. I stopped frequently to read the wall posters. I counted the lighted windows. Suddenly I realized something: I was happy.

# 21

I REMEMBERED what Mama had told me outside the courtroom—that my clothes were at Elena's, that I was to go there first. I remembered her new address.

The stairway was dimly lit, the walls a dirty yellow, the apartment building silent: everyone was still asleep. Somewhere a radio muttered. I heard an alarm clock go off.

I lingered on each landing, forcing myself to wait. Finally, I stood before a door that said, 'E. Arlyuk.' Footsteps on the other side of the door. Voices. I rang.

Lyolia* in a bathrobe. 'Aha! So you decided to show up after all. I was getting tired of waiting.'

The same old Lyolia. Kindly, nearsighted eyes. Bantering tone, as though to say: No sentimentality, if you please. I embraced her. Under her bathrobe she was wearing only a slip. There was about her a heady fragrance, a white softness of skin. I felt as though I had swallowed a shot of vodka. I could hardly hear what she was saying, while I babbled on crazily. A skinny kid—her son, of course—stared sleepily at me.

'Into the bathroom with you,' Lyolia commanded, 'you revolting sight, you incredible scarecrow. Change in the bathroom. Here are your things. They've been waiting here for months.'

The mirror in the bathroom confronted me with a ridiculous mustache, black stubble, distracted red eyes.

Dressed in my suit, complete with shirt and tie, I sat drinking hot aromatic tea out of a fine glass. Lyolia would not let me use the phone.

*Diminutive for Elena.

'Compose yourself first. We can't have Maya and Lyena seeing their papa in this state. How long since they've seen you? Three years. Lyenochka was four years old. Now remember: you've come back from an official trip.'

I phoned home. Gleeful voices on the other end of the wire. Mama, naturally, burst into tears.

Lyolia packed my prison things in a suitcase. 'Here, don't forget this box of candy. It's a present you bought for your daughters. The barbershop opens at eight. Get a shave first. You can't go home looking like a bandit.'

I put on my uniform and went out into the crowded, noisy early-morning street. In the barbershop mirror the foamy lather gradually gave way to a gaunt, grinning, vaguely familiar face.

The same old room; the same old furniture. The bright voices of the girls. Maya had grown up so!—talkative, affectionate, with her hair falling in two black braids down her back. She was ten. Lyena, our little one, was like a Japanese doll. Mama was much thinner and older-looking; I would not have recognized her if I had passed her in the street. Nadia was also thin and a little stooped; she was doing her best to be gay, but I could see that it had been hard for her, what with Mama and the girls. They had been evacuated to Kazan during the German attack on Moscow; they had had to sell almost all their belongings for bread and milk. As for my father, he hadn't changed a bit: still convinced that everything was going well and getting better all the time.

My old friend Boris Suchkov, on the other hand, was unrecognizable. He came by an hour later—smooth-shaven, perfumed, imposing in a stylish fur coat, and his words had a patronizing ring. 'Well, we'll have to do something about you, put you to work. Don't rest up too long, and go easy on the bottle.'

He had been named director of a publishing house specializing in translations of foreign literature and was full of plans. 'We're going to bring out hundreds, thousands of books. We must catch up on everything that slipped by during the war. We'll have to be first in the whole world, of course, in all spheres of culture.'

The names of the leaders of our government dropped casually from his lips: 'The day before yesterday, when I was reporting to Malenkov ... I got a call from Alexandrov about this; he said Comrade Stalin had expressed a personal interest. . . . So I took it up with Voroshilov—you know, he's a plainspoken sort. . . .'

For more than a month I lived in a state of turmoil: meetings, parties, drinking bouts. In the intervals I discussed proposals for finding work. Abram Belkin insisted that I take up teaching. There was an offer of a post on the magazine *Soviet Literature in Foreign Languages*. A phone call from the Institute of Foreign Affairs suggested that I lecture in German on German literature. An old colleague in the Theatrical Society invited me to return to work there, in the Shakespeare department. 'You'll be my commissar, like before the war.'

Another old acquaintance ran into me at a trolleybus stop and embraced me, whispering emotionally, 'I know all about it. . . . so glad to see you.' He took down my number. 'We *must* get together, there's so much I want to ask. . . .'

And there was something I was to learn. Isaac Markovich Nusinov seemed to have shrunk and darkened over the years, and his beard had turned gray. He questioned me about the camp, and particularly about those who had been there since 1937; then he told me that anti-Semitism was on the rise and had reached the Party apparatus—even the Central Committee.

'Not long ago,' he said, 'I was called in by this young, well-fed bureaucrat, who proceeded to explain that we had to limit the number of Jews in the ideological cadres—that this was required by our Leninist-Stalinist national policy, and was something that I, as an old Party member, ought to be able to understand. I told him that while I had been a Party member for thirty years, I'd been a Jew for sixty, and I had never found that one interfered with the other.'

Professor Yakov Mikhailovich M, who had also lost weight and had aged, complained irritably about the squabbling and self-seeking at the university—and the anti-Semitism. He had a thick file to show me: a program he had drawn up for the study of foreign literature; a denunciatory article by one Demeshkan, a graduate student, a girl who, falsely and with evident anti-Semitic intent, claimed that he had given undue prominence to such writers as Heine, Zweig, Feuchtwanger, etc.; his own letters to the Central Committee refuting these allegations; and the statements of two other girl students, both members of the Komsomol, that Demeshkan had tried to persuade them of the necessity of fighting against the 'dominance of the Jews' at the university and in literature in general.

I told him that I thought all this came of several objective circumstances. For one thing, we had recently joined to our territory the bourgeois, westernmost regions of the Ukraine, Belorussia, the Baltic states and Moldavia, and Demeshkan, it seemed, hailed from those parts. For another, Fascist propaganda had found some fertile soil among us during the first years of the war, when the Hitlerites were still winning, and weeds are a hardy growth.

The first time I had heard of anti-Semitism in our midst was in a Latvian division at the beginning of 1942. That summer, when I was back in Moscow for a few days and paid a call on Belkin at the editorial offices where the *History of the Patriotic War* was being prepared, Isaac Mints (the future academician)* told me how they had tried to dissuade him at the university from appointing an old non-Party Jewish professor to a vacancy; how he had written to the Central Committee about this incident and several others like it in the Commissariat of Public Health; and how Stalin himself had written in the margin of the letter, 'Anti-Semitism is a symptom of Fascism.' Mints, whom I recognized later to be an obsequious and weak-kneed timeserver, had appeared to me then as one of those Old Bolsheviks who always went to the heart of the matter and, whatever their personal difficulties, believed unswervingly in the Party and the triumph of its ideas.

He had explained—and I had agreed with him, sharing his views—that the war had brought about a new sharpening of racial and class antagonisms, which in turn were complicated by the wartime need for nationalistic, patriotic, great-power propaganda, a need that was both tactical and strategic. One had to understand this—while, of course, struggling against the inevitable deviations and excesses. All this was quite natural.

Now, five years later, I still saw things that way. (Even ten years later I was of the same view.) The unhappy tales of Nusinov and M I simply took to be the grumbling of tired, affronted old men who couldn't see things objectively now because of the injustices they had been made to suffer. M even inveighed against Boris Suchkov, who had been asked by the Central Committee to go over his complaint against Demeshkan. Talking to M about it, Boris Suchkov waxed indignant about the girl's slimy denunciation; he seemed to have all the facts and to understand everything clearly. Then he wrote an 'on the one hand ... but on the other hand' kind of report. And after that he wrote an article in the magazine *Culture and Life* repeating Demeshkan's lying accusations. This was base of him and difficult to understand. I knew Boris and believed that he was honest, sensible and brave. He had written Rudenko† defending me. Of course, I had noticed his new

*In 1974 Mints was awarded the Lenin Prize for *The History of Great October*.
†Roman Andreievich Rudenko, then Deputy Chief Prosecutor of the U.S.S.R. Rudenko, who headed the Soviet prosecution team at the Nuremberg trials, is today Chief Prosecutor of the U.S.S.R.

manner—a certain stateliness, lordliness; a sort of studied meaningfulness. Still, I told myself, M had been a bit unstable before; I recalled his polemics with others. Perhaps he was exaggerating again; and Boris probably knew something substantive, something important, that neither M nor I was aware of.

At any rate, I felt, all this wrangling about anti-Semitism, no matter how unpleasant and vexing, didn't have anything to do with the main problems before us. Disorder was spreading—poverty, food shortages and hunger throughout the land. How many cities in ruins! How many villages burned down! And now the enmity of our former allies; the infamous policy pursued by President Truman; the battles in Greece and Indochina; those monstrous atomic bombs. . . . I grabbed at every paper I could, to read about these changes in the world.

And our own pressure on Turkey. It seemed that in the fall of '45 some of our Georgian and Armenian academicians had published letters demanding 'reunion' with areas of Turkey that, they said, had once been part of the ancient kingdom of Urartu—a demand, in short, for the annexation of the Bosporus. This was scarcely better than the old territorial demands of Hitler and Mussolini.

Then the affair of the Leningrad magazines. I was dismayed by Zadanov's speech and the ruling of the Central Committee.* Why such rancor, such crudeness? What harm could there be in Akhmatova's verses, Zoshchenko's satires, Khazin's parodies? How could Hoffmann have suddenly become a reactionary? But these were the decisions of the Central Committee! Hence, it was absurd to object to them. One could not, after all, set oneself up against the Party over some literary tiff. . . .

I was drunk with my long-awaited freedom and with my hopes and projects. Still, I didn't become a blind and deaf loyalist. Although I often couldn't or wouldn't see or hear or think about some of the things going on around me, I couldn't forget what I had learned in the prisons or forget the people I had left there. I painstakingly carried out all their commissions. I tracked down Edith's mother and daughter through the Red Cross. I paid a call on Tonya's mother, a silent old woman with a pursed mouth who lived in a grubby old house in a

*In 1946, Andrei Zhdanov launched an official campaign for cultural conformity, with the satirist Mikhail Zoshchenko and the poet Anna Akhmatova as the principal targets. Two Leningrad magazines were shut down for publishing 'harmful' material. The Leningrad satirical writer Alexander Khazin also got his lumps, while the German romantic writer Amadeus Hoffmann (1776–1822) was identified as the 'mystical and decadent' inspiration of Akhmatova's poetry.

rubbish-strewn yard, and who heard me out mistrustfully without asking a single question.

'All right, all right, I know who Uncle Vasya is. I'd like to see *him* do anything for her. All right, I'll send her the onions, all right. . . .'

Thus I exculpated myself before my still imprisoned comrades while I strolled about Moscow, listened to Mozart at the Conservatory,* gloried in brightly lighted buildings, ate and drank at parties, and went where I pleased.

In the mornings I would open my newspaper and read all about my Socialist Motherland, the freest country in the world, and all about the uprisings in Africa and the unemployment in England and the United States, and in the evenings I would meet with my friends and tell them about the people I had met in prison and reminisce about the war. And I listened to what they told me. In Germany, the dismantlement program was proceeding with rapacious destructiveness: whole factories stripped of equipment, superb machinery ripped up by the roots, only to be dumped, messed up, left for rusty scrap. In the Ukraine, famine had set in. Would it be 1933 all over again? In Moscow, Leningrad and other cities robberies were on the rise and there was shameless speculation and a brisk trade in second-hand German clothes and other items, 'trophy' weapons, Soviet medals and Party cards. In Kiev, there was an attempt at a pogrom. A demobilized flier wanted to get back into his apartment, which had been taken over by some flourishing townsfolk. They began shouting at him: 'Kike! Where did you buy your medals?' He opened fire and killed one of them. The funeral turned into a demonstration reminiscent of the Black Hundreds.† In the Baltic states, armed bands were still active, while in western Ukraine there were whole areas under Bandera's‡ control. The Americans and the English were supplying him with weapons and dropping agents by parachute. In Poland things were even worse. And again and again in our conversations, the atomic bomb.

My happiness in being free and no longer hungry, my daily joys and pleasures, and the joys to come that I was already savoring, thinking of the books I would write and the new cities and new countries I would see—all this could not suppress my doubts and anxieties. Against these

*The concert hall attached to the Moscow State Conservatory.

†Black Hundreds: anti-Semitic, anti-intellectual armed bands of prerevolutionary times that often took part in pogroms.

‡Stepan Bandera, Ukrainian nationalist leader of an anti-Soviet uprising in the Ukraine in 1945–47.

I would automatically employ the comforting formulas of our 'material- ist dialectic': 'When you chop down a forest, the chips fly'; 'bad means to achieve good ends'; 'the road of progress isn't like Nevsky Prospekt';* 'barbaric means to overcome barbarism.' I wanted to believe that everything would turn out all right. We had made it through the war; and Stalin, of course, was a genius; and even if he was mistaken in some particulars, he was, in the main, sagacious and wise. He had bested Hitler and he would best these new, less fearsome, adversaries. Our borders now ran along the Elbe; and in China, Red armies were on the move. I believed because I couldn't give up my belief, and because I wanted to believe. And I was gladdened by anything that helped to sustain my belief and my hopes.

On February 10 there was a birthday party for my friend Abram Belkin. Boba, as we called him, placed me at table next to a tough- looking worthy in naval uniform, with silver shoulder boards.

'I want you to meet my cousin Misha,' said Boba with a sly ex- pression. 'You'll find you have a lot to talk about.'

Misha turned out to be deputy prosecutor of the Baltic Fleet. We took to each other right away. He questioned me at length about my camp and prison experiences and told me how he had once saved a man unjustly accused of murder from the firing squad. Later, both the worse for drink, we took the same subway home. Nadia and I had to get off first. Misha shook my hand warmly and said, 'I'm very glad to have met you. I'm very glad for you. You're a good fellow. Boba loves you very much. But I must say the people who handled your case were rank amateurs. Frankly, I wouldn't have put up with such amateurish- ness if I had been your prosecutor.'

I didn't follow what he was saying. The train was pulling up to our station. Misha, still smiling pleasantly, repeated, 'I'm very glad for you. But if you'd been in my hands, you'd have ended up with five years at least. These Article Fifty-eight cases—you've got to bear down on them.

I didn't have time to respond. I suddenly wanted to shove my fist in his face and swear, prison style, 'Fuck your mouth, fuck your rotten soul!' But Nadia was pulling me to the door. He waved agreeably, and I kept quiet.

One of the first things I did following my release was to apply to the Party for reinstatement as candidate-member. The interrogator at the

*The main street, straight as an arrow, of Leningrad.

Party commission of the Central Political Administration showed friendly interest in my case during our initial meetings. But each time I phoned to ask if he knew when the commission would meet to consider my request, his manner became increasingly more distant. Finally he asked me to submit the full text of the acquittal. To obtain that, I had to apply at the office of the tribunal.

Walking down the familiar corridor of the familiar building, I felt an unexplainable quiver of alarm. A figure in black was being conducted, propped up by the elbows, by a brace of guards. In the office the stern young women and discourteous men with silver shoulder boards eyed me as a curiosity. They brought others into the room.

'Is that him?'

'That's the one.'

I was able to obtain an excerpt from the acquittal, but for the full text I had to come another time. Again I was assailed by that demeaning sense of anxiety; again I was the center of their stares. They told me to come back in a few days.

But the very next day I was called before a meeting of the Party commission.

The commission sat in an old building on Frunze Street that in earlier years had housed a cadet academy, then the Revolutionary Military Soviet. White columns. Red carpets. At a long table, a row of army and navy officers aglitter with shoulder boards, medals, service ribbons, buttons and braid. I was placed in a chair. The commission chairman reported on my application, reading in a flat voice from an account of my case that could have been written by Zabashtansky himself. Then came their questions.

'How could you have interceded for the German Fascists? How could you have forgotten their depredations?'

'What did you think you were doing when, instead of carrying out your military assignment on enemy soil, you got into disputes with our own command and made difficulties for our soldiers and officers?'

'Your military mission was to undermine the enemy troops, but it seems you undermined our own Soviet troops instead. And after that you want your Party card back? Maybe you'd like a medal too?'

When I tried to answer, they wouldn't listen but leafed through their papers or talked among themselves. When I referred to the tribunal's decision, someone snapped:

'The tribunal absolved you of *criminal* responsibility. That's not the same as recommending you for Party membership. And where's the text of the decision? Oh—you haven't submitted it. . . .'

I tried to stick to facts: how it was that the people who slandered me were able to fool the Party meeting and how they were finally exposed.

'He calls them slanderers—good Communists who did their best to straighten him out!'

'What do we have here? First you presume to attack the decisions of the Soviet government and the high command, and now you have the audacity to demand that we give you back your Party card.'

I insisted that I hadn't made those attacks; that this was slander, exposed by the sworn testimony of Major Goldstein, who was present during the conversation when, according to Zabashtansky's lying report. . . .

'Naturally, Goldstein sticks up for him,' said a blond, square-faced colonel. 'So we're to believe a Goldstein, I suppose, while a front-line *Russian* officer is to be dismissed as a slanderer.'

'Shame on you!' I cried. 'Goldstein is just as good a Soviet officer as Zabashtansky, just as much a front-line soldier. I never expected to hear that kind of talk here!'

'Order!' The chairman tapped his pencil on the table. 'You lectured the Germans,' he said to me, 'and now do you propose to give the Party Commission of the Central Political Administration a lecture on humanism?'

They sniggered, laughed, guffawed.

'I think we can do without your lectures, thank you. What can you add to what you've said? Of a substantive nature, that is.'

I tried to repeat the essence of my final statement before the tribunal. My voice sounded strained and foreign to my ears, but for several minutes I made them listen. They were silent and did not interrupt. I concluded with an emotional vow: I had never been afraid to admit my mistakes or wrongdoings, but in this case I was without guilt in word or thought; I lived—and to my dying day would continue to live—for the Party of Lenin and Stalin.

The chairman said, 'You may go.' He added that the commission interrogator would let me know the decision the next day.

The next day the interrogator's voice on the phone was coldly official. 'The Party commission has postponed its decision pending receipt of the full text of the military tribunal's decision in your case.'

I went back to the tribunal office. The same corridor, the same rooms, the same military and civilian personnel, but something subtly different, something guarded and hostile behind their curious stares.

A frowning, polite captain led me into a side room. 'Wait here, please.'

I had a quick premonition of what would follow: they would come in with an order for my arrest. What did I have on me? Thirty rubles, at most; not even a full pack of cigarettes.

Someone else came in. 'The decision of the tribunal in your case has been set aside in response to the objections of the chief military prosecutor as lacking in sufficient grounds. The case will be tried before another tribunal.'

'What does that mean? Am I under arrest?'

'No. There has been no decision of that nature. But you must sign an undertaking not to leave the city.'

'And when will the new trial take place?'

'That has not been decided as yet. Probably quite soon.'

Hurrying home, I began digging through my papers and books and putting aside material to be destroyed—Nazi German newspapers and magazines I had brought home on visits from the front; our own publications of the 1920s; books by such latter-day 'enemies of the people' as Isaac Babel and Boris Pilnyak; letters and outlines for articles that could seem suspicious to some investigator. All this I tore up into little pieces and flushed down the toilet or buried surreptitiously in an old pan. I tried to couch my explanations to Mama in hazy terms, so she wouldn't start crying again and scaring the girls, who had come home from school. Nadia came back from work and began helping me. Mama ran off to the attorney.

There were phone calls from friends and acquaintances. Something about work for me, or invitations to the theater or to birthday parties. What could I say?

'Yes, yes, of course I'll think about it.' Or, 'Thank you. Yes, of course, I'll be there, if I'm free.'

If I'm free . . .

That night I couldn't sleep; my ears were attuned to the slightest sound in the room where the six of us lived—my parents, the two girls, Nadia and I—partitioning off the room's seventeen square meters with a wardrobe, a buffet, a screen and other makeshifts. Several times during the night I got up and went to the kitchen for a smoke, going cold each time I heard an approaching automobile.

What if I simply got dressed and left? I still had some money. I still had my prewar passport;* in fact, I'd had it renewed since my release. I could go to the railway station and leave. I could go east, or

*The reference is to the standard identification document for Soviet citizens.

north—wherever my fancy took me. I could join some team of geologists. I could work as a male nurse. They wouldn't start a nationwide hunt for me; they did that only in cases of espionage or terror or counterrevolutionary activity. There, far away, I could start a new life. I would change my name, claiming that I had lost my papers. I would live in the backwoods; I would write. And then I would reveal myself. Here, I would say, are my books: *The Foundations of Communist Ethics* and *Why Fascism Won in Germany*.

And what would happen to Nadia? They had recently offered to make her chairman of the trade union committee where she worked; she was a Party member; now they would accuse her of helping me escape. And they would accuse my father as well. What would they do to them? What would they do to those of my friends who had come to my defense? If they don't throw out a dragnet for me, won't they go even harder on those close to me?

And if they catch me, how will I be able to prove my innocence? And even if they don't catch me, isn't running away worse than suicide—an admission of guilt, a confirmation of what all those bastards had been saying about me?

No, I couldn't run away. I couldn't run away from myself.

Six weeks had passed since my release. My attorney was reassuring: They weren't likely to arrest me; chances were that they wanted to reformulate the acquittal in such a way as to bar reinstatement in the Party and leave no grounds for action for slander against my accusers. Still, we should try to strengthen our case for the new trial; were there any new witnesses to be found?

I did know someone who would have a file of our front-line newspaper *For the Motherland*. I went to see him and got a copy of an article of mine on East Prussia. The article was a compendium of shrill, chauvinistic phrases, distinguishable from Zabashtansky's efforts only by its pretence at style and its gingerly references to the German working class.

I also went to see a newsreel cameraman who had seen our broadcasting unit at work in Graudenz; he had been present when the division commander, Major General Rakhimov, had read out his Order of the Day thanking us for our decisive help in the taking of the fortress and recommending us for military awards.

Then there was Mikhail Kruchinsky, a Civil War veteran who had vouched for my character when I was detained in 1929 in Kharkov, and who had fought again in this war and had been seriously wounded at Stalingrad. When I told him of the new trial, he offered himself as a character witness.

I came around to thinking that the issue was solely one of formulation —that certain influential patrons of Colonel Zabashtansky's and General Okorokov's were concerned for the honor of the uniform and wanted the tribunal to rule that, all other considerations aside, they had acted correctly under wartime conditions.

I, however, wasn't about to weaken my own position. I had done that once before. The Party commission of the Central Political Administration had reminded me that on March 17, 1945, at that Party meeting in Poland, I had admitted my alleged mistakes and, when asked 'why Zabashtansky and Belyaev would say what wasn't so,' had kept repeating: 'They misunderstood me . . . they misunderstood me. . . . I don't know why.' Neither at that preliminary meeting nor at the meeting of the full Party membership the next day had I called them slanderers. I had been so afraid of being accused of picking a quarrel! I had wanted so badly to be quit of all that: the Political Administration, the baldheaded general with his clinking spurs, the seekers after 'trophies' and medals with their gilded shoulder boards—all those insolent, self-satisfied, insatiable henchmen of a victory they had done nothing to win. I had wanted to leave for the front, to be among real troops, where the war was still being fought; I had hoped that there I would be rid of the spoilers and would not have to lie or adapt myself to their squalid ways. But most of all I had wanted to get out of the army: the war had almost ended; the time had come to think things through and arrive at an understanding of what had happened and why.

Out of fear of being made to seem a petty squabbler, out of a desire to get away, I had done no more than defend myself, and had thus played into the hands of those who dealt in political denunciations. I had helped them drive me into prison. I would not repeat that mistake now. I would not concede them one syllable of the truth. In March 1945 that emptyheaded toady Vladimir Mulin had talked me into it: 'Don't get into a fight; don't go attacking the lieutenant colonel. Make a partial admission of your mistakes; he'll meet you half way. They'll give you a reprimand, and you'll soon be back in their good books.' This time I wouldn't make terms with scoundrels. Two years in prison and camp were perhaps deserved punishment for having lied and lowered myself to such agreements.

Or maybe, I reasoned, I had simply been inept? Maybe, if I had to lie, I should have lied more craftily and purposefully, so as to confuse them and turn them one against the other? But I could not have done that under any circumstances, because I would have stopped being myself.

And I also reasoned: There is the ethics of the microcosm, and the ethics of the macrocosm. On the 'macro' level—in class struggle, revolution, war—the only operative law is the law of expediency; the goal justifies any means, so long as they are effective. But on the 'micro' level, in relations between people, we need firm and definite moral laws and tenets—truth, unselfishness, compassion. This blend of Christian Communism and pragmatic common sense became my faith for many years.

My days and evenings were taken up looking for new witnesses and new documents. I made a collection of old articles of mine, published and unpublished, and of others' comments on my scholarly work. I tried not to meet people I knew whom I couldn't tell about the setting aside of the verdict; they might think there was 'something there after all.' I gave less thought to finding a job; it wasn't likely that I'd be allowed to teach pending the trial. At night I would wake up, gasping with terror, imagining a voronok* driving into the yard, men coming up the stairs. . . . During the day I was often overcome by a melancholy fright: what would happen the next day, or the day after? At the conservatory, looking at the program of coming concerts, I would think: Will I still be free on this or that evening?

On the evening of March 17 I stopped by at a pharmacy on the way home. Maya was suffering from an infection of the inner ear, and we needed more cotton and bandages for compresses.

I badly wanted to be closer to my daughters, but we saw each other in snatches, mostly with company present. I had hoped to see more of them during their summer vacations. In the camp I had begun to write something for them—*The Stories of Grandfather Neposyed*, a kindly old eccentric who accomplishes a kind of magic that puts little children inside books like *The Odyssey, Don Quixote, Gargantua and Pantagruel,* and the novels of Tolstoy and Dickens. My stories were meant to excite their imagination and make them want to read those books themselves.

That night, when I came home, I hardly had time to close the door behind me when the doorbell rang and two men in dark overcoats entered.

One of them, without removing his hat, said, 'Good evening. Here,
*From 'voron,' or raven: slang for police wagon, like the English 'Black Maria.'

if you will. An order for your arrest. There won't be any search. Just give us your papers, whatever's on you.'

Mama clasped her hands and began to reason with them—that I had been acquitted, that I loved my country and the Party even more than my parents and family, that our little girl was seriously ill.

'Don't worry,' the man said. 'It'll all be cleared up. You can give him something to eat if you like. Put some things together. He can change his clothes if he wants to. The neighbors don't have to know anything. We'll sit and wait.'

Trying to sound cheerful, Nadia told the children, who were in bed behind the wardrobe, 'Papa's going on an official trip with these two men, and he's coming back soon.' And she began to pack my bag.

Mama pushed plates of food at me across the table. I forced the food down, trying to eat slowly, and had a swig of vodka. One of the two men sat at the door. The other sat at the table and kept looking at his watch.

I changed into warmer underclothes.

When I said good-bye, Maya, all feverish, half-asleep, embraced me with her hot, thin little arms. 'You'll be back soon?'

'Soon. I'll try. Get well.'

Mama was biting her lip. Nadia was being brave. 'Remember, we're with you everywhere and always, and everything will be all right.'

Going down the stairs, one of the men walked ahead of me, the other behind me. A car stood in the courtyard, with a man at the wheel. They put me between them in the back.

We drove in silence across Moscow.

## 22

THEY TOOK me down to the basement. The cell was cold and grimy; they seemed to have used it for storing coal.

A young fellow in a torn military coat sat hunched on a bunk. He stared at the sack Mama had filled with food. I gave him some of it. He ate greedily, like a starving pup. He said that he and his comrades had been taken prisoner, sent to Germany and enrolled in a division composed of Russians and Ukrainians.

'I know all about it,' I said. 'SS volunteers.'

'Oh, sure, volunteers—at the end of a big stick!'

I slept that night with an arm around an SS man, both of us shivering in our clothes, huddled together for warmth.

In the morning they took him away. A few hours later they came for me.

'Hands behind your back.'

I felt my right wrist caught in an iron clamp.

'By what right?' I demanded. 'I am an officer, acquitted of all charges. Even when I was under investigation, I was never handcuffed!'

'You're being transported in an open vehicle. The orders are handcuffs.'

I sat in an open truck, my back to the cab. One by one, the varied structures of the Moscow subway system—dull-rose brick, iron statue, soaring column—receded before my eyes. Buildings, streets, people, traffic—everything faded, fell away. With each lurch of the truck the handcuffs cut painfully into my wrists.

We turned into Chekhov Street. That meant Butyrka* again.

We stopped for a red light. A drunk began clambering aboard. 'How about a lift, soldiers? Drop me off at—'

*Familiar name for the Butyrki prison.

'Get away—not allowed!' The guards pushed him out.

'Why not?' Then he saw me. 'Ah, you're rounding up the Jews. Good, good . . .'

He stood shouting merrily after us as we drove on.


A familiar courtyard. We stopped. The handcuffs came off.

In the outer office a gray-faced captain looked up. 'Repeater? You say they acquitted you? Well, they made a mistake. They'll correct it.'

He wasn't gloating; he didn't look particularly mean. I remembered the Baltic Fleet prosecutor: 'These Article Fifty-eight cases, you've got to wring them dry.' My acquittal had been an anomaly, a departure from the norm. The prison captain was only expressing his love of order: the mistake would be corrected.

'*I* believe I'll be acquitted again.'

He shrugged. 'Believe whatever you wish.'

A windowless room next to the one I had sat in before they let me out. How long ago was that? Seventy-two days? Seventy-three? It seemed like yesterday. And, at the same time, as though in another life.

The interlude was over.


After a trip to the shower room and the storage area, where I was given a mattress, a mug, a blanket, a sheet and even underwear—Butyrka was becoming more affluent!—I was placed in a cell with a German V-2 rocket specialist. In the next five weeks we were joined by a succession of Russian returnees from German war-prisoner camps. Then I received a signal: five onions and four heads of garlic in a food parcel from home. That meant that my trial had been set for April 5. I spent the remaining days going over what I might be asked this time and working over my final speech.

The session was held in a large hall. The three-man tribunal—a fat black-haired colonel; a thin, graying major; and a youngish captain—sat on a platform at a long table covered with a cherry-red cloth. To one side of them stood a dais, with a bench, behind a low barrier; I was placed there. Just below me the white mane and stooped shoulders of my attorney. Directly opposite me the prosecutor at his table. Squarish head, short hair, square glasses, strong chin, his bulky frame packed into his uniform, with silver shoulder boards and shiny boots.

The witnesses sat on rows of benches; as the last time, they were asked to leave the room after the preliminaries and were called in to testify one by one.

Zabashtansky was the first. Clearly, he had profited from the previous trial. Anyone, he remarked by way of introduction, could make a mistake recalling details so long after the event—what day it was, what time of day, who was the senior officer on one occasion and who commanded on another. That, he said, wasn't really the issue. The important thing was the situation that was created when a man, as though blind to the grandeur of victory and the heroism and suffering that had brought it about, as though having eyes only for the occasional ruffian who tumbled a German woman or the odd soldier who scrambled for booty—when such a man distressed and offended our soldiers and officers by delivering untimely lectures about all kinds of humanism, raking up dirt, and equating these unavoidable derelictions with the conduct of the entire army.

Sadly, he testified to the damage inflicted on the work of our section by my 'gloomy attitude,' lack of discipline, self-indulgence, demoralizing talk and disrespect for authority.

'It got so bad that, for instance, he would say, "Our *Voyentorg\** is the most fearful organization on earth, after the Gestapo." And he said it in public, with Poles present—civilians we had invited for a film showing. When I reprimanded him later, he made light of it. "Can't you see I was joking?" he said. "Where's your sense of humor?" And another time, at a Party meeting, he said, "We won not because of our personnel sections but in spite of them."'

At those words the general on the tribunal sat up and began scribbling on his pad.

The fat colonel, the chairman, conducted the session unhurriedly, without raising his voice. After Zabashtansky was through, he let me speak.

I reminded the court that the witness had twice been caught lying at the previous session.

The thin general interrupted. 'The witness spoke of your statements about the *Voyentorg* and about our personnel sections.'

'Yes, and that perhaps was the only time he told the truth. I did say those things, jokingly.'

'Jokingly? And you still think they were jokes?'

'Of course they were jokes! Maybe stupid and out of place, but jokes. How else can you interpret statements like that?'

'Then you admit they were harmful, anti-Soviet statements?'

'No, because they were made jokingly, and about certain specific

*Abbreviation for the system of Soviet army stores, notorious at that time for their poor organization, paltry stocks and discrimination against the lower ranks.

units, and not against the Soviet government. Just as in *Krokodil**
you'll find some individuals and organizations lampooned.'

In the pause that followed, my attorney looked up and whispered,
'You put your foot in it this time. You know who this general is? He's
head of the personnel section of the Moscow Military District. You'd
have done better to deny the whole thing.'

Belyaev said what he had said the last time, but more calmly and
confidently. Remembering the questions with which I had tripped him
up at the first trial, he said maybe I hadn't spent all that much time saving
Germans and arguing with our soldiers and officers, but my general
attitude had been gloomy and demoralizing and this had affected him
and made his work all the more difficult—which was why the mission
to East Prussia wasn't carried out as well as it could have been.

Nina and her husband, Georgi, had little to say this time; their testimony, if anything, was favorable to me.

Galina gave a few direct and concise answers and was gone.

My friend Ivan Rozhansky reiterated his good opinion of me and
was excused without being questioned at all. I objected. Why, I asked,
didn't my attorney take full advantage of this witness, who had exposed
Zabashtansky and Belyaev so thoroughly the last time? The chairman
shrugged my objection aside: all this was in the court records; if I
wanted to, I could bring it up in my final statement.

The next witness was new: a major who had succeeded Belyaev as the
principal of the anti-Nazi school. He had been discovered by my
attorney, who regarded him as an invaluable addition to the defense.

The young major plunged into a brisk account of how Belyaev had
neglected the administration of the school while he busied himself with
sending on the booty that he had brought from East Prussia, which
included several carpets and wardrobes and two pianos.

The prosecutor broke in. 'What has that got to do with this case?'

The young major, flustered, said that Belyaev wasn't trustworthy:
he had abandoned his wife and two children and was living with
another woman; he wasn't making his alimony payments, about
which his wife had written three times to the Central Political Administration. He, the witness, had copies of these letters on him.

'What is the relevance,' the prosecutor asked, 'of all this gossip?
Who invited this witness?'

My attorney said haltingly that he had called the witness in order to
shed light on Belyaev's character. He had thought that that would help
the court evaluate the credibility of the prosecution's principal witness.

*The Soviet satirical magazine.

The prosecutor, with a show of distaste, said that he was dismissing the witness, whose testimony only wasted the court's time. 'We are dealing with serious political accusations. We aren't interested in the private lives of the witnesses.'

This was the prosecutor's first real intervention in the trial. Up to that point he had only asked me a few questions about the 1920s, about Mark Polyak; he wondered what it was about the Trotskyist slogans of the day that had attracted me. I answered truthfully but cautiously, choosing my words carefully; the prosecutor took them down. He was courteous, and only the cold, enigmatic eyes behind his glasses put me on my guard. Now, dismissing the witness, he allowed a burst of irritation to break through—unless he simulated it for the tribunal's benefit.

I too was irked by this tattletale. But what disturbed me even more was the tone of my attorney's responses to the prosecutor. He seemed to be afraid of the man; he was positively ingratiating.

Several of my old friends had volunteered to speak up for me when they learned that I was to be tried again. The first of these, Mikhail Arshansky, now told the tribunal that he had known me well for many years and was intimately acquainted with my attitudes and viewpoints, which had always been imbued with Party spirit.

The prosecutor asked how he could know of the attitudes and viewpoints that had produced the charges against me, since he had served on a different front.

Mikhail replied that he had heard about these matters in detail from comrades who had served with me; moreover, we had had long talks when both of us were on leave in Moscow in January 1940; and on the basis of all that, and of our lifelong friendship, he was sure that the charges were not only false but absurd.

He praised me, with simple, unaffected words that made such familiar concepts as country, Party, the duty of a Communist and an officer, sound new and fresh.

Mikhail Kruchinsky, true to his word, was there to testify about my early days in Kharkov. The Civil War veteran said that I had come from a 'real, patriotic, Soviet family.' He had had occasion in 1929 to talk about me with his friends in the prosecutor's office in Kharkov and in the Ukrainian branch of the GPU; they had all agreed that my brush with the authorities, when they had considered holding me, at the age of sixteen, as a Trotskyist, had been nothing but a boyish escapade, lasting no more than several weeks. I had fallen under the influence of an older relative, and in the years that followed I had rehabilitated myself fully by my work.

The prosecutor asked what the Comrade Colonel knew of the essence of this case. Had he been at the front with the defendant? No? Then all this was hearsay, rumor?

The court adjourned until the following day.

'This case,' the prosecutor began the next day, 'is highly unusual. Never before have I encountered anything like it.'

He spoke in measured, dispassionate, reasonable tones. The session was held in the same large office where the first trial took place in October. Arnold Goldstein was on hand to reiterate his crucial testimony, but he had arrived late and the tribunal decided not to hear him.

'A great deal of good has been spoken about the defendant,' the prosecutor went on. 'There is no cause to doubt this testimony, although it should be noted that all these commendations are expressed in generalities and relate to different periods from the one when the actions that have been construed as crimes took place.

'But even if we are to accept all this testimony as true, does it follow that the defendant should be acquitted? Folk wisdom tells us, "He to whom much is given, from him much shall be asked." If the man in the defendant's box were a rank-and-file soldier or an ordinary worker or a farm laborer from some kolkhoz . . . but, of course, such a man, if he were to blurt out some gross stupidity out of ignorance, would not be held responsible under Article Fifty-eight. The man before us, on the other hand, is a scholar, a writer, an army major, a figure of considerable authority. That is clear if only from the number of people—also scholarly and authoritative—who have come to his defense. In judging the words of a man like that, we must apply more exacting criteria.

'The defendant denies many of the charges and tries to blacken his accusers. But he himself has admitted that he made anti-Soviet jokes. Take what he said about the cadres. What cadres, comrade judges? The cadres of our heroic, victorious army. Comrade Stalin has said that everything turned on the cadres. Even here, the defendant persists in treating his coarsely slanderous anti-Soviet statements as a joke. Yet from a man of his calling, position and authority, such statements were especially pernicious. Joke indeed!

'One might object that these were isolated, random lapses, that the man had had too much to drink—although we know the folk saying "What's on the tongue when drunk is on the mind when sober." And when we're dealing with educated and clever people, what is on their minds must interest us much more than what is on their tongues. And, in this case, these anti-Soviet statements were not casual slips of the tongue.

'In his youth the defendant was involved with the Trotskyists. When we consider his remarks and his behavior during the years of the Great Patriotic War, we cannot help but see a direct link to what he said and did in nineteen twenty-nine. A straight line—a bridge, as it were—connects nineteen twenty-nine with nineteen forty-five. For what was the defendant occupying himself with during those early years when our Party, our entire people, poured all their energy into the Socialist reconstruction of our economy and of our whole life—those glorious, heroic and difficult years of struggle against the kulaks, of collectivization, of the first five-year plans? Why, he was on the side of those who surreptitiously defamed our Party and our great leader; of those who tried to sow doubts about the building of Socialism; of those who spread calumny and threats and pointed the weapons of the terrorist-murderers who had entered into a conspiracy with the imperialists and the Fascists, the deadliest enemies of the world's first Socialist country.

'One might object that he was young; he didn't know any of this; he was after something quite different. I accept that. I even believe it. But this young man wasn't an illiterate besprizornik;* he read Marx and studied foreign languages. And he was so smart, you see, that he wouldn't listen to *us*; he couldn't put his trust in the Party or in the great Stalin or in the truth of Socialism. Instead, he put his trust in a gang of the Party's deadliest enemies—in their rhetoric and their demagoguery. That could have been passed off as accidental: he had been misled. And he had his defenders—like the worthy old-timer we heard from here. But now we can see that it wasn't accidental. It was no accident that he was twice expelled from the Komsomol because of his Trotskyist past. It is no accident that he sits today in the defendant's box. During the Party's fierce struggle against counterrevolutionary Trotskyism, he revealed his sympathy for the Trotskyists. During the Patriotic War against German Fascism, he revealed his sympathy for the Germans—his Germanophilism. It is impossible not to discern in this a definite system of thought—of ideology. We have seen how his friends and acquaintances believe and respect him. That means that his anti-Soviet attitudes and statements could be particularly dangerous and have particularly harmful consequences.

'Hence, the acquittal that was handed down on the basis of a purely

*Besprizorniki: The bands of homeless children who formed a criminal element in the cities after the years of revolution and civil war.

formalistic and superficial examination of this complex and unusual case was a mistake—a serious political mistake.

'Hence, in the interests of the Party, the government and the army; in the interests of all the honest Soviet citizens who are connected in one way or another with this case—who were deceived because they were too trusting or had a mistaken view of the demands of friendship; in the interests of the defendant himself—he is still young and can still reexamine his past and reform his ideology and psychology; for all these reasons, the defendant cannot go unpunished.

'At the same time, with due consideration for everything that has been presented here and for all the mitigating circumstances, keeping in mind that our Socialist jurisprudence aims first and foremost at rehabilitation, and proceeding from the relevant articles of the Criminal Code, I believe a comparatively light penalty would be in order: five years in corrective-labor camps, followed by a three-year loss of civil rights.'

My attorney's very voice betrayed his uncertainty. Stringing lifeless words together, he jumped from one subject to another, leaving his thoughts half-completed, searching through his papers: 'Here we have convincing evidence . . . here we have an undeniably positive characterization. . . .'

'The Comrade Prosecutor,' he said, 'is, of course, perfectly right in his evaluation of the, so to speak, objective meaning of the case, its significance in a general historic context, from a political and Party perspective. On the other hand, I ask the tribunal to weigh the evidence that puts the defendant in a different light.'

Whereupon, in a heightened, declamatory style, he read lengthy excerpts from some of my friends' letters and statements—choosing, I thought, the least telling portions—as well as from my articles.

'The Comrade Prosecutor,' he resumed, 'spoke of Germanophilism. But that is not, with us, a punishable offense. People say Ehrenburg is a Francophile. Very well, the defendant is a Germanophile. I will admit that he leaves much to be desired in the way of political steadfastness and moral stability, that he made mistakes which led to his exclusion from the Party. But dismissal from the Party is not, by itself, grounds for criminal prosecution either. As a Communist, I understand that his errors and his improper statements made the dismissal inevitable. More than that, I agree that to some extent he is guilty of acts proscribed under Article One Hundred Ninety-three, Section Two, of the Criminal Code, in that he did not see to the accomplishment of his military assignment in East Prussia. At the same time I believe I can justifiably ask the tribunal to acquit him of the charges under Article Fifty-eight, Section Ten.

'Inasmuch as the defendant's actions and words were not deliberately aimed at undermining the Soviet social system, I believe it to be compatible with my conscience as a Communist to ask the tribunal to take all these circumstances into account, and also to consider where the defendant could be most useful to society—and in that regard, the Comrade Prosecutor himself recognized his positive qualities. While conceding the partial truth of the charges, I request that the defendant be acquitted of criminal responsibility—though not in such form as to disavow the condemnation he deserves on political and Party grounds.'

'Defendant, you have the last word.'

Listening to the prosecutor and to my attorney, I had to reformulate the speech that I had rehearsed for so many weeks. I decided to divide my final statement into three parts.

First, I replied to the prosecutor, trying to speak as calmly and confidently as he had.

'The prosecutor did his best to portray me in my youth as a collaborator with the enemies of the people. But he must know that this is not true—that my adolescent involvement with the Trotskyists lasted only a few weeks at the beginning of nineteen twenty-six. He must know that after that I took an active part in those same glorious deeds he talks about—collectivization, the first five-year plan—and became a member of the Komsomol. The prosecutor speaks of some kind of bridge between my youthful transgressions of nineteen twenty-nine and the crimes imputed to me by my calumniators sixteen years later. But where are the foundations of this bridge? He did not cite a single fact. And yet my whole life during those sixteen years is an open book. Everything can be checked: what I did, where I worked, what I wrote, what was written about me and my work.

'The prosecutor reminded the tribunal several times that I was twice expelled from the Komsomol. Why did he neglect to remind the court that I was twice reinstated? I was reinstated because there were comrades who knew the truth about me and refuted the false and lying accusations made in each instance by the same libeler, Boris Kublanov. Open my file: there you will find Kublanov's lies rejected by the Komsomol regional committee in Kharkov in nineteen thirty-five, rejected again by the Komsomol central committee in Moscow in nineteen thirty-eight, and, in spite of that, repeated by him in a letter to *Red Star* in nineteen forty-three. Seven years later, the lies of Kublanov merge with the denunciations of Zabashtansky, two lines of slander cross, and a case is born.

'Where, then, is this bridge that is evoked by the prosecutor? In my writings, perhaps? Did anyone, at any time, find any ideological errors in my writings? Someone did try to, once, in the spring of nineteen forty-one. A member of the Komsomol committee at the Institute of Philosophy, Literature and History complained that several pages of my dissertation on Schiller were given over to polemics with the Nazis. He accused me of a "primitive anti-Fascism," incompatible with the policy, then in effect, of friendship with Germany. Never were there any other suggestions of political or ideological error on my part. Where, then, are the foundations of this bridge? In the fact that I volunteered for the front when I could have had a deferment? In the fact that throughout the war I refused to be promoted to higher posts in the rear areas? In the fact that my political and ideological work at the front persuaded my superiors to accept me into the Party and honor me with awards?

'No, because there is no such bridge, no such guiding system of anti-Soviet ideology. My whole life attests to that. It has been proved by the written and oral testimony of men and women of unimpeachable civic and Party credentials. Why, then, does the prosecutor ignore their truthful testimony and erect an illusory bridge on the words of proven liars?

'I listened carefully to the prosecutor's speech. From the way it was constructed and presented, it was clear that he is an intelligent and educated man. That means he cannot believe what he asserts. I simply cannot understand, and it disheartens no less than it astonishes me: Why does he feel he must say what he cannot believe to be true? Why does he ask for a chastisement that he cannot regard as being either just to me or useful to the Party or the state?'

I then took issue with my attorney. I said that I could not accept that kind of defense. I was not asking for leniency; there could be no question of any partial admission of the charges, since there was no guilt. I objected to the term 'Germanophile'; this was a bourgeois concept, whereas I was true to the principles of proletarian internationalism, so well expressed by the words of Comrade Stalin, 'Hitlers come and go, but the German people remain.'

I was encouraged by the attentive stillness, the eyes of my friends, the intent gaze of the prosecutor. He sat motionless, elbows on the table, his chin resting on his hands.

'At the last trial I asked not for mercy but for justice. The decision then was just, and nothing has happened since to bring it into question. Therefore, I want to utilize my final statement before this court not to defend myself again but to accuse. I accuse two men present here—Zabashtansky and Belyaev.'

They sat, staring at the floor, to my left, separated from me by a guard and an empty chair. I was pleased to see Zabashtansky redden at my words and Belyaev squirm and look about apprehensively.

'I accuse them of a double crime—a crime against the person, and a crime against the state.'

This concluding portion I had memorized long before, culling and polishing every sentence.

'They committed, and are continuing to commit, a crime against the state because, for two years, they deprived it of the services of a political worker who, toward the end of the war and, subsequently, in the occupied territories, could have been of more use to the country and the Party in one week than they can be in their entire lives—the lives of self-seekers, slanderers and careerists. They committed, and are continuing to commit, a crime against the person by the deliberate and malicious bearing of false witness, in making trumped-up political charges against an honest man devoted to his country and his Party, thus consigning him to a cruel, undeserved ordeal and his family to mental anguish.'

Speaking those words, I felt my throat tighten. What was this—tears? They would think that I was putting on an act. I stopped abruptly. 'That's all. I ask not for mercy but for justice. I do not defend myself—I accuse.'

Everyone was asked to leave while the tribunal deliberated. I was led to the far end of the corridor. My attorney came up, looking embarrassed.

'You shouldn't have gotten so upset,' he said. 'You must understand . . . I am a Party man. . . . The prosecutor liked your final speech very much. He said nice things about you: "coherent, literate." . . . You must understand . . . he has his own obligations. . . .'

Three hours passed. I had glimpses of Nadia, Mama, my father. They nodded and smiled.

Toward evening we were called back. Again, as the last time, everyone remained standing.

The chairman read slowly from the verdict. The import of his words was immediately clear. In conclusion: 'three years' detention in corrective-labor camps, followed by two years' loss of civil rights.'

# 23

SOME TWENTY men sat on benches along the walls. There was something about them that was different from the prisoners I had been accustomed to seeing. A few looked like elderly peasants. The others were like a sampling of city people—laborers, mechanics, office workers.

One of them was in military uniform. I sat down next to him. 'What front were you on?'

'Volkhov front,' he said, with quiet dignity.

I noticed a young man, completely naked, covered by a piece of dirty cloth, staring vacantly ahead.

'Lost his clothes gambling,' my neighbor explained. 'Young punk.'

I had been transferred to this room after three days in a transients' cell—why I did not know. I gathered from the remarks around me that we were waiting for a 'buyer,' whatever that meant.

A group of prison officers entered, paper folders in their hands. They were accompanied by a man in civilian clothes who looked like a foreman and spoke with a businesslike air.

'New camp,' he said. 'Good one. Not far from Moscow.'

He was the 'buyer,' my neighbor explained—a respresentative of a labor camp rounding up a work force.

I found myself in a large closed truck with about thirty others. We drove for several hours.

The newly erected barracks were surrounded by forest and smelled of tar. The camp commandant, a captain by rank, sat behind his desk, the visor of his cap pulled low over his peevish eyes.

'Scholar, eh? But what can you *do*? Know how to use an ax? If you don't, you'll learn. If you don't learn, you don't eat. You'll croak. Get it?'

That's how I became a carpenter. Nikolai, my uniformed friend, was in the same team. We were taught how to make planks out of tree trunks. But, except when the camp authorities came by, the team boss, himself a prisoner, did not expect to get much work out of his wards.

I had been slow to realize why. They were all thieves, including my alleged war hero (now reduced to prison garb), and working was against their code.

'What are you breaking your ass for, Major?' Nikolai said. 'Let those muzhiks sweat. That's all they're good for. But you are a warrior, a scientist. Sit down with us—have a cigarette, tell us a story. This brigade chief's an old hand—he knows how to get along with people.'

'People,' in their language, meant 'thieves.' A 'real man' meant an authentic, professional, 'lawful' thief, otherwise known as 'blue blood' and 'honest crook,' as distinct from 'trash,' 'minors,' 'Stalinist thieves' and other lower elements of their order.

A month later I was called into the medical section. My records showed that at Unzhlag I had been a male nurse. They gave me the job of medic at a penal colony being formed at a gravel pit somewhere on the banks of the Volga.

About a hundred of us zeks were sent to establish the colony. We traveled for more than twenty-four hours by barge. When we arrived at the site, Nadia was waiting for me on the riverbank. She had arrived at the base camp with a food parcel right after we left, and beat us to our destination by hitching rides.

The officer in charge of the contingent, a Kirghiz, wouldn't permit a meeting at first. 'Nothing's been arranged. . . . I don't have any guards to spare.' Then he relented and took Nadia and me to a hillside where he let us sit together for half an hour while he sat discreetly at a distance.

The new colony was erected in a hollow at the foot of a steep, sandy cliff. Two huge tents with wooden floors accommodated about seventy men each. A partitioned-off space at the end of one of the tents served as the infirmary. A low ridge hid us from the Volga. The whole area was encircled by two rows of barbed wire.

I lived and worked in the infirmary. My hours began at 5:30 A.M. I would see those who had asked to be excused from work by reason of ill health, and those whose sick leave was up. From 7:00 to 9:00 the infirmary was open to ambulatory patients, and after 10:00 I made my rounds of the bedridden.

The head guard, a foulmouthed lieutenant, stopped me on the second day. 'What's the matter with you, doctor? You out of your fucking mind? You've given sick leave to fifteen men. Who's going to get the work done?'

'Citizen commander,' I said, 'I've excused only men who are crippled by illness and who have high fever. They can hardly walk, much less work. Suppose I refuse a man sick leave and he dies in the pit. It won't look very good for you, will it?'

'Yeah, you're right. Just think, what a crock of shit we got here. They've given me a bunch of goners and cripples, and I'm supposed to give them a hundred tons of gravel a day. Look, doc, do your best with these jerks—may they be fucked in the mouth and hung up to dry!'

Later in the day, there was usually some free time. I could read, lying on the grass at a spot near the infirmary where the breeze from the Volga blew away the smell of chlorine. Sometimes I would be joined there by one or two of these thieves, or by Misha, a lawyer given two years for 'bribery' after he interceded on behalf of his imprisoned father, also a lawyer. Misha told me that he had been a classmate of Stalin's daughter, Svetlana. He spoke fondly of her. One day, he recounted, Svetlana brought a book of Esenin's poetry to school, and it was passed from hand to hand.* The teacher discovered this 'harmful book' in the possession of one of the students and confiscated it. There was an investigation. Everyone kept mum, of course. Then Svetlana went up to the teacher and said, 'This is my book. I got it from Papa.' And everyone dropped the whole thing.

The thieves in our camp held a secret conclave and, departing from custom, decided to form their own work team. Except for the obstinate Lenya the General and one or two who were really sick, they marched off every morning to the gravel pit. They balked at working in the afternoons (although on sunny days they'd stay on at the pit to sunbathe), yet they fulfilled or overfulfilled their daily quota. This was because of the prodigious work of one of their number, Karapet the Bomber, a short, broad-shouldered Armenian. Good-natured, helpful and always smiling, Karapet actually enjoyed working. With sweat streaming from his bare, muscular, copper-red torso, he would push his heavy-laden wheelbarrow on the run, calling out happily, 'Make way for the Bomber!' The other thieves took perverse pride in his

*The late Sergei Esenin (briefly husband to the American dancer Isadora Duncan), whose popularity in the prerevolutionary and early revolutionary years was followed by official obloquy. More recently, his poetry has been rehabilitated, and an official cult of Esenin has been established.

records. But one of the 'minors,' Goga, took an intense dislike to the Bomber.

One day he cheated the Bomber at cards, and the Bomber refused to play. 'A thief, when he plays with another thief, plays honestly,' he said.

Goga cussed him out—another infraction of the thieves' law. Goga called him a fat-assed mule, which Karapet took as a slur on the Armenian people.

'Shut your dirty mouth, punk,' he growled, cuffing Goga with a massive paw.

Goga began screeching. 'He hit me! He hit a thief! Scum! Bitch! Break him!'

To be 'broken,' in their parlance, was to be found in violation of the thieves' law and deprived of the rights and privileges of their world. A broken thief lost his natural right to 'pluck the pigeons' (i.e., help himself to whatever he wanted in the outside world); he no longer had a right to every other thief's assistance when in trouble; and, in fact, he was no longer immune to violence or death at the other thieves' hands. The elders, in this case, refused to break the Bomber, but Goga wouldn't be mollified, and he was supported secretly by the other minors, who felt that their leaders, in forming a work team, had entered into a compact with the 'vipers,' the thieves' term for the camp authorities. As for the Bomber, they regarded him as practically a 'strikebreaker,' soiling the honor of the 'blue blood.' But none of them dared to argue openly with the chiefs.

At last, to my relief, the head of the medical section at the base camp arrived on an inspection tour.

Alexander Ivanovich X* was a man just under forty, with a slight hump. A priest's son from Kuibyshev on the Volga, he was assigned to the medical corps at Gulag directly after graduating from medical school. By the time I met him, he had spent ten years working in the camps.

Alexander Ivanovich, on arrival, regarded me with skeptical curiosity. He quizzed me and appeared to be satisfied that I had a certain pains-taking knowledge of the causes and treatment of pellagra, scurvy, dystrophy, dysentery, tuberculosis and other illnesses relevant to our work. But, apparently, he had also been bemused at a distance by the zeal shown by my written reports to his office. The stock explanation was simple: who wouldn't rather work with thermometers and pills

*The author does not give his surname; Ivanovich, of course, is his patronymic.

◇ 217 ◇

than with shovels and wheelbarrows? But that hadn't tied in with my tiresomely frank admissions of ignorance: my reports brimmed with questions, appeals for fresh instruction, reminders of questions still unanswered, and descriptions of all my mistakes of commission and omission, which had to be corrected with their help, at once. A camp-wise charlatan hanging onto a soft berth would never have undermined his own authority that way.

The doctor was accompanied by a base-camp supervisor who proceeded to yell at our officers and, entering the infirmary, at me.

'What is this—a sanitarium, a health resort? Eighteen sick leaves in one day! Some medic! So scared he unloads in his pants and signs sick leaves for every faker in sight. Or maybe they grease your palm, eh? You want to be sent to the pit yourself or have your sentence extended?'

My temper snapped. 'Citizen commander! I won't permit you to insult me or pin something on me! Let the head of the medical section see if I signed a single phony sick leave. I was sent here to treat the sick, not drive them out to hard labor! This is a *Soviet* camp, not Maidanek!'

Alexander Ivanovich cut in. 'No hysterics, please. No one's trying to pin anything on you. I'll look into the matter myself.'

He approved all my sick leaves; only one of my patients had let me down. Lenya the General had come to me muttering, 'Damn syphilis is crawling out again,' and had shown me the red sores on his member. Scared by these symptoms of a disease about which I knew next to nothing, I treated him with zinc ointment and disinfectant and ordered him isolated in his barracks as much as possible. But when Alexander Ivanovich looked at these same symptoms, he grunted, 'Let me have the iodine.'

'Hey, doctor,' Lenya the General protested, 'that burns!'

'I'll show you what really burns if you play any more tricks like that. What did you put on there—manganous?' He turned to me. 'Did you give him any manganous?'

I hadn't, but I had given it to one of his buddies to be dissolved and taken internally against dysentery; and I now learned that grains of manganous, when applied to sensitive tissue, can cause unsightly ulceration.

Lenya the General wasn't put out by the discovery of his ruse to get out of joining the thieves' work team.

'Sorry, citizen doctors,' he said, groaning from the sting of the iodine. 'Only this damn syphilis *is* sitting inside me, and that's the truth.'

'He's probably lying,' the doctor said, 'but we'll give him a Wassermann to make sure. Meanwhile, off to work with him.'

Alexander Ivanovich and the supervisor went back to the base camp, taking the more seriously ill with them.

I was attending to the usual midday business at the infirmary when I heard shouts. 'He killed him! He killed him! Stop him!'

There was a burst of automatic fire.

I ran out. Karapet the Bomber stood bare-chested by the kitchen, his face running with blood, calling out almost gaily, 'Fuck you! I'm all right! . . . Fuck you! I'm all right!'

Goga, grabbed from behind by Uncle Vasya, was trying to break free. His face was white and his eyes were wild. He had an ax in his right hand.

The sentry was yelling and waving his submachine gun. The cook dashed about shouting, 'Help! Murder!' A small crowd stood back. Uncle Vasya was shouting, 'Take away his ax! What are you standing there for—bastards, cowards! Can't you see he's cracked up?'

Coming up from behind, I jerked the ax out of Goga's hand and threw it over the barbed wire. I ran up to the Bomber, who kept repeating, 'Fuck you! I'm all right!' There was a deep gash on his left cheek and another on his left forearm. With the help of two others I led him into the infirmary.

He had been attacked while sleeping by the woodpile and had grabbed the ax away from Goga. Goga had pulled a second ax out of the woodpile when Uncle Vasya stepped in.

I placed a tourniquet around the Bomber's mighty shoulder, but the bandages I wrapped around the forearm were immediately soaked in blood.

There were shouts outside. 'Doctor wanted at the gate!' I ran to the gate.

'What's going on in there?' the lieutenant asked. 'Is he still alive?'

'Yes, but he's got to be taken to the hospital at once. I've got nothing to sew him up with. He'll bleed to death.'

The hospital was in the base camp. The zeks at the gate fell still, listening. The guards bunched up behind the lieutenant.

'Where am I going to get a vehicle?' the lieutenant said. 'We won't have one before evening.'

'Then take him to a civilian hospital. There must be one around here. Or he could be dead in two hours.'

'He won't die. He's as strong as a bear. First we've got to tie up that murderer.'

Goga had squirmed out of Uncle Vasya's grasp and, pulling a third ax out of another hiding place, had run into an empty barracks, threatening to kill anyone who went in after him.

'You, doctor,' the lieutenant said, 'and you, overseer, and some of you others—go tie up the bastard, or he'll kill you all.'

A sullen murmur came from the crowd.

'Carry out the order!' the lieutenant snapped. 'Or I'll consider this collective resistance and open fire on the whole camp.'

'Citizen commander,' I said, 'your order is illegal. My duty is to tend to the sick. The overseer's duty is to assign work. Arresting murderers is *your* duty, and you cannot shift that duty onto the zeks. No one is offering collective resistance. And your threat is illegal. You yourself know that no one can violate the law and go unpunished. I repeat, the zek Arakelian is seriously wounded and needs immediate surgery or he will die. I will submit a written report, giving the exact time when I said this, and all these men here, the zeks and the guards, will be witnesses.'

Sounds of approbation came from the crowd. 'That's right, doctor. . . . Those vipers—a man's life to them isn't worth more than a dog's. . . .'

Senka the Leg emitted a piercing whine. 'What is this? Where are we, on Russian soil or in Fascist Germany? A man is dying for no good reason, and the commander threatens to kill others as well? Who can do things like that? Only vipers, executioners, curse their souls—not Soviet people!'

Whipping himself into a frenzy, he fell down and began beating his fists and feet on the ground. 'I spilled my blood at the front for the Motherland, for Stalin! And now a Russian soldier wants to shoot me down! For *what*? For *what*?'

Several of the other thieves joined in. 'They've driven the man out of his mind. . . . Is there no law here? . . . We'll write to the prosecutor, to the commandant of all the camps. . . .'

The guards' dogs set up a nervous barking. The lieutenant stood red-faced and confused. He said curtly, 'Get the wounded man here. But if that other one with the ax comes out of the barracks, we'll open fire.'

I turned to Lyokha the Bald. 'Do something! You were boasting that you have your own law. . . .'

'Stop worrying, doctor,' Lyokha said soothingly. 'Goga isn't coming out. What you said to the vipers—that was good. Now take care of the Bomber. Leave Goga to us.'

They took the Bomber by motorboat to a hospital in Kimry, half an hour away. I wasn't allowed to accompany him.

'You're the doctor,' the lieutenant said, 'but you're also a Fifty-eighter, and that means no leaving the zone.'

Several days later the base camp sent us about thirty more men, including a new medic. I was being transferred back.

One of the new men had a deep hole in his forehead, grown over with skin—the result of a severe fracture of the skull. Another suffered from prolapse of the rectum. I pronounced them both unfit for work, and they returned with me.

I reported to Alexander Ivanovich. The doctor heard me out and said, 'Didn't you see my signature on their papers? Didn't it occur to you that I might have known what I was doing when I sent them there?

'The hospital in this camp,' he continued, 'is crammed with people who are treatable. That man with the hole in his head and the other with the prolapse are not responsive to any further treatment, and I don't want them taking up space. There, in the colony, they would have been let off from work from time to time, and they could lie on the grass and rest. The regime is easier there, and the food is better, and there's more room. Here the trusties are going to keep them hopping. So you see, you had to barge in with your principles, and you've only made it worse for them. That's called being extra kind to someone—at his expense.'

Goga's trial took place a month later in the camp dining room. The judges and assessors sat behind a long table covered by red cloth. Uncle Vasya and I had submitted written testimony, at the interrogator's request.

The Bomber, called to give evidence, answered the prosecutor's questions with 'I don't know. . . . I didn't see. . . . I was asleep. . . .'

'Listen, Arakelian,' the prosecutor said, 'this man came close to killing you, or at least crippling you for life.'

Goga sat impassively in the defendant's box.

'And yet you cover up for him. Why do you refuse to tell the truth when you know who hit you with the ax?'

The Bomber gave him one of his most good-natured smiles. 'Citizen Prosecutor, please, don't get mad. You see, this is a simple matter.

This Goga, who is he? A thief. Who am I? A thief. We have the same law. And you, Citizen Prosecutor, who are you? A viper. And the Citizen Judge is also a viper.'

The prosecutor frowned. The presiding judge, a woman, said, 'Arakelian, do you realize what you've just said? I could have you punished for swearing, for insulting the court.'

The Bomber looked hurt. 'I'm not swearing—I'm saying what is true. The thief has his law; the viper has his law. A thief cannot squeal on another thief to a viper. If he does, he's not a thief; he's a bitch.'

Goga shouted, 'Good for you, Bomber! Stand up for the law! Fuck them in the mouth, the vipers!'

The defense attorney made a long and fiery speech about the defendant's unfortunate childhood, his inadequate moral and political upbringing, the influence of the criminal milieu. He argued that the attempt was made in a state of acute excitation.

Goga's final statement was brief.

'Citizen judges, I have confessed in all sincerity—I hit him, but I didn't mean to kill him. Let me drop dead on the spot if I did. I only wanted to frighten him. Then I got frightened myself when I saw the blood, and I went off my rocker. What do I ask? I ask you to look: What kind of a young life have I had? My father died for his country. Mama died of internal complications. From strangers I've only had scorn. My nerves are all shot. I ask you to have mercy.'

The court gave him seven years.

# 24

IN AUGUST the camp authorities permitted another meeting with Nadia. She told me that the Supreme Court had voided my sentence—*for excessive leniency!* The court had also found a procedural error: a three-year term for a crime committed before the end of the war fell under the postwar amnesty, a circumstance that the tribunal had overlooked. There would have to be yet another trial. The best we could hope for now was a sentence of no more than four years—just long enough to escape the provisions of the amnesty. An acquittal seemed out of the question.

Thinking about this brought on a weight of impenetrable sadness. At times despair tightened like a knot. But there were the sick and the dying all around me—so much distress, so much misfortune, so much irremediable suffering, that my troubles seemed far more bearable than theirs.

In that summer of '47 the number of zeks in our camp grew to six or seven thousand. More than two hundred patients were housed in the three yurts and single wooden barracks of the hospital, and more than a hundred prisoners applied at the dispensary each day. The medical personnel consisted of Alexander Ivanovich, his woman assistant, two nurses, a woman dentist who came every other day (all of them free citizens working for the camp), two medics who were prisoners and lived in a barracks some distance away, and me. After Alexander Ivanovich left for the day—he tried to be out of the camp before nightfall—I was left in charge.

'The mortality rate here is normal,' Alexander Ivanovich said to me. 'Only five dead last week. That's less than one a day, on the average. Difficult situation, you see. New camp, so they keep sending us shipments from the older ones. Whom do they give us? Ballast, rejects, the goners, the incurables. Our commander protests, but they know they won't get theirs back. I write letters to the administration. We're not supposed to have to cope with a hundred beds in this camp. There should have been a separate hospital, a special staff.

'Mortality is going to go even higher, of course. Lousy diet. Infections. Dysentery we'll manage somehow, but dystrophy, scurvy, pellagra, heart disease—that's going to be more difficult. Come winter, the goners are going to die like flies.'

At the front I saw many deaths. I myself might have killed—how many times we had to fire at a barely visible enemy!—and at Graudenz I gave commands to our artillery over our sound truck. I buried my comrades in the forest clearings of Staraya Russa* and in the cemeteries of Belorussian and Polish villages. In the winter of 1941–42 I saw our soldiers rest, eat and smoke sitting on the corpses of German soldiers frozen solid and sprinkled with snow. I saw a grotesque row of German corpses stuck into snow banks—some straight up, legs apart; others head down, legs up in the air—by some ruffians from transport. In the summer of 1944, on the fields and roads of Belorussia, I saw the German dead in their blue-gray uniforms hideously swollen in the heat; I saw our own men hanging by their necks from telegraph poles, in their soldiers' shirts or in ragged mufti, barefoot, with placards on their chests: 'Traitor to the Motherland'; 'Fascist accomplice, murderer of women and children.' And later I saw German soldiers, the eagles and epaulets ripped off their gray tunics, strung up with the signs: 'I showed cowardice before the enemy'; 'I let the Bolsheviks into Germany'; 'I am a traitor.' I saw the bodies of raped women in East Prussia and the charred corpses of our soldiers in a house blasted apart by a bazooka. In Unzhlag, watching a dead prisoner being carried out to be buried, I saw the guard at the gate pierce the body through the sackcloth with an awl—to make sure, on orders, that the prisoner wasn't pretending to be dead in order to get out.

But the ones I remember most clearly and most painfully are those who died in this new labor camp named 'Great Volga'—those whose temperatures I took, to whom I brought medicine, vainly trying to delay their death. Actually, the first man who died in my presence I don't remember seeing alive. Soon after I was made medic, before I even had time to get to know anyone, an oldish man down with scurvy died in the yurt for the seriously ill. He died late in the evening. They brought his body into the dispensary. I was alone and ran to Alexander Ivanovich's office in another barracks to telephone him at home. The

*An area between Moscow and Leningrad.

doctor lived in a cottage not far from the camp. The voice on the line was either sleepy or drunk.

'Died? So what? What are you shouting from the housetops for? I can't resurrect him. You could have waited till tomorrow with your good news. You're a medic, not a miss who's scared of the dead. What to do with him? Hmm . . . yes; can't leave him on the floor by the door . . . outpatients before the work shift tomorrow morning . . . people stumbling all over him. Can't put him out in the open—not allowed. Guardhouse won't take him. Y-y-yes, a problem.

'And you can't solve it yourself? And what if I was away or at someone else's house, what would you do? You don't know. What's the head on your shoulders for? You're an educated man, a Ph.D., why can't you think of something?

'No, we can't put him in the storehouse. Maybe the bathhouse. Better still, the boiler room next to it. No, can't leave him there—too hot, and it's summer. Besides, those bathhouse attendants could kill you there, and what am I going to do with two corpses and one medic less?'

'Tell you what, take him to the dental office—no visiting hours there tomorrow. What do you mean, no room for stretchers—stick him in the dentist's chair. And something else: got to get the cause of death, got to have a biopsy. Cut a piece of mucous membrane from his mouth. Don't know how? What are you talking about?—you won't be cutting up a live man; he's not going to complain. Only you've got to do this officially, so that everything's in order. Go get Alexei; tell him I ordered you and him to get some tissue from his oral cavity for testing —from several spots. He'll probably know how to do it better than you. Go ahead, do what I say and stop making all this noise about it.'

Alexei, one of the other two medics who lived in another part of the camp, was shaking when I got him over. 'Cold,' he said, 'and I don't like stiffs. Maybe he has some kind of infection. Just don't cut yourself; there's this poison in corpses—you know? Finish you off in no time.'

With the help of another orderly, we managed to sit the corpse down in the dentist's chair. It wasn't quite stiff as yet and squirmed about eerily. Putting on rubber gloves, Alexei held the jaws apart with a pair of dental pliers while I cut bits of flesh from inside the cheeks with a scalpel and placed them in a glass jar.

Musa, the quiet Georgian, lay in the yurt for the most serious cases, breathing with difficulty and gazing at us, when we attended to him, with grateful eyes.

'Thank you, doctor. Big thank you.' He spoke with the accents and word patterns of his native mountains.

His illness, when we got him, had been diagnosed as pleurisy. But the swelling on his chest grew day by day. Alexander Ivanovich decided to puncture it. The big needle caught between his ribs. Musa moaned, as quietly as he could.

'Hold out, *katzo*,'* the doctor encouraged him. 'Just a little more.'

Almost half a pail of gray liquid drained out. Musa began to breathe more easily.

'Good . . . good . . . Thank you, doctor. Big thank you.'

Back in his office, the doctor said, 'He'll live for a few more days. We'll have to open him up and take a look. I've never known cancer like this.'

He unlocked an iron safe and took out a handful of ampuls. 'Inject him with these three times a day. Only go easy on the dosage. We'll need it for the others.'

The relief from the drainage was short-lived. Musa's breathing grew strangled. After an injection his chest cleared briefly. He would thank me quietly and fall asleep.

The next day, in the evening, he became talkative.

'Doctor, I will die soon. Send a letter to my house. My father is there, and my mother and my wife. Address is here.'

'What are you saying, my dear friend? You will live. You will live for a long time. They will reduce your sentence, and you will go home.'

Musa, from what he told me, had been a truck driver in his village, with the job of taking produce into town, and in the city of Ordzhoni-kidze he had tangled with a Russian policeman—'bad man, very bad man'—who made a practice of picking on Georgian truck drivers. The policeman made the mistake of telling Musa to go fuck his mother, and Georgians, Musa explained, 'cannot listen when any man speaks bad words about your mother.' Musa struck the policeman and was given ten years for 'banditry.'

Musa was surprised to hear that I had never been to the Caucasus.

'You must go to the Caucasus, doctor. You come to my village— very good place. Big mountain. Many mountains. High, high the snow lies. Clean, clean the wide air. We have forest. We have fields. We have many sheep. You can eat well.'

He closed his eyes and smiled. Sitting by his bedside, I fell involuntarily into his way of speaking.

'Sleep, my friend, sleep. When I finish my sentence, I will go to see

*Katzo: 'Friend' in Georgian.

you in your house. We will go into the mountains. We will eat the shashlik and drink the wine. We will sing the songs of your land.'

There were a score of other patients in the yurt, but none of them took it amiss that we gave most of our attention to Musa. The young orderly, Seva, a prisoner who had been nursed by the doctor through a bout of angina, would wake me up at night. (I had a partitioned-off cubbyhole of my own in a neighboring yurt.)

'Quick—*katzo* is hardly breathing!'

I would hurry over and give him another injection.

The last hour of Musa's life, I sat by his side. By this time three injections in a row had no effect. He breathed more and more painfully. His eyes seemed to be turning into stone. But now and then their black pupils quivered.

'Speak, doctor, please speak. Am I dying now?'

'You won't die, Musa. Hold out a little longer. Just one or two more days. Then you will be better. Then you will get well. You will go home to the mountains. You will go home to the forests, to the fields, to the clean air.'

'Speak, doctor, speak.'

Again and again I stuck my needle into his parchmentlike skin.

'Thank you,' he would mumble each time. 'Speak ... house ... mountains ...'

I spoke, and did not notice when he died, his eyes open as though transfixed by a vision of his distant home.

Our day at the hospital was strictly organized. From 6:00 A.M. to 9:00 A.M. we took the patients' temperatures, gave injections, handed out the prescribed medicine and performed other chores. I then gave Alexander Ivanovich a case-by-case report. In the afternoon we transferred the chronically ill to outpatient treatment, signed out those who had recovered, received new patients and examined new arrivals. After the nurses' departure came the evening routine. One thing I never learned was how to give intravenous injections: I was afraid. In Unzhlag, when I had just begun my medical training, I saw one of our nurses give an intravenous injection to a young woman thief. The lively, rosy-cheeked patient suddenly fell back, hiccupped, paled and stiffened. Death was ascribed officially to thrombosis of the aorta brought on by an advanced case of syphilis. But our doctor-instructor, Uncle Borya, thought that it was probably something else.

'You know how good that nurse is at giving injections,' he explained to us. 'She used to say she could find a vein with her eyes closed. Well,

I'm afraid she was overconfident. Just one tiny bubble of air in the syringe is enough to cause an embolism—and that means instantaneous death.'

Remembering what had happened then, I didn't dare now to try my hand at intravenous injections. To compensate for this, I threw myself all the more zealously into the other evening tasks: cupping, mustard plasters, injections, enemas.

One evening I was attending a patient for whom the doctor had ordered a sodium phosphate enema. The labeled bottle in which we kept that solution was almost full, and I gave him the whole amount. He groaned piteously and ran out to the toilet. I turned to the men who needed cupping, but I could not find the benzine.

'Where is the bottle of benzine?' I asked the young orderly.

Seva said that the bottle was dirty and he had poured the benzine into an empty bottle, a clean one—the bottle labeled 'Sodium phosphate solution.'

The urge to kill the orderly was suppressed by the realization that nothing should be said or done to make the patients suspect that something terrible had just occurred.

Summoning the residue of my sometime instruction in the Stanislavsky Method, I clung to the role of a busy, competent medic. As though catching sight of my victim, who was back in bed, prostrate and ashen, I asked him how he felt, nodded wisely, and said, 'We're going to have to clean you out more thoroughly than that.'

Seva and I, between us, must have sluiced a whole pail of tepid soapy water through his intestines. After he recovered, we made him eat quantities of rice boiled with cod-liver oil and drink glasses of tea with milk and sugar. The patient said that he didn't feel too bad, except that he just couldn't face another plateful of rice. That night I hardly slept, jumping up at every sound and creeping back to the yurt to see if the man was all right.

Alexander Ivanovich took my news calmly. 'No harm done. You acted in time. But even if you hadn't done anything afterward, nothing too awful would have transpired. Most of the benzine must have come out by itself. The only real danger I can think of is if you had decided to inspect what was happening by holding a lighted match to his asshole.'

The boy looked no older than twelve: a little skeleton inside a tight casing of light gray skin; eyes all pupils, with only a trace of whites; boils from the neck down.

It turned out that he was sixteen—a kolkhoz kid sentenced for 'stealing collective-farm property.' He had been caught going home from work with some wheat, peas and beets hidden in his clothing.

'Everybody was hungry,' he told us. 'Mama and my brothers and my sisters, and I was the oldest. Papa? The Germans killed him.'

They had given him three years. But in the camp he had stolen a pair of shoes from another zek. He had simply lifted them when the barracks were empty and had taken them to the men in the fields, admitting that the shoes were not his and offering to exchange them for bread.

Ivanko (his name) was tried in the camp dining room, sentenced to five more years and placed in a punishment barracks. The bulk of the inmates there were 'lawful thieves,' and they ran things their way, 'confiscating' most of the food rationed out to the other prisoners. Ivanko had been there for almost a month before Alexander Ivanovich discovered him in one of his periodic visits. The boy was suffering from acute undernourishment and pellagra.

'Another week,' said the doctor, 'and he'd have— We've got to be very careful. No overeating. No fresh bread: dry it out first. And only small portions several times a day.'

We placed him in the yurt where I had my cubicle. He ate frantically, swallowing convulsively, licking the plate dry, his sunken eyes fixed in an unseeing stare. He did not talk to anyone but lay on his bunk, his head under his blanket, sitting up only when he smelled food being brought in. After a week or so his strength began returning; the boils began drying up; soon he was able to sit out in the sun. He even tried to help distribute the meals until we caught him sneaking food from the others' plates; he then offered to collect the empty plates and would lick each one diligently.

One day the 'shepherds'—prisoners deputized by the camp authorities to maintain order—found him eating the garbage piled up behind the kitchen. The head trusty was disgusted. 'A dog wouldn't stick its nose in that stink! The commandant told us to pour chlorine over all garbage. That'll stop these jackals—you know how chlorine burns?'

I tried to talk some sense into Ivanko. Seeing that I wasn't getting very far, I commandeered his pants. Nevertheless, he was caught again at the garbage dump. This time he was brought in by a guard, who threatened to report him for 'running bare-assed around the camp.' I got around the guard by slipping him a pack of cigarettes and promising to have the boy strapped to his bunk if necessary.

'You idiot!' I yelled at him. 'If you don't die of food poisoning from the refuse, you'll be put back into the punishment barracks. Have you forgotten what it's like there?'

He stared at the floor, sniffling and muttering, 'I won't any more . . . honest to God . . . Give me something to eat. . . . I'm hungry.'

We took away his shirt and gave it back to him only after lights-out. In the daytime he lay naked under the blanket.

One night I was awakened by some noise. Ivanko was lying across his bunk, shaking violently with spasmodic laughter.

One of the patients said, 'He's having a fit. He's been at the garbage again. Told the orderly he was going to the toilet, and came back chewing on something foul.'

'When was this?'

'Maybe half an hour, an hour ago.'

Chlorine poisoning! I looked up the instructions in our handbook for nurses.

Ivanko's twitching arms and legs were becoming hard as wood. I gave him an injection of atropine and of a camphor compound, and the spasms weakened. He stopped laughing and began moaning and grinding his teeth. I woke up the day orderly, Gosha, a working lad from Tula who had received a year for a drunken fight, and the two of us had to use all our strength to force Ivanko's jaws open and pour a warm soda solution down his throat. He choked and vomited a thick, putrid black stream smelling of rot and chlorine. We labored over him, with more solutions down his gullet and up his rear, until his breathing became more even and his paroxysm ceased. His pulse was weak but regular. Toward morning I arranged to have one of the prisoners who could leave the camp without supervision tell one of our nurses to bring some milk. She arrived with a bottle, and we warmed it and managed to get Ivanko to swallow a few gulps.

Alexander Ivanovich examined him carefully and said, 'You did more or less right. No use washing him out any more. That chlorine must have been inside him for an hour before you got to him. The spasms mean that the poison's in the bloodstream. He'll die, of course. If not today, then tomorrow. Killed himself, the cretin. We could keep his heart going for a little while, but what's the use? Leave him in peace.'

'I was taught we must do everything possible to keep a patient alive so long as there's a spark of life.'

'You weren't the only one taught that. The laws of medicine! The physician's code! All that's fine in the normal—well, comparatively normal—world out there.' He made a weary gesture with his long, dexterous arm. 'But in here, we have other kinds of laws. That's something you should have realized by now.'

'I wasn't taught out there but in Unzhlag. My teachers were doctors who were prisoners themselves. But they upheld the laws of medical ethics. To decide whom to keep alive and whom not to—that's the same as deciding whom to sentence to death as "worthless." That smacks of Fascist eugenics. It's against my principles.'

'Some principles, pushed too far, become folly—stupid, suicidal folly. It's lucky for you that I don't have anyone at the moment to take your place.'

His long, oversized head on his hunched narrow shoulders was skewed to one side, as though he did not trust himself to look at me. I could see that he was piqued.

'Keep on butting your head against the facts and they're going to break your skull,' he said. 'And your ribs as well.'

We stood in his office, looking at each other.

'All right, damn your soul,' he said; 'if you're in the mood for experiments—'

He gave me three handfuls of ampuls, of different colors—American, English and German. 'These are for the heart. These are antispastic. These restore breathing. Inject him with one of each every two hours. Then we'll see.'

Seeing my beaming expression, he shrugged. 'We'll see how long you can keep him alive. Maybe this experiment will be of some use to someone, somewhere. More likely it's just nonsense, a waste of time, art for art's sake. You are a high-principled fool, and your superior is an undisciplined softie.'

I poked Ivanko with my needle for three days and three nights. He was in a coma all the time. We made him swallow warm milk; Alexander Ivanovich helped the nurses prepare a vitamin-fortified chicken soup; in one way and another we poured almost two liters of various solutions into him. We packed his little body in hot-water bottles, and his limbs grew softer, his pulse a bit stronger. At night the young orderly would wake me up at regular intervals. 'Time for injections.'

On the fourth night, shaking me awake, he cried, 'The little jackal is smoking!'

Ivanko lay on his side, eyes half-opened, puffing on a cigarette. One of his bunkmates said that the boy saw him rolling some makhorka and asked for a puff.

I could have kissed his wizened little face. All around us there were friendly voices. 'Hey, little jackal . . . Come alive?'

We gave him some cod-liver oil and warmed the rest of the milk. He drank greedily.

'I can't swallow,' he complained. 'Sore.'

I gave him an injection, and he fell asleep.

In the morning Alexander Ivanovich's strong, sensitive hands explored the boy's puny chest, stomach, back.

'Sore,' Ivanko responded. 'It's sore there . . . and there . . . and there. . . .'

'Well,' the doctor said, 'your Lazarus has truly risen from the dead. Stinks like hell, but he'll live. No more injections. Feed him carefully. Watch him. He wasn't what you'd call a powerful intellect to start with, and now he's mentally retarded as a result of this, and probably for life. That's your contribution to humanity. Satisfied?'

A few days later Ivanko was able to sit up, and even tried to get out of bed. He was still weak but resumed eating with the same old gluttony. We gave him his dried-out bread in four daily portions and fed him rice and oatmeal, jello made of concentrated fruit juices, and other special treats in place of the regular balanda. He accepted it all as his due and became irritated and demanding when '*my* food,' as he came to call it, did not arrive in time or in sufficient quantities.

'Give me my bread! All of it! Give me my soup, fuck your mother! Give me my kasha . . . give me!'

Gosha, the young orderly, lost patience with him. 'Once a jackal, always a jackal. Not a word of thanks. Only bares his teeth. He'll bite your hand off if you let him.'

I tried to explain to Ivanko that he'd get all his bread, only not all at once. He glared at me with his small, unblinking eyes, and I could see the hatred in his smoldering black pupils.

'Took away my bread, the vipers.'

Suddenly he grabbed a boot standing by his bunk and heaved it at me. 'You—kike! Give me back my bread, you kike, fuck your mother!' He was still so weak that the shoe barely reached my shoulder.

The other patients were outraged. 'Who are you throwing your shoe at, you screwball? . . . He dragged you from the grave—you'd be dead if it wasn't for him. . . . He gives you his own rations, you scum. . . . He should have let you croak.'

Gosha looked as though he was about to attack him with his fists. Ivanko got scared and shut up. I told the room that the boy wasn't himself—the poison had affected his mind—and we should all have compassion for him. But sitting in my cubicle, smoking and trying to read, hearing the patients on the other side of the wooden partition telling Ivanko that he ought to apologize, that the Jews were not really such bad people, I gave in to feelings of humiliation, hopelessness, anger and a dull sorrow for myself and for the boy.

Well before he was to be sent off to another camp he was pretty much recovered; we had to take his clothes away during the daytime as before, and the orderly was instructed to accompany him if he claimed that he had to go to the toilet at night. Alexander Ivanovich dictated, and I took down, a detailed report on the history of the case. The doctor concluded that the boy was psychologically damaged and recommended that he be released before completing his full sentence.

The last I saw of him was when he was led off to join a batch of prisoners in transit to his new destination—a small, cropped head on a thin neck sticking out of a dirty padded cotton jacket (on a hot August day); unsteady legs weighed down by a pair of dilapidated reddish-brown boots too big for his feet. Gosha gave him a bundle 'for the road'—some dried bread, cookies and sugar. Ivanko grabbed it and, without saying thank you, without even nodding good-bye, hobbled after the guard.

Sasha the Captain was the deputy chief trusty. Given a year for disorderly conduct after a drunken restaurant brawl in Moscow, where he had been employed as a construction worker, Sasha intended to stay on after serving his sentence and hire himself out to the camp authorities as a free laborer. 'The pay's all right,' he said, 'and it's not far from home, and there's discipline—keep me out of trouble.' Sasha wore his prison jacket with flair—collar up, a sailor's belt tight around the waist. The belt was what gave him his nickname, though he'd been just a sailor in the fleet. The war with Japan landed him in Korea. 'Some of the fellows had it soft out there,' he recalled. 'Those Japanese and Korean women—mmm!—first class! As for me, all I got was my ass frozen off. It hardened my body, but it ruined my disposition.'

He used to come by and sit with me, telling me about doings in the camp. I took a liking to him and he, I thought, to me.

One day, after completing my evening rounds, I returned to my cubbyhole and found my civilian suit gone. The padlock on the door of the wooden partition had not been forced. Gosha, who took great pride in his friendship with me, swore that he hadn't left the yurt and hadn't given the key to anyone. Yet neither the small window nor the ledge under the window where I kept my books and papers showed any sign of entry. Gosha was upset and yelled so the whole yurt could hear that he would give everything he had to anyone who helped him catch the jerk (a man who stole from his fellow prisoners was not deemed worthy of the honorable title of thief).

Inside the camp—in the barracks, the yurts, the dining room, the bathhouse, the 'streets'—our lives were under the direct control of the trusties. These were prisoners who had been given light sentences for rowdyism or absenteeism or petty larceny or the like. Sasha the Captain came at once with two other 'shepherds.'

Sasha conducted the investigation like a seasoned detective. He was particularly severe with Gosha, although I said at once that there could be no question of the boy's guilt. Finally he said, 'This was pulled by some experienced filchers, but from among the minors. Only a minor could get through that window, and only an experienced burglar could do it without leaving a trace. You have friends among the thieves. Speak to them nicely. They'll find out who did it, if they want to.'

With Gosha and my criminal friends on the job, we soon discovered that some of the minors had been seen selling clothes to the cooks. That evening, at dinnertime, Sasha and two men with staves, with Gosha and me in tow, visited the barracks shared by the cooks with some of the other more privileged inmates. The barracks orderly and a few others lying on their iron cots looked at the long staves and at my white coat but did not say anything. Sasha asked where the cooks slept; he lifted a mattress, then another. There lay my jacket and pants.

He called over to the orderly. 'Whose cot is this?'

'Semyon's.'

'Do you see this?'

'I see it, but I don't know anything about it.'

'No one leaves the barracks until Semyon gets back.'

We stepped outside.

'I know this Semyon,' Sasha said. 'Mean bastard. Thinks he's God almighty. Wangle an extra plate of gruel and he'll have it in for you. Now we're going to get him.'

His eyes sparkled. The excitement of the chase communicated itself to Gosha and me. We didn't have long to wait. The head cook, a burly, rosy-cheeked fellow of about thirty, greeted Sasha with a grunt.

'Salutations, shepherd. You taking doctors into your flock now?'

Sasha replied in the same vein. After a while the cook excused himself, saying that it was time for bed.

'Pleasant dreams,' Sasha called out. 'Oh, just one minute—I meant to ask you something. This medic here had his suit stolen. We heard someone in your barracks bought some clothes. Know anything about it?'

'No, never heard of it.'

'Wait, wait. Maybe, if you think a bit, you'll remember something? Maybe you could tell us where to ask?'

'How can I tell you anything when I don't know a damn thing about it?'

'And what if we find the stolen clothes in your barracks? What will you say then?'

'I won't say anything because I don't know anything. I stand over that stove eighteen hours a day. I don't have time to be listening to who bought and sold what.'

'Well, let's go inside and take a look.'

'And who gave you permission to make a search? You got a written order from the commandant?'

But he followed Sasha inside. At the sight of the two men with staves, his cockiness evaporated.

Sasha said harshly, 'For the last time, before witnesses: Do you know if anyone here bought stolen property? You don't? Then we'll look. Whose cot is this?'

Semyon's voice jumped. 'That's against regulations!'

'Never mind that. Where do you think you're going?'

Gosha and the two shepherds barred his way at the door.

'Is this your cot?' Sasha asked.

'Mine.'

'All these things yours?'

'Mine.'

'And this'—Sasha lifted the mattress—'is this yours too?'

'This? I never saw it before. That's where I kept *my* suit! Now someone put someone else's things there! Son of a bitch! Took my stuff away and gave me someone else's! I'll catch him, I'll bash his head in! Maybe this is yours?'

'Yes,' I said, 'it's mine.'

'Well, Captain,' he turned to Sasha, 'then you look in his barracks— maybe you'll find my suit there. I don't want anything that doesn't belong to me, but I want my clothes back.'

He carried on like that, more bold-faced every minute, until I couldn't restrain myself any longer and hit him in the mouth. He stood blinking for a few seconds, then collapsed theatrically on the cot. 'What are you beating me for?' he wailed.

Sasha nodded to the other shepherds, and they lifted him up by his elbows. 'Quiet,' Sasha said. 'Let's go for a little walk.'

They took him to my cubbyhole and went to work on him. Sasha punched him in the stomach and the sides. He struck him on the back of the neck with the edge of his palm. His men hit him on the calves with their staves.

'Who did you buy the suit from?'

Semyon said that someone had brought it to him in the kitchen and he had taken it without looking and had given the man some bread, kasha and makhorka. He said that he hadn't owned up at first because he was scared.

Sasha chopped away with short, vicious blows, his finely shaped lips curled with disdain.

'Stop moaning, scum. Who sold it to you? The truth now—cut the crap.'

Gosha got in a lick, but they pulled him away.

'Not on the face,' Sasha said. 'Leaves a mark.'

The cook slipped down off the cot. They pulled him up and stood him against the wall. His head lolled as though he had passed out. I held a bottle of ammonia to his nose. His eyes settled on mine. 'And you call yourself a doctor.'

Sasha, a cigarette between his lips, jabbed him in the solar plexus. The cook choked and turned blue.

I didn't object to this beating, or step in, even though they were beating him in my cubbyhole. I didn't call for pity or compassion or feel pity myself. It was repugnant, nauseating, like opening up a corpse, and at the same time frightfully interesting. ('So that's what they're like, these "third degrees."') This cook, this brazen operator who doubtless spent his days cuffing the kitchen workers and the helpless goners, was disgusting. But with every blow, ill feeling toward Sasha— toward his coldblooded, studied, almost gleeful brutality—grew in me as well. He and his helpers landed their blows calmly and calculatingly and only pretended to be angry in order to whip themselves up. They, and my gentle Gosha, who exulted in the success of the chase and hated the cook with an innocent hatred, filled me with fear and distaste, all the more so since I was becoming distasteful to myself, taking part in torture and unable to interfere—not wishing to, perhaps. All the same, I stopped Sasha several times: 'Let me ask him; let me explain to the son of a bitch. . . .' And I tried to scare the battered man, predicting terrible agonies, threatening him with injections after which he himself would beg for death. All the while, Sasha prompted him with the minors' nicknames: 'Maybe it was Gray Hair? Gold Tooth? Or Blockade? Thorn? Cossack? Redhead?'

The cook shook his head, 'Don't know . . . don't remember . . . Kill me—I still don't know. . . .'

Sasha's fist and stick had a stronger effect than my eloquent threats. Wiping his tears and sweat, the cook at last confessed that he had bought the suit from the minor Lyoshka, known as Thorn, and had paid him three hundred rubles in cash. He sat on the floor, propped against the wall, wheezing painfully. I gave him a sedative.

'Fixing me up, you shit? First you cripple me, then you fix me up?'

The two shepherds brought in Lyoshka—fidgety, pimply, thin as an eel. Seeing the cook, he let out a shriek. 'Don't beat me!'

Sasha poked him under the ribs, and he began to cry like a baby.

Gosha and I knew him. We had cured him only recently of scurvy.

'Scum,' Gosha said. 'Parasite. He took care of you, and you steal from him!'

'I didn't steal! Let me rot if I—'

'Then your partner stole, and you helped him through the window. Who's your partner?'

'I don't know! I'm not going to be a viper! I don't know!'

The cook jumped up and began pounding the boy with his fists, demanding his money back. We dragged him away. He kept shouting, vowing vengeance, until Sasha kicked him out of the door.

They went easier on the boy than on the cook, but I couldn't look on. His howling filled the yurt. I heard the patients' voices. 'Why are they beating the kid? . . . Hey, you shepherds, screw your mouths! . . . Hey, doctor, what are *you* doing there?'

The kid finally named his accomplice. He showed how he had climbed through the window while the other stood outside. He swore that he had lost the cook's money at cards. In fact, he said, it was his earlier gambling debts that had forced him into stealing.

Sasha decided to stop there. The kid's accomplice was in the punishment barracks. The cook wouldn't say anything. 'It's not in his interests. If he gets the camp officials into this, there's no telling how far it can go. The lawful thieves wouldn't like that either. We want order in the camp. That means we must keep the thieves in their place. But they're pretty strong right now, so we've got to move carefully.'

That day my friendship for Sasha the Captain reached a turning point. I saw him in a new, unpleasant and rather frightening guise. This handsome young man—'one of the boys'—had a vicious streak. He could be a good companion—sensible, generous, game for a lark. But, after coolly weighing the pros and cons, he could also betray, rob and kill.

He felt that I was becoming more withdrawn but could not understand why. He tried several times to clear the air.

'Let's have a heart-to-heart talk. Looks to me like you're scared of me or something. I'm your friend, believe me. I don't care if you're a Fifty-eighter. I can see through people better than any investigator. I trust you. Can't you understand?'

Another time he said, 'I'm being aboveboard with you. I'm no informer for the Oper. I've got my own informers. I know things about you that maybe you yourself don't know. As for your boss, he's a smart one. But he can guess wrong too. All these thieves he's letting into the hospital. Knows how to get his palm greased, eh? Stop shaking your head—what do you know? Only we bitches, as the thieves call us, we're going to make it hot for the thieves pretty soon. More and more bitches among the new arrivals, did you know that? Explain that to your boss. When there are three men and two of them start fighting, the third one keeps out of it if he's got any sense—or else backs the stronger man. You understand?'

I passed the message on to Alexander Ivanovich, glossing over Sasha's allegations of the doctor's corruptibility. But the doctor caught on.

'That's nonsense,' he said. 'There's no favoritism in this hospital. I'd be on your guard if I were you. These thieves don't have any conscience, as some people have no ear for music, but the bitches are even worse. Your Sasha the Captain—don't trust him for a minute. For that matter, you're not obliged to trust me either. And all this is a huge bore, as far as I'm concerned, and I don't know why I'm wasting my time on you. Report on the patients!'

# 25

NEW COLUMNS of prisoners, twenty or thirty or more at a time, arrived almost daily from the other camps and the Moscow prisons, and our dispensary became more and more crowded. Besides taking care of outpatients, we had to examine each new arrival, and every new batch meant several more cases for the hospital. I became more and more tired and groggy; my head ached constantly and I was kept going by aspirin and caffeine. Sometimes I would give in to a dismal indifference: whatever I did was all in vain; nothing would change, nothing would get any better. Help a goner today, patch him up a bit, and tomorrow they'll chase him out to work and the next day he'll collapse again.

An apprehensive tension stole over the camp. A prisoner had escaped. The guards and the shepherds were on edge. Men late for roll call were hurried along by kicks and blows of the stick. Less than a week later another prisoner broke out during the night—and from the punishment barracks at that. A minor in solitary took apart a couple of floor planks with an iron crowbar and dug through the brick wall of the foundation. The guards on the lookout towers did not catch sight of him until he crawled under the outer ring of barbed wire.

I ran out to the sound of automatic fire. Orange tracers streaked across the starry sky. A woman's voice shrilled, 'There he goes! He's heading for the Volga!' Some of the sharpshooters were women.

Lilac beams of light tossed about. A siren wailed. A man's voice: 'What are you shooting at the sky for, you dumb broad? Shoot him down! Hey, you in the white coat!' That was for me. 'Back into your barracks, or we'll shoot! All of you—back!'

At roll call the next morning the guards announced that the escapee had been shot while trying to swim across the river and had drowned. A week later one of our patients, another minor, got a postcard in the mail, postmarked Orel. 'I am going off for a rest, although my health is good,' the escapee wrote. 'Greetings to all my friends.' The card had somehow got past the camp censors. The addressee must not have been on the censors' special list.

Vakhtang was brought into the hospital with a severe case of scurvy. One of his legs was gnarled; the other was on its way; his gums bled. With his reddish hair and light blue eyes he didn't look like a Georgian, although his speech left no doubt that he was; and with his good-humored air, devoid of the slightest trace of the watchfulness I had learned to recognize in our criminals, he looked even less like a 'lawful thief.' Yet he was carried in by a few of our leading 'professionals,' who enjoined me to do well by their buddy.

I massaged his bad leg. He gritted his teeth and tried to smile. Afterward, getting his breath back, he said, 'Doctor, *genatzvali*,* I saw you somewhere before. No, not in the camp—before that.'

'Maybe in your dreams—or in the movies. Only it wasn't me.' I was familiar with the thieves' ways of smelling you out.

'No, doctor, don't think I'm giving you a line. Where did you live? Where were you during the war?'

It turned out that we had actually been in Graudenz at the same time. Vakhtang had been General Rakhimov's driver. He had seen me several times. He remembered how our group had returned with the German general, and how Rakhimov had praised us before his men.

Vakhtang, it also turned out, was not really a professional thief. Wounded by the same German shell that killed General Rakhimov, he made friends in the hospital with some 'professionals' in uniform and agreed to help them collect some 'trophies.' They got hold of a Studebaker truck, piled it high with booty, including quantities of food and vodka, and bounced across Poland for two months, drinking, carousing and plundering.

'But nothing messy, *genatzvali*, not a drop of blood. They were all real men, *katzo*, all honest thieves. That's when I began to respect them. They aren't bandits—they'll take your things, they'll take your money, but they won't take your life. And things and money aren't to keep but to share, so that all their friends can live happily, *genatzvali*. If they like you, there's nothing they won't do for you. Your fraier†

---

*A multipurpose Georgian term of endearment; roughly, 'my good friend,' 'my dear,' 'darling,' etc.

†'Fraier': untranslatable camp slang for anyone who does not belong to the thieves' world.

can live a hundred years—yesterday, today, tomorrow, everything's the same. Screw him in the mouth, he'll say thank you and offer you his ass. He'll sell his wife for his wages, and his son and his friend. But a real man—one day he lives like a prince, the next day he's in jail, the third day maybe he's in his grave, or maybe he's living again, better than a general, with friends to drink with and beautiful women to love. No, doctor, *genatzvali*, better that I live one day like a real man than a hundred years like a fraier.'

A little later he said, 'Is your mother still living, *genatzvali*? And your father? And you have a wife and children? Then I ask you, as one soldier to another: Swear on their health that you'll tell me the truth. Swear! All right. Now answer me: Can you cure me? You're telling me the truth? All right. Thank you.'

I asked him why he insisted on so solemn an oath. He dug under his shirt.

'You see this, *katzo*?' He held up a dagger. 'Sharp as a razor. When I fell sick I told myself, Vakhtang, maybe you will live, maybe you will be a real man, with a beautiful wife and good children. But if you become a cripple, with crooked legs and a crooked back and no teeth, then, *katzo*, you cannot go on living. To hang by the neck is a miserable death. Swallowing powders is a woman's way. But a good dagger—' He held the point against his neck. 'One slash and you die like a soldier, like a man.'

Alexander Ivanovich said that Vakhtang was too far gone for pine brew to help. Onions and garlic would be good, but we didn't have enough of them. Even vitamin pills might not do the trick. 'Now if we had a ten percent solution of ascorbic acid . . . Ten cc's in the buttocks twice a day, and we'd have him on his feet in a week. But that's one thing they won't send me, no matter how often I ask. Everything gets done according to plan, so all the ascorbic acid goes to the camps in the north and the far east. You see, they didn't plan for scurvy in our camp.'

A thought struck me. Nadia worked in a factory that produced vitamin pills. Maybe they produced ascorbic acid too.

Alexander Ivanovich jumped at the idea. 'What's her phone number? I'll telephone her myself. If she can bring over, say, two hundred grams of the stuff, we'll arrange a two-day visit for you.'

Nadia arrived with a jar of white powder. The authorities gave us permission to spend two evenings and two nights together in a special room for twenty-four-hour visits. The room had curtains on the window, wide bunks, a table, a chair, and a hook inside the door. A prisoner granted a twenty-four-hour rendezvous would take his mattress, blanket and pillow with him, sent off with the bawdy best wishes of his comrades.

We began the injections the same day. In less than a week Vakhtang and the other scurvy patients—bent over, shaky on their legs, spitting blood—were walking about, good as new.

One morning I saw Alexander Ivanovich, red-eyed and hung over, drop a pinch of the powder in a glass of water, stir in a spoonful of soda, and drink, smacking his lips. 'Have some?' he asked. 'Fizzy, and pleasant to the taste.'

'No, thank you. I don't have scurvy.'

'That's true. And against idiocy it's ineffective.'

Two weeks later Vakhtang came into my cubbyhole while Gosha and I were having dinner and emptied a sack of apples, tangerines and dried fruit on my bunk.

'Parcel from my mother. This is for you and Gosha. If you don't accept it, you'll plunge a dagger in my heart.'

Vakhtang became the night orderly. But he set a condition.

'You see, *genatzvali*, I've been accepted as a lawful thief. Now an orderly, no matter what you say—don't take offense, *katzo*—is sort of a bitch's job. Of course, this is a kind of special hospital. Alexander Ivanovich is a just man. And you are like a brother to me. Still . . . I will do anything you tell me, *genatzvali*. Only let everyone know—I'm just a patient, I'm helping you out. After all, we were on the same front; you treated me and fed me. But I beg you: no titles, no bureaucracy.'

In August they brought us several women patients. We made room for them in a kind of corridor between the yurt for the seriously ill and the yurt for the dispensary. Freckle-faced Anya was a nurse by profession. Recovering quickly from a bout of malaria, she became my assistant. Bashful Zina fell to washing the floors the first day in. But Alexander Ivanovich told me: 'Keep her away from the others. Syphilis, advanced stage.' We got her a separate cot; the others slept on bunks. Valya, with braids the color of straw, had worked in a sewing factory in the Moscow area; they found her going home one day with two spools of thread in her pockets. An antipilferage campaign was on at the plant, and they gave her seven years for stealing state property, though she swore that she had simply forgotten to leave the thread behind at work.

Mila, slim but well-formed, seemed younger than her twenty-six years. She had dark eyes, pale olive skin, a vivid mouth with a full lower lip, and a straight nose almost in line with her forehead, like the drawings on ancient Grecian vases. Her abundant chestnut-colored hair fell to her shoulders. She was from the Crimea.

'Papa was a sea captain. Mama was a fisherman's daughter from Balaklava, and her mother was Greek. I was born in Sevastopol.'

Mila graduated from acting school just before the war and married the director of a traveling repertory company.

'Anatoly was very talented. He could play the piano, the violin, the guitar, the mandolin, the accordion. He could act all kinds of roles—heroic-romantic, comical-farcical, traditional-classical.'

Under the German occupation her husband gave concerts with her as singer—sometimes in German hospitals and officers' clubs. For this they were sentenced after the war under Article 58—he to ten years, she to five, of which she had already served almost three.

We were attracted to each other. After lights out, after Vakhtang and the nurse Anya would leave my cubbyhole, Mila and I would find ourselves alone.

'Don't talk to me like that. Don't look at me like that. Stop—don't! Please don't. Aren't you ashamed of yourself? I'm not what you think. Enough now! I'm not made of stone either. No . . . no . . . not now. Suppose someone comes in? You don't love me, anyway. No, I don't believe it, you just— *Oh, my dear* . . .

'You won't look down on me now? Yes, you will; you'll think I'm like the other camp trash. You love me? You're just saying it. But . . . do you *still* love me? And with Anya you also— No? Not even once? You're not lying? And with Shura? Don't answer—I won't believe you anyway. After all, she's very good looking, much better looking than me. No, don't say she isn't or I won't believe anything you say. She's a real queen of diamonds, and you're king of spades, so she's your taste. Only don't believe anything she says. She's—she's—you mustn't even *look* at her! Give me your word! And please don't think I'm jealous. After all, I'm not jealous of your wife—I know you owe her everything.

'I'm a fool. I loved you from the beginning. You know when? When you came to us the first time and talked so politely to all of us. You said to me, "You're Article Fifty-eight, so we're members of the same union." You made jokes without being fresh—no vulgarities—just like a real doctor. And when did *you* begin to love *me*? Don't lie—you didn't even notice me! I was all skin and bones. But now I'm a little better. My ribs don't stick out, anyway. But do you find me, generally, attractive? You do? What do you like most about me? My eyes aren't too bad, it's true, but that *mouth*! I've got a *ridiculous* mouth; it's like a doll's mouth. Don't say no—I know it is! And my smile isn't an interesting smile, and my laugh is like a child's laugh, or as if I'm pretending. When I was on the stage, you know, I trained myself not to smile too much and not to laugh. Seriousness becomes me.'

I didn't try to conceal from her that I would soon be tried again and expected nothing good to come of it. But if they gave me five more years, she would be freed only a year and a half before me, and if she wanted to, if she tried to, she could find me—we could find each other. She promised. Neither of us put much faith in it.

'Bad business at the BUR,' said Sasha the Captain, coming around one night. BUR was the acronym for the punishment barracks. 'Cut off one of the zek's heads and stuck it on a pole outside the door. Just like old times.'

The trusties discovered the head in the darkness but wouldn't go inside the barracks, which was always locked for the night.

'If they cut off a head, they've got axes and knives in there. Let them sleep with a headless corpse until morning. We'll see about it then.'

Not long afterward, there was a battle between two newly arrived groups—a bunch of thieves and a crew of 'bitches' who had tangled in another camp. The guards on the watchtowers fired into the air, but the fight went on until a detachment of armed guards burst into the camp. Sasha gave me a lively account of how the combatants hacked away at each other with axes, knives and bits of glass and bashed each other's heads in with bricks and shovels. Three men were killed and a dozen were seriously injured. They were taken to a prison hospital in Moscow.

'Who knows how many died on the way? But we couldn't put them in your hospital. They'd start fighting all over again.'

One day two shepherds came for me. 'Quick, come with us. There's an old man—tripped and fell.'

A gray-haired oldster lay on the floor of one of the barracks.

'Got frightened and fainted dead away,' said one of the shepherds. 'Take care of him. Give him something.'

Angry voices came from a corner. '*Frightened*, you say? You beat him to death, you vipers. . . . Killed him, the bitches, and now they're calling for a doctor!'

The old man was dead. A thin trickle of blood came from the corner of his mouth.

I asked, 'Why is he on the floor? Why the blood? What happened?'

'Nothing happened. We came in for inspection, and there he was.'

'He's lying,' came from the corner. 'They beat him with their sticks.'

'Shut up,' a sturdy blond shepherd flung at them. 'Did *you* see anyone beat him? Or *you*? Then stop making a racket, or we'll fuck you in the mouth and hang you out to dry. And *you*—what are you, a doctor or an investigator? Treat him, and stop spreading panic or you'll be sorry.'

'There's no one to treat. He's dead. He was one of our outpatients. He was supposed to stay in bed, not move. Whoever got him out of his bunk killed him.'

'No one touched him. You trying to start something? Go on, give him an injection. If he dies on account of your shooting your mouth off and not doing your job, we got plenty of witnesses.'

'He died before I came here. The autopsy will show that. And what he died of—the autopsy will show that too. Take him to the morgue.'

Sasha came around the same evening. Things were getting worse and worse, he complained—worse than at the front.

'At the front at least you know who's your enemy and who's your friend, but here you don't know what to expect, from what quarter. Some night some raggedy-ass kid will lose everything at cards in some barracks and will start betting with blood. You know what that means? He loses, he's got to pay by spilling blood—the first man he sees when he goes outside the next morning. So here you're walking along and some little shit-head you've never laid eyes on is slinking after you with an ax. They tell us to maintain order; they let us have sticks, but what good are sticks against knives, axes, crowbars? They're not human beings, those thieves—they're worse than animals. A snake won't attack you first, only if you step on it, but they—

'Take yourself. You treat them, you feed them, but how do you know some kid hasn't staked your life on a deal of the cards, that an ax hasn't been honed for you already? Who's going to stand up for you? The commandant? He's as nervous as a virgin. With all this trouble he's gone off his rocker—hits the bottle right in his office and yells at everyone. The Oper in this camp is a sick man—heart trouble—always taking drops. As for us, we do our best, we're being driven out of our wits, and what do we get for it? Take today—another emergency. And what do I hear?—that you have it in for one of our guys. "You killed him," you said, and "You beat him to death." You shouldn't have said that. Can't you understand—we're going around with our nerves exposed. They've got their axes set for us, and you take their side against us.'

He tried to persuade me—and, through me, to persuade Alexander Ivanovich—to cover up the affair by certifying death from a heart attack, without an autopsy.

Alexander Ivanovich was of two minds. 'What will we accomplish opening him up? He didn't have long to live anyhow.'

His chief assistant didn't know what to think. 'This is terrible, just terrible.' She wrung her hands. 'But we can't cover up a murder. We'll answer for it if it comes out afterward. But still, maybe we shouldn't have an autopsy. They might take revenge, you know. And it'll get the commandant into more trouble.'

The medic in charge of the dispensary refused to sign a certificate attesting to death from a heart attack. 'Suppose someone informs on us —says that death was the result of outside causes? What will that mean?—that I have signed a false statement. And that will mean an extended sentence. Let the man who found him sign that if he wants to.'

I said that I wouldn't sign anything without an autopsy; and if these murderers got off scot-free, they would kill again.

Alexander Ivanovich fixed his mournful, sullen eyes on each of us as we gave our opinions. When we finished, he told us all to be present at the autopsy.

Also present, at the doctor's request, was a representative of the camp authorities, a ruddy-faced sergeant who paled when the autopsy began and after a few minutes asked to be excused.

The autopsy revealed three broken ribs and a broken shoulder bone, as well as contusions and abrasions of the head, shoulders, back and sides. None of these injuries, however, the doctor wrote in his report, were the direct cause of death, which had occurred as a result of a massive heart attack growing out of a heart condition of several years' standing.

The sergeant stood smoking outside the morgue. The doctor gave him the autopsy report to sign. Several trusties stood about, as close to us as they dared.

The sergeant said loudly, so they could hear, 'So it turns out he died from a heart attack, not from anything else?'

'He died from a heart attack,' the doctor said, 'but before that he was beaten up. Whoever beat him up contributed to his death. To what extent they contributed is a question for the judicial experts. And who contributed—that's for the investigation to decide.'

Sasha came into my cubbyhole that evening and remained standing.

'Do you think you did a good thing today—cut up that old man, and now there's going to be an investigation?'

'We had to open him up, under the law. The old man's bones were broken. That's something you can see from the skeleton a year later, even ten years later. It's not unusual for a case like this to be reopened, the body disinterred, and the fact of murder established.'

'I know all that. I've read books. I've been to the movies. And you keep wanting to live like in the movies and books.

'That old medic in the dispensary—he swears he didn't want to do any cutting or writing. It's all you, he says, always standing on principle —you who kept yelling they had to have an autopsy and sign a report. And I thought you were my friend. Did we ever do you any harm? Did we ever stand in your way? We know about you and your cutie— did we ever say anything about it? But you want to drag your "principles" into it! All right, now you'll see some principles of another sort, and you'll be sorry. Only I'm afraid it'll be too late.'

Three shepherds came into the yurt. 'Why isn't everyone asleep after lights out?'

'Shh!' I whispered. 'Stop shouting. This is a hospital.'

'Whorehouse, not a hospital! Who's that smoking in bed?' The taller of the three turned to the other two. 'Get his name. We'll report him.'

They gripped their staves threateningly.

'Stop shouting,' I repeated, 'or I'll write a report too—that you busted in and disturbed the whole ward on account of two men who are smoking because they have insomnia.'

'That's right, medic, you do that—you just keep on writing until you get your hands chopped off.'

Out of the darkness, hobbling on a crutch, Vakhtang advanced on the intruders.

'What's all this racket? Why aren't we patients allowed to sleep? Why, dear doctor, do you allow outsiders in here?'

'Who are you—a patient?' the head trusty asked. 'Then go lie down, or we'll stretch you out so you won't get up for a while.'

Vakhtang's voice rose. 'Who'll stretch me out? You, you miserable bitch? You'll be stretched out ahead of me—in your grave, you filth, you half-wit, you bloodsucker!'

The patients were sitting up in their bunks. Some of them got out of bed. A couple of the men were pulling the boards from their bunks. I armed myself with an iron poker.

There was noise all around. 'What's going on? . . . What's the row? Shepherds . . . vipers . . . bitches . . . won't leave us in peace even here.

'. . . You—you tall one—stop shaking your stick. There's an ax after you—been after you for a long time.'

One of the men was searching demonstratively under his bunk. 'Here, here it is. Now you'll get it.'

Banging the poker on the floor, I shouted: 'Quiet! Everyone quiet! No hysterics! Everyone back to bed! And you three—out! I've got men here with heart conditions. If anything happens, it'll be your fault.'

The patients chimed in. 'That's right, doctor . . . Get them the fuck out of here. . . . Stamp them out, the lawless bitches.'

The trusties left, swearing. The tall one said to me at the door, 'Listen, faker, you don't have much time left. Better write your last letters.'

Alexander Ivanovich winced. 'Well, I warned you. Now figure out how to save your neck. To start with, no reports, please. I'll have a chat with the security officer. You can't expect any help from the commandant. The camp's in a state: war between the thieves and the bitches. Two more men killed last night. A trusty strangled in the toilet, stuck head down in the hole. And the goner beaten to death with the shepherds' staves by the garbage dump. The trusties have gone berserk, and the commandant's backing them up. How many thieves do we have in the hospital?'

We counted six among the serious cases, four or five in my yurt, and several others housed in the wooden barracks for outpatients. The doctor instructed me to take two of the latter into my yurt—the security officer had heard that they were first on the list to be killed.

'Lock the doors at night. Don't let in anyone except the guards. If only they'd get you out of here!'

Alexander Ivanovich knew that I was up for a new trial.

That day Mila came running into the yurt for serious cases, her eyes wide with fright. 'Sasha the Captain's looking for you,' she said. 'He's waiting outside your yurt.'

Sasha, cap askew, stood leaning gracefully on his stick. 'We must have a talk.'

I led him into my cubbyhole. He sat down. 'What have you written?' he asked.

'Nothing. So far.'

'Whom have you told about it?'

'Alexander Ivanovich.'

'And what did he say?'

'He'll talk it over with the Oper. There's something like a war on.'

◇ 248 ◇

'You're damn right there's a war on. Those thieves, those underworld rats—they killed another of our fellows last night.'

'I heard. And who beat that sick man to death at the garbage dump?'

'We're looking into that, and we'll hand down punishment. Although I know for a fact that nobody wanted to kill the bastard—just scare him a little; but he was so far gone, he just curled up and died. Can you compare that to when they stake a man's life on a game of cards, when they sharpen their axes and lie in wait, and then attack—a whole pack of them against one man? Isn't there a difference?'

'Sure, but yesterday your fellows told me they were going to kill me. So they're lying in wait too. And I'm not even part of your war.'

'Yes, you are. It was because of you they cut up that old man and started the investigation. And you're hiding thieves in there, helping them pretend they're sick.'

'That's not true. I'm not hiding anyone. Even if I wanted to, I couldn't accept anyone as a patient. The doctor decides these things, not me. And the investigation is under way not because of me but because your fellows killed that old man and broke his ribs. And now you want to kill me. Only don't think I'm going to offer you my neck—don't think I'm going to say, "Go ahead, dear guardians of the law, hack away to your heart's content." No, if I go, some of you guys are going with me—more than one throat's going to be slit before you slit mine. And you can be sure I'll accept any help I can get—from the devil himself.'

'Don't get excited. Stop yelling. If we wanted to kill you, I wouldn't be here. Let's have a proper talk. You know I have nothing against you, even though you rejected my offer of friendship.'

We talked more calmly. He wanted to know if I intended to report on his men and if the hospital was becoming a base for the thieves. I told him that I hadn't intended to take any action unless I thought the hospital, or I, were in danger of being attacked, and I assured him that the doctor wasn't hiding thieves in there but only taking in the sick. We ended on a friendly note. I treated him, as of old, with some cod liver oil and vitamin pills. Before leaving, he whispered:

'Listen—this is for your ears only. After lineup, don't wander off alone. We've got some new bitches—I hate them as much as I hate the thieves. Both dogs of the same breed, though they're snapping at each other. Some of them are the cook's buddies. Remember the cook? So keep your eyes peeled.'

Toward the end of the day Vakhtang came up to me, looking worried. 'The bitches plan to attack the hospital tonight.' He named the thieves marked out for killing; they included the two we had transferred from the barracks to my yurt. 'You, *genatzvali*, you stay in your room. Close the window. Turn out the light. Better still, *genatzvali*, spend the night with Mila—the window there is even smaller. You're on the list too.'

After dark, groups of quiet figures appeared outside both yurts. They sat down, smoking, making hardly a sound.

'You go, take the night off,' Vakhtang told me. 'If anyone needs you, we'll know where to find you.'

Mila had one of the lower bunks. She was awake, tense with fright. I had told her about my morning talk with Sasha. She had seen the strange men appear, had heard the whispering, and did not know what to think.

We lay in the darkness, listening. She pressed herself against me. 'I won't let you go ... they'll kill you,' she murmured, her breath coming faster, her body growing softer, more tender.

Alexander Ivanovich was gloomily hung over. 'All your principles, all your humanism—it's all a lot of shit. Do we have any spirits?'

'Only denatured alcohol.'

'Give me the denatured alcohol. And don't look at me like a priest at a Jew. Give me the carbolic. Good. Now some gauze.'

He ground the carbolic into powder, sprinkled it on the gauze, and poured the alcohol through the homemade filter. He repeated the process twice. Then he threw a few crystals of potassium manganate into the alcohol, added a saline solution, stirred and poured the concoction into two measuring cups.

'Cheers. And here's some valerian to kill the smell. *In vino veritas*—that is God's truth, and all the rest is a lot of shit. What do you think—why am I drinking with you during working hours? How to explain that from the standpoint of your principles? You don't know? There's a lot you don't know yet. But this I'll explain to you. I'm saying goodbye. You're being transferred. Tomorrow. I wish you—what can I wish you that won't be just empty words? I can't abide sentimentality. I wish you to stay alive and well, and not to give way to despair, and to remember that so long as there's life, everything that was wrong can be made right. And you can wish me ... not to become a drunk, an alcoholic, and, generally speaking ...'

'Generally speaking, thank you, Alexander Ivanovich, thank you from the bottom of my heart! I wish you health—physical health and spiritual health—and I too believe that there's nothing in life that can't be fixed.'

I was in my cubbyhole, going over the patients' records with the nurse Anya, who was to take my place, when Sasha poked his head in. 'Let's go out for a minute.'

We left the yurt. Vakhtang and two of his friends followed close behind.

'Your bodyguards.' Sasha sniffed. 'And you said you were neutral.'

'So I am. They're my patients, and they don't want me killed.'

'Who's going to kill you—me? What the fuck I want to do that for? Fuck 'em, anyway. You know about the transfer?'

'What transfer?'

'Stop playing games. They're pulling you out tomorrow. What are you going to be—freed? Retried? Whatever it is, it'll be better than here. You think everything was quiet last night because of your guests? Balls. Because me and my fellows put the leash on the other bitches. They had their axes and crowbars all ready. They would have cut your yurts up into ribbons and all of you into mincemeat. We kept them in check. Not because of any pity for your scum, either. It would have looked bad for us, that's why. Anyhow, tonight you don't have to be scared. I'll come around in the evening to say good-bye.'

He came with two shepherds right after lights out. 'Well, doctor, how about a farewell drink? You must have something put away. Nothing? Really? Well, it'll have to be cod-liver oil again, then.'

I took them to my cubbyhole and gave them some cod-liver oil and vitamin pills, and some sweets left over from my last parcel. Sasha said that the authorities had decided to put an end to the war. The trouble-makers on both sides were being shipped off to other camps. 'Let them strangle each other with their bare hands on the way.'

After he and his men had left, Vakhtang came in to announce a party. There were six of us crammed into the narrow space. Anya was there. And the Bomber, who had been brought back from the gravel pit and made a hospital orderly. Mila brought a sleepy-faced Valya. Vakhtang placed a bottle on the floor, spread a newspaper on the table, and laid out some bread, fried fish and nuts, a few Georgian candy sticks and a can of chubs in tomato sauce.

'Today,' he began in an undertone, 'we are saying good-bye to our dear friend—'

Vakhtang toasted our 'beautiful women, our comrades in arms'; he toasted me; he toasted those present and absent; he toasted friendship —'the main thing in life, whether in prison or at liberty.' We sat on the bunk or on the floor. The women left the vodka to the men; Mila only touched the rim of my glass with her lips. All the fears, experiences, feelings, half-formed thoughts of the past few days were clotted in my breast. What would happen to Mila? She pressed herself against my shoulder. Her thin, strong fingers gripped my arm. Vakhtang became emotional and called me his best friend, who had saved his life.

There wasn't much time left for Mila and me to be alone with each other. She cried. I could not free myself from my load of thoughts. First I would caress her with exaggerated ardor—to think that this could be the last time I would ever touch a woman! Then I would whisper tender nonsense, promise to remember, to write, to find her wherever she might be. I knew that I was lying, and, to even it up between us, I made her promise to be faithful to me.

When I woke up, Vakhtang was knocking at the door. Mila was sitting at the table, writing. It was her farewell letter. She brought it to me at morning lineup, slipping it inside my pocket, together with a loaf of bread. Pretty words about love, parting, pain, such as you read in books or hear in popular songs. She begged me never to forget; she promised always to remember. The words were artificial, but her tears had been real.

A score of us were placed in a three-ton truck, along with five guards with submachine guns and a police dog. We drove through the forest. The white birches were tinted with September yellow. The morning was cool and overcast.

The thieves and the bitches were taken off the truck at our first stop in Moscow. Three of us were left, and one guard. There was still a trace of daylight when we drove up to the Butyrka. The familiar green gates closed behind us. 'Forward,' came the familiar greeting. 'Hands behind your backs.'

# 26

A PARCEL from home contained fifteen onions and ten heads of garlic: the trial was set for October 15. Lyena's birthday. The same date as my first trial a year earlier. A good omen? A bad one?

There was a shortage of prison guards, and I was taken to the trial by the officer in charge of order in the court—a trim, swarthy army captain with rows of service ribbons, graying hair and a trace of Armenia in his speech. Once again I was led, propped up by the elbows, along that corridor where Nadia and Mama stood waiting, with their long-suffering smiles and martyred eyes. Once again, that familiar courtroom, the judges' table on a platform, the defendant's bench behind a railing to one side. The prosecutor was a tall, plump, rosy man in shiny boots. The chairman of the tribunal was a bilious-looking colonel who seemed either irritated or bored. Two other judges, with blank faces and glistening shoulder boards. The court secretary, very young, holding a thin little pencil. My lawyer barely said hello; he seemed despondent and fussed about with his papers, avoiding my eyes. The only witness in the courtroom was Ivan Rozhansky. The only others present were my army captain and a young lieutenant, his assistant for the day.

The secretary read the verdict of the military court setting aside the earlier acquittal. I asked that additional witnesses be called; my lawyer gave the motion limp support; the prosecutor objected, saying that there was enough evidence on record; the court agreed with him. I asked that statements in my defense submitted since my last appearance in court—affidavits offered by friends who had known me at the front and before the war—be accepted in evidence. My attorney again joined halfheartedly in my request. The prosecutor made a lengthy and incomprehensible speech, preening himself on the modulations of his voice and the roundness of his sentences. Throwing his head back, then craning forward, raising his voice, then lowering it, he spoke flowingly of 'judicial practice,' 'procedural necessity,' and other legal concepts, both 'on the one hand and on the other.' I didn't understand a word, but the chairman agreed with him, and my second motion was also denied.

The presiding judge and the prosecutor then questioned me in tandem. 'How can you assert that ...? How could you have condemned those heroic ...? How could you have discredited ... slandered ...?'

My lawyer asked me what I had been decorated for and why I thought this or that prosecution witness bore me ill will.

I saw before me the dull, indifferent faces at the judge's table. But the court officer and the young lieutenant listened attentively. I spoke for them. Let these two, at any rate, know my story, hear my truth.

They called up Ivan Rozhansky. He repeated everything that he had said at the earlier trials—the lies spread by Zabashtansky and Belyaev, the single-minded way they had concocted the accusation.

The session was suspended. On the way back to prison the court officer asked me what fronts I had served on and told me about his own wartime career—from private on the Dnestr to lieutenant at Stalingrad to captain at the taking of Vienna.

'If it were not for my lack of education, I'd have gone further. But I only had eight years of schooling, and not somewhere like Erevan* but a rural school in the mountains. I was a shepherd. Wanted to be a veterinary. Of course, war—that's a school too, of its kind.'

'Go on, go on, drive around a little,' he told the chauffeur. 'The man's going back to prison—let him have a breath of air. You spoke well, Major, and you spoke the truth, I could tell. Your friend the captain, he speaks softly, thinks before each word—you could drive ten sheep through one of his pauses. But he speaks well too, and also the truth. The prosecutor speaks smoothly, like on the radio, like reading a newspaper, but I could tell—he says a lot but doesn't think about what he's saying.'

'That's called oratory,' the lieutenant offered.

'Oratory! Who the hell needs it if it's to put a man in jail? You, Major, did you let yourself be captured? No. Did you run away from the front? No. Did you cook up any self-inflicted wounds to be pulled out of action? No. Were you wounded? Yes. Were you decorated? Yes. How long were you at the front? Almost the entire four years.

*Capital of Armenia.

◆ 254 ◆

Then why are you being tried? Because you called a looter a looter? Because you didn't want them to rape German women? You should have been thanked for that, not put on trial. Now if you cussed out your superior officer—that's a different matter. He was a bastard, no doubt about it. Still, authority supports authority. So let them give you a reprimand, a demotion, even a dishonorable discharge. But imprisonment? No, they can't—they won't do that.'

The next day we were called up in the afternoon. The captain greeted me like an old friend. Nadia and Mama weren't there in the corridor. (Later I found out that they had been told there wouldn't be a session that day.)

Ivan was back on the stand. The secretary read excerpts from Zabashtansky's and Belyaev's testimony, and the prosecutor asked questions meant to trip him up. The presiding judge leaned forward, as though ready to pounce, and fairly shouted:

'We want straight answers! At the Party meeting at the front you did not object to expelling him from the Party—yes or no?'

'No,' Ivan said. 'But I didn't vote yes either.'

'No buts! Don't forget you're testifying before a military tribunal. Don't forget you're responsible before the Party and the courts for your every word! Answer directly: you wrote a letter to the chief prosecutor defending a man whose dismissal from the Party you had not opposed.'

'That's right.'

'Then how is one to understand your attitude, Comrade Captain Rozhansky? On the other hand, you don't object to his expulsion from the Party—and not for some trifle, some drunken brawl, some minor infraction, but for hostile political statements of the most serious nature, statements that under the front-line conditions of the Great Patriotic War were tantamount to crimes. And then you go and write a letter in his defense and give testimony in court that can only sow confusion! What do you call that, may I ask?'

I could not restrain myself from saying loudly to my attorney, 'Why don't you object? This is against the law. He's pressuring the witness.'

The lawyer glanced fearfully at me over his shoulder. 'Keep still. You're only doing yourself harm.'

The chairman, without a look in my direction, bore down on Ivan. 'Answer! What would you call such behavior?'

Ivan stood there. Alone. He rubbed his hands calmly, as if he had just laid down the chalk at a lecture.

The prosecutor on his left chimed in: 'Doesn't it seem your

behavior could be described, so to speak, as double-dealing, considering we're both Party members?'

'Double-dealing in relation to the Party,' shouted the judge, 'and bearing false witness in defense of a criminal in the legal sense. Answer —what made you do it?'

Ivan raised his head and looked steadily at the judge. 'I can't accept that—uh—construction. No, I—uh—can't accept it. I didn't vote at that meeting. But why I didn't vote I explained the last time. I thought I was obliged to follow orders. Then, when I learned of his arrest, I wrote to the chief prosecutor. And I wrote what I knew to be the truth.'

'You mean at the meeting you didn't know what the truth was?'

'I knew, but—'

'Then why didn't you vote against the expulsion? How do you explain *that*?'

'I made a mistake. And later I corrected my mistake.'

'And who told you to? Who advised you? Or, maybe, *ordered* you again?'

'No one. I myself. My conscience. My Party conscience. It was my moral duty.'

'And so you reaffirm your testimony in favor of the accused? You reaffirm it despite the decision of the Military Collegium of the Supreme Court, which twice set aside any lenient view of his actions?' The chairman was no longer shouting but rapping out each word in a tone meant to be more frightening than shouts.

'Of course I do.'

The judge let out a sigh of exasperation. There was a long silence. 'You are excused.'

Ivan went to the back of the room and sat down.

The prosecutor spoke for more than an hour. Putting on his horn-rimmed glasses, he read reams of evidence from his voluminous file, losing his place, placing meaningless emphasis on some sentences and sliding over others, and breaking off now and then to plunge into some disconnected commentary.

'... For while it clearly follows that the defendant tries in vain to convince us of his innocence, counting apparently on his ability to influence the military tribunal in some measure, in the face of such obvious and concrete prosecution evidence, which not only fully exposes and confirms but, in a certain sense, even strengthens the conclusion of the indictment ...'

He went on, alternating between the evidence and his summation.

'Here I stand, Assistant Prosecutor of the Moscow Military Region Miltsyn—here I stand before you, comrade judges, openhearted, in line of duty, yet the defendant would have you believe that it is not I, the prosecutor, not I, the colonel, not I, Comrade Miltsyn, who is standing before you but someone, in a manner of speaking, quite different— someone whom *he*, the defendant, sees and knows and understands better, if you please, than you, comrade judges, better than the Party, better than the entire Soviet people. But can we allow ourselves to indulge the defendant in these affectations? Can we, for the sake of these— even if, in a certain sense, original—pretensions give up our own Party viewpoint, our Marxist-Leninist and patriotic principles, our devotion to our heroic Soviet people? I rather think we cannot allow ourselves to abandon our viewpoint and our principles, since they are the viewpoint and the principles of the great Party of Lenin and Stalin, which is the intellect and conscience of our era, of our people, and we cannot allow anyone to trample on what we hold most sacred. . . .'

He spoke on and on, and it was clear that he no longer remembered exactly what I was accused of and what crimes I had committed. Perhaps he never knew in the first place, not having had time to study the case. He even appeared to forget about Ivan Rozhansky's testimony, for he said:

'The defendant's obvious guilt has been amply proved by the testimony of numerous witnesses, such as Zabashtansky, Belyaev, Khromushina, Belkin, Rozhansky—'

'But the last three were witnesses for the *defense*!' I exclaimed.

The chairman rapped his fingertips on the table, and the prosecutor, thrown off momentarily, smiled and went on: 'Exactly—witnesses for the defense. And that, in a certain sense, is even more convincing than the testimony of the witnesses for the prosecution. We have seen how the witnesses for the defense have exposed the defendant precisely in what he tries hardest to conceal. We can understand his doing that, of course, from a human standpoint: no one wants to go to prison. In this I see a certain consistency. Our courts are the most magnanimous in the world, and our prosecutors are the most humane in the world, but we cannot leave unpunished—'

He spoke in rolling cadences until I was mesmerized and felt my eyelids droop. At last I made out the final chords.

'And so, proceeding from what we have learned about this rather weighty, complex and profoundly political case, from everything we have heard here, I deem it necessary to ask the court to hand down the maximum penalty under this Article—in other words, in peacetime, ten years' imprisonment, five years' loss of civil rights, loss of army rank, and a motion before the Supreme Court for divestment of all governmental awards.'

My attorney began with cloying praise for the brilliant summation of Comrade Colonel Miltsyn—a speech of exemplary partyness, staunch principle and superb argumentation. But going by the prosecutor's wonderful tribute to the magnanimous and humane qualities of Soviet justice, he asked the tribunal to take into account the large number of authoritative and positive character references submitted on the defendant's behalf, as well as the defendant's military services and injuries and the state of his health, and yet another circumstance—namely, that the guilt in question related to wartime and that the penalty could therefore be lightened in this time of peace. Wherefore he, an attorney, a Communist since 1920, conscious of his responsibility, ventured to ask this magnanimous court to reduce the sentence, bearing in mind the possibility of rehabilitation. . . .

When they let me have the last word, I repudiated my lawyer's defense, saying that I did not admit to any of the accusations made by the prosecutor, since they bore no relation to this case and the prosecutor did not even seem to remember what had been said by the various witnesses.

The prosecutor regarded me with an almost gentle, condescending smile, shaking his pink head and shrugging his fleshy shoulders, as though to say, 'He's not himself, poor fellow.'

I said that the prosecutor's demand was in monstrous contradiction to the spirit and letter of the law and to the best interests of the Party and the government. After that, I repeated everything I had said at the first two trials, but more succinctly and briefly.

The court left the room to deliberate.

The court officer came up to me. He wasn't as optimistic as before. 'Some judge. I didn't know there were judges like that. The way he shouted at your friend. But that captain—he's quite a man. The other one screams at him, and he just stands there like a rock. And the prosecutor—as though he's playing children's games. Spin the bottle—ten years! He's drunk, or has a head injury, or what? Your lawyer—he's a weak old man. He's afraid. What's he afraid of? "I'm an old Communist," he says. All right, then—act like one. And you—you spoke well again. You gave it to both of them—the prosecutor and the lawyer—like a soldier. And the judges—I'm sure now they'll understand. Hell, *I* understand, and I'm an ordinary man, a soldier—and he, the chairman, he's a judge, a jurist, a lieutenant colonel. . . . No, no, they *must* understand.'

The conference was brief. The chairman read the verdict, which began, inauspiciously enough, with the words: 'Having earlier been a member of the Trotskyist cadres . . .' What followed was vintage Zabashtansky. And the conclusion was precisely what the prosecutor had asked for—guilty as charged; a ten-year sentence, plus a five-year suspension of civil rights, and loss of military rank and awards.

'Defendant, do you understand?'

'No, I do not understand.'

The chairman reread the conclusion with the same even, raspy voice. 'Ten and five. You understand now, I trust?'

'I don't understand where justice comes into it.'

Yet, in a way, the verdict was just. I did not understand that then. I came to understand it later.

In reviewing my youth for the court—and on other occasions years later—I was proud of having been part of the events of the 1930s, which I saw as heroic high tragedy. Instead of Fate, the action was moved by 'historical necessity,' in which I believed more ardently than, as a child, I had believed in God. That is why I was proud that I had helped take bread away from peasants; that I, a twenty-year-old city know-nothing, had instructed people who had grown old farming as to how they should live, how they should work, what was good for them and what was bad. And no wonder: I had looked down on them from the pinnacle of the one, true, all-redeeming social science. Of course, I had never regarded them as condescendingly and inimically as did my more militant comrades, who saw these 'country hicks'—especially those who did not join the kolkhoz and were tagged as 'cheats,' 'turkeys' and 'Hindus'*—as a pernicious kulak element or, at best, as ignorant boors lacking in class consciousness. I had learned from childhood to value hard work, and the respect for calloused hands shown by most of my contemporaries was largely genuine. But private property was seen by us as a wretched and despicable sin, the basis of a 'petit bourgeois outlook.' So I was convinced of my ideological superiority to the peasants and was ashamed of feeling pity while we robbed them.

Everything was simple and clear: I belonged to the one and only

*'Indiuk' ('turkey') and 'Indus' ('Hindu') were a colloquial variation on 'Indkhoz,' a Soviet contraction of 'Individualnoye khoziastvo,' or 'Individual farm-ownership.' Calling an 'individualist' a 'turkey' and a 'Hindu' made it easier to hold him up to scorn.

righteous Party; I was a fighter in a just war for the victory of the historically most progressive class—and hence for the ultimate happiness of all mankind. Therefore, I had to be ready to sacrifice my life at a moment's notice, and to demand any sacrifice from my comrades and friends. And, of course, I could not show mercy to the enemy or have pity for 'neutrals.' In the sacred struggle being waged by many millions of people, the fate of one person—or of a hundred thousand—was mathematically insignificant. In battle it is sometimes necessary to sacrifice a few men to save the company, a company to save the regiment, a regiment to save the army, an army to save the nation. And for the victory of the world revolution, it was permissible to sacrifice whole countries and peoples—Poland, Finland. . . .

This is what I thought; that is what I believed; that is what I wanted to feel.

In arguing as I had with the spokesmen of the new chauvinism and of 'sacred revenge,' in disputing their attempts to justify looting and rape, I was convinced that I was defending the ideas and principles of Marxist-Leninist internationalism and the true interests of my government, my Party and my army. I was always annoyed when they said that I was playing Don Quixote in the name of some abstract morality: there was nothing abstract about it to me, feeling as I did that morality was always determined by specific social conditions—by class, by party. Even in the most oppressive times in prison and camp, I felt myself a fragment, still, of the Party that had cast me out, an acolyte of the government that had reduced me to a slave. I was ready to fight for them again and again, to spend myself in labor at their behest, to brave any dangers—even death. I did not understand in those days—I did not want to understand—that the Zabashtanskys and the Belyaevs, with their enmity toward me, and the investigators and the prosecutors, with their distrust of me, really did exemplify what had become of 'partyness' and government, and that I should have taken pride in their unwillingness to count me one of their own.

Many more years would have to pass, many more illusions would have to be broken, many more self-deceptions would have to be overcome before I would begin to understand that my accusers were essentially right—that all my insistence on doctrinal text, all my clinging to ideals hopelessly alien to the reality around me, were indeed the product of an intellectual, 'petit bourgeois' upbringing, the real reason I did not and could not become the companion of my persecutors.

But I came, at length, to understand. I came to understand that my fate, which had seemed so senselessly, so undeservedly, cruel, was actually fortunate and just. It was just because I did deserve to be punished—for the many years I had zealously participated in plundering the peasants, worshiping Stalin, lying and deceiving myself in the name of 'historical necessity,' and teaching others to believe in lies and to bow before scoundrels. It was fortunate because the years of detention saved me from taking part in still newer villainies and deceits, and because what I experienced, discovered and rethought in the prisons and the labor camps helped me later. Gradually I was able to free myself of the sticky web of dialectical sophistry and syllogism which can transform the best of men into villains and executioners. Gradually I lost my awe for those ideas which, in 'capturing the masses,' can become ruinous to whole peoples.

The judges and the prosecutor left. My lawyer said in a hurried whisper, avoiding my eyes, 'We'll appeal. . . . Let's hope . . . perhaps a reduction of sentence . . .'

The captain brought Ivan over. 'Say good-bye. Maybe for a long time. I never thought anything like this could happen. Ten years—for nothing. Condemning a man like wetting two fingers when you take a leak.'

He repeated that phrase several times. Why two fingers?

Ivan and I embraced. Never had I seen him look so sad.

In the car, the captain told the chauffeur, 'Drive around Moscow for a while. When is he going to see the place again?' He had him pull up to the curb at Mayakovsky Square, then on Gorky Street, then on Manezh Square. 'Look at the city,' he said. 'You're a Muscovite, aren't you? You love Moscow?'

He went into a store and brought me a bottle of beer and some apples and candy. 'Drink the beer here, in the car, and put the rest in your pockets.'

We arrived at Butyrka. The guards receiving the prisoners looked surprised: the captain stretched out his hand to me with a flourish.

'Good luck, Major. Good-bye, Don't give up. If you survived the front, you'll survive anywhere!'

'Thank you, Captain, thank you! Good luck!'

Keys clanked against belt buckles. Keys grated in locks. Around me ebbed and flowed the discordant noises of the prison night.

# Afterword

THE WELCOME in the apartment on Red Army Street in Moscow was always the same, and remains unforgettable. Ring the bell, wait a moment, see it open to reveal a giant man, 6 feet 3 inches at least, with a thick and bristly white beard under a large nose and a grin.

'Oh!' he would shout each time. 'Dear one, how are you? Come in!' Always a kiss or a hug, always the feeling that this giant has been waiting in his book-lined room hoping for nothing so much as a visit from *you*, and now his fondest wish has been realized. I haven't rung that bell for more than two years, but I have it on excellent authority that the reception is still the same.

Lev Kopelev is the giant behind the beard, and he is not parsimonious with that greeting. He gives it many times every day; his apartment is surely one of the busiest in Moscow. In the course of a month it is visited by an extraordinary range of people, from distinguished Soviet academicians of international repute to pilgrims from the remote Soviet provinces who have heard of Kopelev and have come to see if he is real. Many of the visitors come to see Kopelev's wife, Raisa Orlova, a distinguished translator and critic of American literature. Together Kopelev and his wife preside over a remarkable salon, one of the centers of literary life in the Soviet capital.

'Salon' may be the wrong word; it has the wrong connotation. The small flat on Red Army Street would not fit the Parisian image of a salon. The furnishings are spare and practical; the most striking feature of the place is its books and photographs. Kopelev's room is almost entirely lined with books, but their titles are blocked out by row upon row of photographs: some grinning snapshots, some stilted, formal portraits which you can sometimes have taken at Moscow's photo shops, reminiscent of the pictures boys and girls bring home from school. These are Lev and Raya's friends—more accurately, a tiny fraction of their friends—constant reminders of the most important element in the Kopelevs' lives, people.

Much of the socializing in that flat goes on around a narrow table in the kitchen. I met some of the most interesting people in Moscow at that table while drinking tea and eating open sandwiches of cheese and Russian salami. On special occasions there is a bottle of something, wine or vodka or breathtaking Georgian cha-cha, a homemade spirit which Lev brought back from trips to Tbilisi.

Lev's health has not been good in recent years; he is under stern orders not to drink, and he usually respects them. He is also forbidden to smoke, but the reader of this book will not be surprised to learn that Lev's love of tobacco periodically proves stronger than his will power. His favorite gambit is to sneak a drag on someone else's cigarette while Raya is out of the room or looking the other way. If he is caught, his eyes twinkle like a small boy's. Please understand, they seem to say; I cannot help myself.

The bustle of people in and out of the Kopelev apartment is more or less constant. Children and grandchildren, neighbors and colleagues, students and friends of friends, visitors from abroad—the stream has no end. Lev is a one-man cultural exchange program with both Germanys, East and West. Heinrich Böll is a close friend who always comes to call when he is in Moscow. So do many East German writers and scholars, all of whom marvel at Lev's perfect German and his detailed knowledge of their literature. The Kopelevs also have countless American friends, some of them—like Lillian Hellman, whose foreword graces this volume—dating from the war years. Styron, Updike, Arthur Miller, and Herbert Gold are among the dozens of American writers who have visited Lev and Raya.

The most basic family joke is the telephone, which never stops ringing. I remember once trying to get through on the telephone for two days without success. Finally I drove over to see if the phone was out of order. No, not at all, Raya explained. Elections to the Academy of Sciences were coming up in a few days, and Lev was on the phone constantly, politicking for his friends and against those he deemed unworthy.

That politicking demonstrated Lev's unusual status in Moscow. He is a friend to many of the best-known dissident intellectuals of recent years, including both Alexander Solzhenitsyn and Andrei Sakharov, but it would be misleading to categorize him as a dissident. He has not cut himself off from Soviet society as many of the dissidents have; on the contrary, he maintains friendships with many members of the official *intelligentsia* (though some who were once friends now shy away from Lev as too controversial, too outspoken). Both Lev and Raya have maintained memberships in a number of official organizations. Dozens of their friends have emigrated in recent years during an unprecedented exodus of writers and intellectuals, but the Kopelevs have never dreamed of leaving. (One who left is Lev's daughter Maya, mentioned in this book, who now lives in America with her husband, Pavel Litvinov, grandson of Maxim Litvinov, the young Soviet Union's commissar of foreign affairs during the 1930s.)

Lev is a fierce patriot; he took me to task on many occasions for failing to understand more sympathetically what his country, and particularly its creative intellectuals, have been through, and what they have nevertheless accomplished. More than once I saw him sharply contradict disenchanted Russians who simultaneously despaired of their government and overpraised America and the West. The Watergate affair was a philosophic comfort to Lev; he thought it proved his point that no country or system could guarantee the virtue of its politicians.

Unfortunately, Kopelev's brand of patriotism is not appreciated by some of the officials who govern intellectual life in Moscow. Because of his friendships with controversial Soviet citizens and foreigners, and because he is unable to hold his tongue in the presence of a self-evident injustice, no official journal or publishing house will publish his work (mostly literary essays). Occasionally he is invited to a university or institute to give a lecture. While I was in Moscow (1971–74), his translation of Brecht's *Galileo* occasionally appeared at the Taganka Theater. But most of Lev's recent work has been published in Germany. This book of memoirs, which will be published in every major language of the Western World, will have a much wider readership than any previous Kopelev work. But it will not be published in the Soviet Union. (A Russian edition of Kopelev's original text has been published by Ardis, Ann Arbor, Michigan.)

In recent years the Kopelevs have been the victims of a variety of harassments. For months on end they have received none of the letters and books sent by their many friends and colleagues abroad. Threatening, anonymous phone calls have become a rather routine part of their lives. Once a caller asked Raya if she had made funeral arrangements for her husband. On another occasion someone threw a brick through a window of their first-floor apartment. It is impossible to know who is responsible for this harassment; some of the Kopelevs' friends believe it is the Soviet secret police, the KGB. But Lev and Raya do not make that accusation, and they put up with the harassment with remarkable equanimity. No doubt, after surviving the events described in this book, Lev has a high degree of tolerance for lesser distractions.

.    .    .    .    .

Kopelev's publishers have asked me to bring his story up to date from the point where it ends in this book. I do so, but only reluctantly and sketchily, in part because I don't know all the details, in part because it is not my job to tell the whole story.

Lev finally got out of prison in 1954, but he was not immediately rehabilitated. He spent years clearing his name, both legally and in the eyes of the Communist Party, which finally did readmit him. (In 1968 Kopelev was expelled from the Party again, this time because of his public protest against the persecution of Soviet intellectuals.) Lev felt he had to be rehabilitated by the Party partly for the sake of those—only partially described in this book—who risked a great deal by testifying on his behalf at one or more of his trials. Some of them later suffered for defending a 'criminal'—Kopelev.

Kopelev entered the war as the zealous Communist who appears in this book, but he left prison in 1954 as very different man. I once asked his wife, who had known him before the war when he was married to another woman, what had changed the most from the 1930s to the 1970s. 'Our tolerance,' she replied. Stalin's Communism was a religion, and Lev and Raya were both devout believers. I will never forget the sunny afternoon in the country outside of Moscow when Lev told me that he himself had rushed into battle against the Nazis shouting, 'For the Motherland! For Stalin!' He had meant it, too. Today Lev is a profoundly tolerant man, and a practicing humanist. His values are the values of the early Karl Marx, the humanist Marx who has been compared to an Old Testament prophet.

There is one fascinating and important part of Kopelev's story which I must mention here, though he will be angry with me for bringing it up. That is his relationship with Alexander Solzhenitsyn. ('Not important,' Lev would say.) As was mentioned in Chapter 7 of this book, Kopelev and Solzhenitsyn met in a 'sharashka', a scientific institute staffed by prisoners. In the postwar years Stalin was able to exploit many talented Soviet citizens who happened to be in prison for transgressions like Kopelev's by placing them in these institutions. Solzhenitsyn has memorialized the sharashka in which he and Kopelev met in *The First Circle*, in many ways his most interesting novel.

Anyone who has read and enjoyed Kopelev's book should turn to *The First Circle* and read it again, keeping in mind that Kopelev was the model for many characteristics of the character Solzhenitsyn called Lev Rubin. Rubin is the brilliant linguist and philologist who persistently defends Stalin and the Soviet system despite the fact that they are responsible for his wholly unjustified imprisonment. Rubin's stubborn faith sounds very much like Kopelev's in this book, which is no surprise.

Ironically, the world might never have known *The First Circle*, or even the name of Alexander Solzhenitsyn, were it not for Lev and Raya Kopelev. Solzhenitsyn was not freed until 1956, and he then began a new life as a provincial schoolteacher. At home, largely for himself, he began to write, acting out an ambition that had been with him since adolescence. *One Day in the Life of Ivan Denisovich*—surely the most important book published in the Soviet Union in modern times—was written by that reclusive schoolteacher.

Unlike virtually every other major Soviet writer of the postwar period, Solzhenitsyn was an utter stranger to the Moscow literary establishment. He turned to the Kopelevs—who then, as now, had a wide circle of friends—for help.

Lev and Raya both knew Alexander Tvardovsky and his colleagues on the editorial board of *Novy Mir* (*New World*), a monthly literary magazine which, under Tvardovsky, was the most interesting and important journal that has been published in the U.S.S.R. since the Stalin era. The Kopelevs were both smitten by Solzhenitsyn's short novel and urged it upon their friends at *Novy Mir*. Tvardovsky concurred in their enthusiasm and decided to try to publish Solzhenitsyn in his journal. His success in 1962 launched one of the most dramatic literary careers of the twentieth century.

Solzhenitsyn's books have given millions of non-Russian readers a glimpse of Soviet society under Stalin and since, but Solzhenitsyn's vision is incomplete—which brings me to this book. There is a real danger that Western readers will rely too much on Solzhenitsyn to convey the nature and texture of Soviet life during this painful era. His books are invaluable, but others—the present volume is an outstanding example—are equally important.

In his dedication Kopelev writes that this book would not have been written without Raya, and that is true. It was she who, when he came out of prison in 1954, insisted that he tell her everything that had happened to him. At first Lev was reluctant, but finally he told her the story. She was overwhelmed by it and insisted that he put it down on paper. Again he was reluctant, but she persisted and he finally agreed.

This English translation is not the complete book that he wrote. More than a third of the original has been cut at the urging of the British and American publishers, who felt that Kopelev could best find a wide readership in the English-speaking world if the size and price of this volume could be kept moderate. What has been cut, in effect, is detail: portraits of people Kopelev met during his adventures, more anecdotes and stories. (The Russian edition published by Ardis is unabridged.)

In my opinion the essence of the original Russian work—and the essence of Kopelev—are well preserved in this volume. Most important to me is the portrait Lev draws of the true believer, the ardent, literal-minded Stalinist who let nothing—not even the most obvious facts—alter his faith. Stalin's enormous accomplishments (and equally enormous crimes) during the 1930s would have been impossible without hundreds of thousands, perhaps millions, of such true believers. So Kopelev's story is not only an emotional human tale; it also helps explain one of the most astounding periods of all human history.

—ROBERT G. KAISER

Washington, D.C.
December 1976